A STUDENT'S GUIDE TO HEARSAY

SECOND EDITION

Clifford S. Fishman
Professor of Law
The Catholic University of America
STUDENT GUIDE SERIES

STUDENT GUIDE SERIES

1999

QUESTIONS ABOUT THIS PUBLICATION?

For questions about the **Editorial Content** appearing in this volume or reprint permission, please call:

Mark Landis, J.D. .... (800) 424-0651 ext. 300
Steve Revell, J.D. .... (800) 424-0651 ext. 321
Outside the United States and Canada please call .... (212) 448-2000

For assistance with shipments, billing or other customer service matters, please call:

Customer Services Department at .... (800) 533-1646
Fax number .... (518) 487-3584

Copyright © 1999 By Matthew Bender & Company Incorporated
Publication dates: 1st Ed.
All Rights Reserved. Printed in United States of America.
No copyright is claimed in the text of statutes, regulations, and excerpts from court opinions quoted within this work. Permission to copy material exceeding fair use, 17 U.S.C. § 107, may be licensed for a fee of $1 per page per copy from the Copyright Clearance Center, 222 Rosewood Drive, Danvers, MA 01923, telephone (978) 750-8400.

Library of Congress Catalogue Number 99–30679
ISBN 0–8205–4132–X

MATTHEW BENDER & CO., INC.
Editorial Offices
Two Park Avenue, New York, NY 10016-5675 (212) 448-2000
201 Mission Street, San Francisco, CA 94105-1831 (415) 908-3200

Statement on Fair Use

Matthew Bender recognizes the balance that must be achieved between the operation of the fair use doctrine, whose basis is to avoid the rigid application of the copyright statute, and the protection of the creative rights and economic interests of authors, publishers and other copyright holders.

We are also aware of the countervailing forces that exist between the ever greater technological advances for making both print and electronic copies and the reduction in the value of copyrighted works that must result from a consistent and pervasive reliance on these new copying technologies. It is Matthew Bender's position that if the "progress of science and useful arts" is promoted by granting copyright protection to authors, such progress may well be impeded if copyright protection is diminished in the name of fair use. (See *Nimmer on Copyright* § 13.05[E][1].) This holds true whether the parameters of the fair use doctrine are considered in either the print or the electronic environment as it is the integrity of the copyright that is at issue, not the media under which the protected work may become available. Therefore, the fair use guidelines we propose apply equally to our print and electronic information, and apply, within §§ 107 and 108 of the Copyright Act, regardless of the professional status of the user.

Our draft guidelines would allow for the copying of limited materials, which would include synopses and tables of contents, primary source and government materials that may have a minimal amount of editorial enhancements, individual forms to aid in the drafting of applications and pleadings, and miscellaneous pages from any of our newsletters, treatises and practice guides. This copying would be permitted provided it is performed for internal use and solely for the purpose of facilitating individual research or for creating documents produced in the course of the user's professional practice, and the original from which the copy is made has been purchased or licensed as part of the user's existing in-house collection.

Matthew Bender fully supports educational awareness programs designed to increase the public's recognition of its fair use rights. We also support the operation of collective licensing organizations with regard to our print and electronic information.

TABLE OF CONTENTS

CHAPTER 7. EXCEPTIONS TO THE HEARSAY RULE: PRELIMINARY MATTERS . . 69

CHAPTER 8. RULE 803: THE "DECLARANT AVAILABILITY IMMATERIAL" EXCEPTIONS 73

PREFACE

"I've already spent 40 or 50 dollars on a casebook and separate rules pamphlet. There are hornbooks and manuals that cover all of evidence. Why should I buy a book that only deals with hearsay?"

Good question. Here are my answers:

1. Hearsay is an important subject. It is a major component of your evidence course; it is one of those subjects that every lawyer should understand.

2. Hearsay is one of the more difficult bodies of law you will encounter in law school. The basic concept is a tricky one; once you've mastered that, you have to deal with dozens of technical exceptions, written and unwritten.

3. This book will help you learn it.

Let me expand a little on each of these reasons.

1. Hearsay is an important subject.

Hearsay pervades everything a lawyer does in a courtroom; it is impossible to try even the simplest case without encountering it. The leading evidence casebooks devote anywhere from 20–40 percent of their length to the hearsay rule and its exceptions; professors spend an equivalent percentage of classroom time covering the subject.

2. Hearsay is a difficult subject.

The hearsay rule itself is simple enough: "Hearsay is not admissible except as otherwise provided by law." But that is the only thing about the rule that is simple.

The legal profession has struggled for more than a century just to come up with a basic *definition* of hearsay. (Look up *Wright v. Tatham* in your casebook.) Even though hearsay is now defined by statute—thank goodness for the Federal Rules of Evidence!—there are numerous "unwritten exceptions" to the definition, as well as eight statutory exceptions to the definition, each of which creates a category of evidence that fits the definition (or appears to), but is classified as *non*-hearsay. In addition, there are 29 statutory exceptions to the hearsay rule,[1] each of which creates a category of evidence that is hearsay but is nevertheless admissible over a hearsay objection. Each of these statutory exceptions has its own requirements, procedural wrinkles, legislative history, and judicial gloss.

To learn this body of law and apply it correctly is a major challenge. Suppose, for example, I want to call W, a witness who will testify, "On March 1, X said to me, 'I'm going out with Frank tonight.'" Under some circumstances, what X said to W is not hearsay; under some circumstances it fits the basic definition of hearsay but is not hearsay because what X said fits within an exception to the hearsay definition; under other circumstances what X said is hearsay, but fits within an exception to the hearsay rule; in still other circumstances, it is hearsay and does not fit within any exception; and yet in other circumstances, it is hearsay but judges disagree as to whether it fits within an exception to the hearsay rule.

---

[1] There are 23 exceptions codified in Fed. R. Evid. 803, five exceptions in Fed. R. Evid. 804, and a "residual" exception in Fed. R. Evid. 807.

Additional complicating factors include constitutional considerations (in particular, the Fifth Amendment privilege against self-incrimination, and the Sixth Amendment Confrontation Clause), as well as the concept of multiple hearsay.

To repeat the basic point: hearsay is a difficult subject.

3. This book will help you learn it.

This book will help you learn hearsay because it breaks down each element of the hearsay definition, and each exception to the definition or to the rule, into its component parts. For example, for each hearsay exception, this book:

- Outlines the policies underlying the provision

- Lists and explains the requirements that must be satisfied for the evidence to fit within the exception

- Explains additional issues that have arisen or are likely to arise

- Explains how a rule interacts with other rules of evidence

- Spells out the procedural and tactical considerations that must be understood to appreciate how the rule "plays" in the courtroom

- Gives review questions and answers so you can test and apply what you've learned[2]

Don't misunderstand: you are not getting a simplified, Classics Illustrated Comics version of hearsay. This book will help you learn hearsay as you want to learn it, to do well on your final, the bar exam, and in practice.

I've been teaching evidence for 20 years, to an average of 60 or so students each year. (Before that, I was a prosecutor in New York City for eight years.) The outlines, explanations, and questions in this book have been tested in the classroom. They have worked for my students; I'm confident they will work for you.

Clifford S. Fishman
The Catholic University of America
Washington, D.C. 20064
1999

---

[2] Along the way, this book also answers other interesting questions, such as, "What do Commander Data, a ham sandwich, the Greek God of wine, the Baltimore Orioles, Leonardo DiCaprio, the speed of sound, and the 'human insect' in *Men in Black* have to do with the hearsay rule?"

(Matthew Bender & Co., Inc.)

ACKNOWLEDGMENTS

I would like to acknowledge, and express my gratitude for, the assistance of The Columbus School of Law of The Catholic University of America. Work on this book was subsidized by a law school summer research grant, student research assistance funds, and that most wonderful of academic fringe benefits, a sabbatical. Thanks also go to Judith Sweeny, Stephanie Michael, Pam Ray, and Michael Pannell for their technical assistance and support. Recognition also is owed to David Stern, David Falk, Patrick Ewing, *et al.*, for making it so much easier this fall (1998) to focus on the job at hand. Finally, I want to thank the hundreds of students over the years whose dedication to learning and to the law has taught me so very much — including, how to teach hearsay.

Clifford S. Fishman
The Catholic University of America
Washington, D.C. 20064
1999

C H A P T E R

1

THE HEARSAY RULE AND ITS RATIONALE

§ 1.01 Rationale Behind the Hearsay Rule: Sometimes Cross-Examination Can Dramatically Reduce the Impact of a Witness's Story

At 2:00 p.m. on February 1, a man wielding a revolver robbed a bank on 10th Street and Metropolitan Avenue. Three months later, on May 1, D was arrested and charged with the robbery. He has retained you to represent him. No one has positively identified your client as the perpetrator; the case against him is based on circumstantial evidence.

On October 1, the trial begins. A jury is selected and the government calls X, Y and Z. Each testifies that he or she was in the bank that afternoon and saw the robbery. Each testifies that the robber wore a three-piece navy blue suit and a ski mask, and stuffed the proceeds of the robbery into a black leather doctor's bag. They testify that D is roughly the same height and build as the robber, but none can identify him as the perpetrator.

Next, the government calls W. After W is sworn, he testifies as follows:

Q. Do you recognize the defendant?

A. Yes, I do.

Q. When did you first meet him?

A. At a party late in January. Someone introduced us, and we talked for a couple of minutes.

Q. Did you see him again sometime thereafter?

A. Yes.

Q. When and where did you see him next?

A. On February 1st, at five minutes after two in the afternoon. It was on Metropolitan Avenue between 8th and 9th Streets.

Q. Describe what happened.

A. I was walking toward 9th and he was walking from the direction of 9th toward 8th. When I saw him, I angled over toward him and stuck out my hand and said, "Hey, man, how're ya doin'?" He looked right at me like he was real upset and then went right by me, without saying a word.

Q. Describe his physical appearance.

A. Well, he was wearing a blue suit and he was carrying a black bag.

Question

Q. 1. Is this testimony relevant? Why?

Ans. If W's testimony is accurate, D was walking downtown (from 9th Street toward 8th Street), away from the scene of the crime (10th Street), a few minutes after the crime was committed. Thus, it is circumstantial evidence that D was at the scene of the crime at the time the crime was committed. Like the robber, D wore a blue suit and carried a black bag. He was in a hurry and seemed upset that W saw (or recognized) him, which permits the inference that D was anxious to leave the area as quickly and unobtrusively as possible.

By itself, this testimony is not enough to convict; still, it is powerful circumstantial evidence that D is the robber—*if* the jury believes W. Each juror began to evaluate W from the moment he walked into the courtroom. They watched him take an oath to tell the truth. They observed his demeanor (eye movement, body language, tone of voice, etc.) as he testified.

A witness's testimony is relevant only if we can make four *"testimonial inferences"* about the witness, relating to perception, memory, narration, and sincerity.

1.   Did the witness accurately *perceive* the events in question?

2.   Has the witness *remembered* the events accurately from that day to this?

3.   Has the witness accurately *narrated* what he or she perceived and remembers (i.e. do the witness's words mean the same to him or her as they do to us?)

4.   Is the witness *sincerely* trying to testify accurately, or is there a reason why the witness might be deliberately lying, or subconsciously shading the truth?

Generally, the best opportunity to assess a witness's sincerity and the accuracy of his or her testimony occurs when the witness is tested by cross-examination. Effective cross-examination might expose weaknesses with respect to any or all of these testimonial inferences. Consider the following cross-examination of W in the robbery case:

Q. What did you say D was wearing when you saw him on the street on February 1?

A. A blue suit.

Q. Three-piece? Two-piece?

A. No, it was one piece. Y'know, with the big zipper up the front?

Q. And he was carrying a bag?

A. Yeah, a black bag. Like if you buy something at a department store, they put it in one of those bags . . .

This testimony exposes problems in narration: when W said "blue suit" and "black bag," he meant something quite different than X, Y and Z meant when they used the same words to describe the robber.

The point is this: there are no guarantees, but sometimes cross-examination can dramatically reduce the impact of W's story.

Now suppose that instead of calling W as a witness, the prosecutor calls Police Officer Y. She is sworn and testifies as follows:

Q. Did anything happen on May 2 that relates to this case?

A. Yes. A man walked into the station house and identified himself as Mr. W. He said, "I read about the guy who was arrested yesterday for bank robbery; I have some information that might be helpful. I first met that guy at a party late in January. Then I saw him again on February 1 at 2:05 p.m. He was coming from the direction of 9th Street toward 8th Street on Metropolitan Avenue, wearing a blue suit and carrying a black bag. When I saw him then, I went up to him and said 'Hey man, how ya doin?' He looked right at me like he was real upset and went right by me without saying a word." That's what Mr. W told me on May 2.

Officer Y is under oath; the jury can watch and hear her testify; and you can cross-examine her to test the accuracy of her perception and memory, examine her choice of words, and probe whether she might have a reason to lie or subconsciously shade the truth. For example, you might ask Y whether

W spoke with an accent which might have interfered with Y's ability to understand (perceive) what W was saying. You might test her memory of what W said by asking when (if at all) she took notes or wrote a memorandum about her conversation with him. Let us assume, though, that Y is an honest, efficient, conscientious officer. She had W write out his statement. Thus, we know precisely what W said to Officer Y, in W's own words. (Perhaps she even had W swear to his statement before a notary.) You proceed, therefore, to ask Officer Y the questions you otherwise would have asked W—designed to test *W's* perception, memory, narration and sincerity—and run into a stone wall, because Y's honest, efficient, conscientious response to virtually every question is, "I don't know."

You have just encountered hearsay. W's statement to Officer Y is hearsay, whether he made his statement orally or in writing, even if it was made in a sworn affidavit.[1]

And you have just encountered the reason for the hearsay rule. W, not Y, is the real source of the information here. Yet, unless *W* comes to court and testifies, it is difficult or impossible to test *W's* perception, memory, narration, or sincerity. This is why the "testimonial inferences" that underlie the relevance of any witness's testimony are often referred to as the *hearsay risks*, because unless W takes the stand and is cross-examined, we run the risk the jury will rely on his testimony without an opportunity to adequately assess whether he perceived accurately, remembered correctly, narrated clearly, and is sincerely trying to tell the truth.

You will encounter the phrases *testimonial inferences* and *hearsay risks* from time to time in this book, in court decisions, and in law review articles and treatises. Both phrases refer to the same thing: perception, memory, narration (sometimes referred to as "communication"), and sincerity.

Since the end of the 17th century, hearsay has been considered such an inherently *untrustworthy* form of evidence that, as a rule, it is not admissible in a trial. W's statement illustrates the primary reasons the law distrusts hearsay evidence:

(1)   The typical hearsay statement was not made under oath.

(2)   The fact-finder does not have the opportunity to observe the demeanor of the person making the statement.

(3)   Most important, the party adversely affected by the hearsay has no opportunity to test, by cross-examination, the perception, memory, narration, and sincerity of the person who made the hearsay statement.

Hence, hearsay is generally not admissible at trial. **Fed. R. Evid. 802** sets forth the hearsay rule:

> **Hearsay is not admissible except as provided by these rules, by other rules prescribed by the Supreme Court pursuant to statutory authority or by Act of Congress.**

§ 1.02   The Federal Rules of Evidence; Legislative History

This book analyzes Article VIII of the Federal Rules of Evidence, and the issues that have arisen or are likely to arise as courts apply the provisions of Article VIII. The Federal Rules of Evidence were enacted into law by Congress in 1975. Since then, the vast majority of the states have enacted or promulgated evidence codes based on the Federal Rules.

Because the Federal Rules are statutory, it is sometimes necessary to refer to the legislative history in analyzing its provisions. Enactment of the Federal Rules of Evidence was the culmination of a lengthy process that began in 1965, when then Chief Justice Earl Warren appointed an Advisory Committee to draft rules of evidence for federal courts. A first draft was issued in 1969; a second draft was issued in 1971. In 1972, Congress decided to deal with the matter by legislation. The Judiciary Committees of the House and Senate each studied and debated the Advisory Committee draft. Some provisions were

---

[1] The major portion of the next chapter is devoted to defining hearsay. If at this point you don't know why W's statement to Officer Y is hearsay, don't panic—we haven't gotten to that yet. For now, just take my word for it.

amended in committee; some were amended on the floor of the House; as to some provisions the House and Senate disagreed, and the dispute was reconciled in a Conference Committee made up of representatives of both houses of Congress. Ultimately, Congress enacted the rules into law, effective January 2, 1975. Since then, Congress has from time to time amended one provision or another. Where necessary, I refer to this legislative history—the Advisory Committee's final draft, the reports of the House and Senate Judiciary Committees, action on the floor of the House, and the decisions of the Conference Committee.

CHAPTER

2

DEFINING AND RECOGNIZING HEARSAY

§ 2.01 Introduction

Knowing that there is a rule against hearsay, students tend to form a mental equation: "Hearsay = inadmissible evidence." This equation is inaccurate. Much evidence that is hearsay is nonetheless admissible, as you will learn in Chapters 3–10. Conversely, much evidence that is not hearsay is inadmissible on a variety of other grounds (e.g. because it is irrelevant or prejudicial) is not properly authenticated, or is excluded by some other rule. As you study these materials and outline your answers to the problems, keep in mind that this chapter does not address whether a particular offer of evidence is admissible. Rather, the focus is on defining and recognizing hearsay.

§ 2.02 The Basic Definition of Hearsay

Fed. R. Evid. 801(c) defines hearsay as follows:

"Hearsay" is a statement, other than one made by the declarant while testifying at the trial or hearing, offered in evidence to prove the truth of the matter asserted.

Thus, the definition has three elements: (1) a "statement"; (2) "other than one made by the declarant while testifying at the trial or hearing"; (3) "offered in evidence to prove the truth of the matter asserted." To avoid missing potential hearsay issues, every offer of evidence should be examined to ascertain whether the evidence fits this definition:

1. Is the evidence a "statement," as that term is defined in Fed. R. Evid. 801(a)?

2. When and where was it made?

3. Why is it being offered?

We will examine each element of the definition in detail. First, however, a brief overview might be helpful.

"Statement" is defined in Fed. R. Evid. 801(a) as "(1) an oral or written assertion, or (2) nonverbal conduct of a person, if it is intended the person as an assertion." The key word in each part of the definition is "assertion." An assertion is something someone says or does in order to communicate a fact or opinion in the hope or expectation that it will be accepted as true or accurate. Obviously, many spoken or written remarks are not "statements" under this definition, because they are not "assertions." A man who turns to a woman as they are slogging along in a January blizzard and says, "I enjoy these sunny summer days," is not asserting, and does not expect the woman to believe, that it is summer, or that the weather is sunny, or that he is enjoying himself.

If words (or conduct) are spoken (or performed) by the declarant (or actor) with the intention of communicating a fact in the hope or expectation that it will be accepted as true, then we have an assertion (i.e. a "statement" as defined in Fed. R. Evid. 801(a)). Otherwise, we do not have a "statement"; and if we do not have a "statement," we do not have hearsay.

The third element of the definition—"offered in evidence to prove the truth of the matter asserted"—requires us to focus on the purpose for which the evidence is offered. Why does the lawyer offering the evidence want the judge or jury to hear it? In other words, why, in the context of this particular lawsuit, is the evidence relevant? For example, suppose it is important to determine when a man and woman first met. She claims it was in January; he claims it wasn't until June. The woman is on the witness stand.

Q. Describe when and how you first met him.

A. It was in the middle of January. I had just gotten off a bus on my way home from work. It was a miserable day—snowing, windy. This man got off right behind me and said, "I enjoy these sunny summer days." I laughed and we struck up an acquaintance.

The woman is quoting the man, but not to prove that what he said was true. The attorney eliciting this testimony isn't trying to prove that it was a sunny summer day. Thus, we do not have to draw the "testimonial inferences" discussed in § 1.01 in order for the *man's* words to have probative value. The hearsay hazards are absent, because we are not relying on *his* perception or memory or choice of words; we are not relying on *his* sincerity. In this particular lawsuit, *what* the man said is not all that important. What *is* important is that he said something (anything) to the woman during a January blizzard, as a result of which they became acquainted. In this lawsuit, his comment to her would have been equally relevant if he had said "Twas brillig and the slithy toves did gyre and gimble in the wabe" (the opening line to "Jabberwocky" in Lewis Carroll's *Alice Through the Looking Glass*). The woman is testifying to the man's remark, *not* to prove the truth of the matter asserted, but simply to prove that the words were said, because in this lawsuit, the mere saying of the words, regardless of whether they were "true," is relevant evidence of a fact of consequence in the lawsuit.[1]

Now consider the second element of the hearsay definition: "other than one made by the declarant while testifying at the trial or hearing."

Assume we are trying a personal injury case involving a collision between a bus and an automobile in a Manhattan intersection. The plaintiff (P), the owner and driver of the automobile, calls a witness, who is sworn and testifies as follows:

Q. What is your name?

A. Winston Smith.

Q. Where do you live?

A. 1984 Orwell Drive, New London, Connecticut, apartment 101.

Q. What is your occupation?

A. I'm a rat exterminator.

Q. Where were you at one o'clock in the afternoon on April 4, 1999?

A. I was at the corner of Broadway and 48th Street in Manhattan.

Q. What was the weather like?

A. Bright and cold.

All of Mr. Smith's answers are "statements," (i.e. they are "assertions"): he claims to be telling the truth, to be communicating accurate information, based on his own knowledge and perception. The attorney eliciting his answers hopes the jury will believe those answers, so Smith's testimony is being

---

1 Needless to say, issues frequently arise as to whether a "statement" is being "offered in evidence to prove the truth of the matter asserted," or whether it is being offered for some other relevant purpose. We will explore these issues in some detail later in this chapter.

(Matthew Bender & Co., Inc.)

offered "to prove the truth of the matter asserted." However, nothing Smith has said so far is hearsay, because Smith is making his statement "while testifying at the trial or hearing." Defendant's attorney can test Smith's perception, memory, choice of words and sincerity by cross-examination. Thus, the hearsay hazards are absent.

P's lawyer continues to examine Smith:

> Q. Did anything unusual occur at that time and place?

> A. Yes. I was looking at a movie poster when I heard a woman shout, "Oh look, the bus is running the red light!" A second later I heard a crash.

Once Smith relates what someone else said, we enter the realm of hearsay. Why does P's attorney want Smith to tell the jury what the woman shouted? "To prove the truth of the matter asserted" (i.e. to prove that the bus ran the red light). Smith is not the source of this information: he has not testified that *he* saw the bus run the light. Rather, the woman is the source of that information. She, not Smith, is the "declarant." She made her statement (assertion of fact) out of court. Her statement is offered to prove the truth of what she asserted. Hence, her statement is hearsay.

Note that her statement poses most of the trustworthiness hazards that make hearsay objectionable.

1.   *Perception*: perhaps the sunlight reflecting off the traffic light made it appear that the bus had a red light when actually it was green.

2.   *Memory* does not seem to be much of a problem here. (It is unlikely that she forgot what she saw in the split second between seeing the event and making her statement.)

3.   *Narration*: perhaps, in the excitement of the moment, she said "bus" when she meant "car."

4.   *Sincerity*: perhaps what she said—or what she thought she saw—was colored by some bias against the bus company.

Since the woman is not on the witness stand, the defendant's attorney cannot cross-examine her about potential lapses in perception or narration or about the possibility of bias. Nor would it do much good to cross-examine Smith about them, because he did not see the accident or what caused it.

§ 2.03   A Note on Vocabulary; Common Abbreviations

The terms we use in discussing and analyzing hearsay problems are quite important. As used in this book, the words "witness," "declarant," "statement," and "testimony" each has a precise definition.

Adverse party is the party against whom the evidence is offered.

Declarant (often abbreviated "DL") is defined in Fed. R. Evid. 801(b) as "a person who makes a statement."

Statement will be used as defined in Fed. R. Evid. 801(a): in essence, words or conduct intended to be an assertion.

Testimony will be used to mean what a witness says while under oath.

Witness (abbreviated as "W1, W2," etc.) will be used to mean a person who has taken the witness stand at the trial or proceeding currently in progress.

In sum, therefore, a "witness" gives "testimony"; a "declarant" is someone who has made an out-of-court "statement."

§ 2.04   "Out-of-Court"

We begin our detailed examination of the definition of hearsay with the second element of the definition, which relates to when and where the statement was made. A commonly used shorthand definition of hearsay is "an *out-of-court* statement offered in evidence to prove the truth of the matter

(Matthew Bender & Co., Inc.)

asserted." The phrase "out-of-court" is adequate to cover most situations, but not all. Hence the wordier, but more accurate, phrase contained in Fed. R. Evid. 801(c): "other than one made by the declarant while testifying at *the* trial or hearing" (emphasis added). The lengthier phrase is necessary, because some "in-court" statements are also hearsay.

Questions

Q. 1. In the bus-auto collision case, assume that Smith testified at a pre-trial deposition as to the positions of the bus and auto in the intersection immediately after the collision, and then repeated this testimony at a trial that ended in a hung jury. Now, with the second trial about to begin, Smith cannot be located.

a. P therefore seeks to introduce into evidence the transcript of the testimony Smith gave at the pre-trial deposition. Is it hearsay?

Ans. Re-read Fed. R. Evid. 801(c). Smith's deposition testimony is hearsay as defined in Rule 801(c), because that testimony was not given at "*the* trial" currently being tried.

b. P next seeks to introduce into evidence the transcript of Smith's testimony at the first trial. Is it hearsay?

Ans. Yes! That testimony was given at an earlier trial of the same case, but it was not given at "*the* trial" currently being tried.

One more aspect of the "out-of-court" element of the definition merits consideration. Again assume we're trying the bus-auto collision case. P calls Ms. Julia Albion as a witness. She testifies that she was on the corner of Broadway and 48th Street at 1 p.m.

Q. And what, if anything, happened?

A. I glanced out into the intersection and I shouted "Oh my gosh, the bus is running the red light!"

The portion of Ms. Albion's testimony in which she quotes herself ("Oh my gosh, the bus is running the red light!") is a statement (i.e. an assertion). P is offering it in evidence to prove the truth of the matter asserted (i.e. to prove that the bus ran the red light). And when Ms. Albion originally made the statement, she was not "testifying at the trial or hearing"; she was on the corner of Broadway and 48th Street. Thus, her prior statement *is* hearsay under Fed. R. Evid. 801(c). Ms. Albion may, of course, testify that she *saw* the bus run the red light; such testimony would not be hearsay. But once she repeats on the witness stand what she *said* on an earlier ("out-of-court") occasion, she is relating hearsay.

To recapitulate: whenever a witness seeks to testify to words that were spoken by anyone (including himself or herself) at any time other than while testifying during the current trial, those words fit the second element of the definition in Fed. R. Evid. 801(c) (and therefore must be classified as hearsay if those words also constitute a statement and are offered in evidence to prove the truth of the matter asserted).

§ 2.05 "Statement"

[1] In General

Fed. R. Evid. 801(a) defines statement as "(1) an oral or written assertion, or (2) nonverbal conduct of a person, if it is intended by the person as an assertion." The Advisory Committee Note on this definition includes the comment: "The effect of the definition of 'statement' is to exclude from the operation of the hearsay rule all evidence of conduct, verbal or nonverbal, not intended as an assertion. The key to the definition is that nothing is an assertion unless intended to be one."

I have divided discussion of this definition into the following: spoken words (both "assertive" and "non-assertive"); written words (both "assertive" and "non-assertive"); conduct (both "assertive" and "non-assertive"); photographs and films; non-human "declarants"; and silence.

[2] Individual Declaration or Narration as a Whole

Cars driven by Falstaff and Fields collided as both were leaving a party hosted by Dion Ysius.[1] Describing the situation a few days later, Falstaff said, "That was quite an ending to quite a party. Ysius kept pouring and wouldn't take no for an answer. I had a couple of scotch sours before dinner, wine with, and a brandy afterward; and you should've seen Fields! He had half a bag on when he got to the party, then he had three martinis before we ate, wine *and* beer during dinner, and two full snifters of brandy afterward. And those cigarettes he was smoking sure looked and smelled funny!"

This might legitimately be considered a single statement—"What went on at Ysius's party." Or it might be considered to be several statements: (1) "Ysius kept pouring"; (2) what Falstaff drank at the party; (3) Fields's condition when he arrived at the party; (4) what Fields drank at the party; (5) what Fields smoked at the party. Which is the proper approach, when deciding the hearsay implications of what Falstaff said?

The answer probably depends upon the particular provision of Article VIII of the Federal Rules being applied. Some provisions within the hearsay definition and some of the hearsay exceptions probably require us to examine each assertion within the narrative.[2] Others may permit an examination of the narrative as a whole.

[3] Assertive Speech

When a person says something it is generally easy to determine whether his utterance is a "statement." Simply look at the words themselves. If they appear to be an assertion of fact (or opinion), they constitute a "statement" under Fed. R. Evid. 801(a), unless unusual circumstances clearly indicate that the declarant did *not* intend them to be an assertion of fact. "I enjoy these sunny summer days" appears to be an assertion of fact until we consider that it was spoken in the middle of a blizzard in January.

[4] Non-assertive Speech; Implied Assertions

Much of what is spoken is not overtly assertive. When a person asks a question, generally the purpose is not to assert, but to obtain, information. "Did the Orioles win today?" "Have you eaten dinner yet?" "Who's at the door?"

Similarly, when a person states a direction or makes a command or request, generally her purpose isn't to assert; it is to direct, order or ask someone to do something. "Place tab A in slot B." "I'll take the red one in a size medium." "Don't forget to pick up my suit at the dry cleaner's."

Utterances are sometimes referred to as "non-assertive verbal conduct." Because they are non-assertive, they are not statements; and because they are not statements, they cannot be hearsay. And this makes sense. If the declarant did not intend to assert anything, we don't have to worry about whether he had some reason to lie or mislead; and this eliminates, or at least minimizes, the "sincerity" hearsay risk discussed in § 1.01.

---

[1] "Falstaff" is a hard-drinking comic character in three of Shakespeare's plays. W.C. Fields was a comic actor who often played hard-drinking characters in numerous movies during the first half of the century. In Greek mythology, Dionysus was the god of fertility and wine. (This cultural note is brought to you by the author free of charge!)

[2] In *Williamson v. United States*, 512 U.S. 594, 600–601 (1994), the Supreme Court held that, when applying the declaration against interest exception (Fed. R. Evid. 804(b)(3)) in certain situations, "statement" meant "a single declaration or remark" (i.e. an individual factual assertion), rather than "overall narrative." (*See* § 9.12.)

Unfortunately, it is not quite that simple, for several reasons. First, human speech is not always clearly divisible into assertions and non-assertions; sometimes people say one thing but mean another. Second, sometimes, even if the declarant really intends to ask a question or make a demand or request, a key fact is so implicit in what she says that, at least according to some courts and scholars, the utterance should be classified as an assertion.

1. Why did the declarant say what he or she said?

If declarant meant his or her words to be an assertion, we have to classify them as such, even though the words themselves seem to be non-assertive.

Sometimes it is easy to tell whether the declarant meant his or her apparently non-assertive words to be an assertion, sometimes not.

(A) After a long and intense romance, F told M that she did not want to see him anymore. This hit M pretty hard, but after awhile, he thought he was getting over it—until he went to a party; and there was F, clinging to her new guy. The next day, M's friend W asked M, "Did it upset you to see F at the party?" M replied, "Does the sun rise in the east?"

Superficially, "Does the run rise in the east?" looks like a question, but here, it is M's way of saying "Yes" (i.e. his way of saying, "I was upset to see F at the party"). If an issue later arises about how M felt on seeing F that night, W's question and M's response would be hearsay.

(B) A father says to his son: (1) "You left your @#$!$^%@*! bicycle in the driveway!"[3] This is a straightforward assertion (i.e. a "statement" per Fed. R. Evid. 801(a)). If this utterance is later offered at a trial to prove where the bicycle was at the time, it is hearsay.

Suppose instead the father says: (2) "How many times have I told you not to leave your @#$!$^%@*! bicycle in the driveway?" Superficially, this appears to be a question, but anyone who has ever been a parent—or a child—knows that the father intends to assert to his son that the bicycle is in the driveway. So this "question" is really an assertion, hence a statement.

Suppose instead the father says: (3) "Get your #$!$^%@*! bicycle out of the driveway!" Here, you could argue that the father doesn't intend to assert that the bike is in the driveway; he's just telling his son to move it. But that is a pretty lame argument, because the assertion that the bike is in the driveway is so clearly implicit in the father's demand. As a practical matter, there is no real difference between (1), (2) and (3); so there is no logical reason why the law of hearsay should treat them differently.

2. "Implied assertions."

If your professor never mentions the phrase "implied assertion," skip the rest of this section, and consider giving her an extra point when course evaluation time comes around. But many professors, and more than a few courts, have spent a great deal of time debating "implied assertions"; it is a difficult issue, and how a court treats it can make the difference between admitting and excluding evidence.

We saw in the third bicycle example that some assertions are so implicit in what the declarant says that as a practical matter, we should treat the utterance as an assertion. On the other hand, you could make a logical argument that virtually every utterance contains implicit assertions. Consider the questions, directions, commands and requests I used as examples at the beginning of this section.

(1) "Did the Orioles win today?" Implicit in this question is the assertion that the declarant believes that the Orioles played today, and perhaps also that the declarant is an Oriole fan.

(2) "Have you eaten dinner yet?" Here the implied assertion is that it is more-or-less dinner time.

(3) "Who's at the door?" This implies, first, that there is a door, and second, that someone is at it, or, at least, that the declarant heard or saw something to make him think that someone was at it.

---

[3] In the previous sentence, "@#$!$^%@*!" might mean "Schwinn" or "Cannondale" or "Trek." But I doubt it!

(4) "Place tab A in slot B." This implies that tab A exists, and that slot B exists, and that tab A will fit into slot B.

(5) "I'll take the red one in a size medium." This implies that the declarant, or someone she is shopping for, likes red and wears size medium.

(6) "Don't forget to pick up my suit at the dry cleaner's." This implies that DL owns a suit, that the suit is at a dry cleaner's, and that the person to whom DL is speaking knows which dry cleaner DL is referring to.

You may be thinking, "Some of these examples are a real stretch." Yes, they are; and that is precisely the point: if the "implied assertion" concept is taken too far, virtually every utterance could be called an assertion, which would vastly expand the impact of the hearsay rule.

So why the fuss? Because sometimes the hearsay risks *may* be significant even where the declarant does not intend to assert anything. Suppose an issue at trial is whether X came to the door of a particular home at 3 p.m., listened for a few seconds, and then left without ringing or knocking. W will testify that DL, her grandson, got home from school shortly before 3 p.m. She asked him, "How was school today?" Before he could reply, the phone rang, and she answered it. A few seconds later, she heard DL call out, "Who's at the door?" This is relevant to show that someone was at the door,[4] but only if we overlook the hearsay risks of perception and narration. Perception: we have to accept that DL saw or heard something which did in fact indicate someone was at the door—that he didn't misinterpret the sound of a lawnmower from across the street, or a shadow caused by a cloud briefly covering up the sun. Narration: we also have to accept that DL said what he meant to say; that he didn't really mean to ask W, "Who's on the phone?" And of course there is always the possibility that DL made up the whole thing, for reasons we cannot guess (but which a skillful attorney might discover on cross-examination).

Courts and professors have suggested numerous approaches to the "implied assertion" question.

(1) Reject the idea altogether, applying the hearsay definition rigidly and literally.

(2) Place the emphasis on what the declarant intended: regardless of the form her words took, classify what she said as an assertion if that is what she probably intended. But if she did not intend to assert anything, it is not hearsay.

(3) Place the emphasis on the hearsay risks: if the relevance of the statement depends heavily on the declarant's perception, memory and narration, classify the utterance as an assertion even if the declarant did not intend to assert anything.

Needless to say, there are variations and spinoffs within these basic approaches.

Which is the "right" approach? Whichever one your evidence professor likes best, of course. In the absence of a clear preference from your professor, I would suggest the second approach, which emphasizes the declarant's intent. If the words look like an assertion, they are, unless the party arguing that the utterance is not hearsay can convince the judge that no assertion was intended. If the utterance does not look like an assertion, then it isn't, unless the party arguing that the utterance is hearsay can convince the judge that the declarant intended his utterance to be an assertion.

We will return to the "implied assertion" doctrine later, when we look at the third element of the hearsay definition, "offered to prove the truth of the matter asserted."

Questions

Q. 2. Which of the following are "statements" as defined in Fed. R. Evid. 801(a)?

---

[4] Even if DL said nothing to suggest that the person at the door was X, DL's utterance is relevant to show that *someone* came to the door; and if other witnesses testify that X was the only person who was walking on that block around 3 p.m., their testimony, plus X's statement, adds up to circumstantial evidence that X in fact came to the door.

(Matthew Bender & Co., Inc.)

Statement 1: "I'm looking for John Henry."

Ans. This is a statement.

Statement 2: "I'm looking for John Henry. Does anybody know where he is?"

Ans. The first sentence is an assertion, hence a statement. While the second sentence is not, it's so closely linked with the first that a judge is likely to consider the entire utterance as a unit.

Statement 3: "If you see John Henry, tell him I'm looking for him."

Ans. This is a directive but contains an assertion ("I'm looking for him") within it, and probably the assertive character predominates.

Statement 4: "Has anyone seen John Henry?"

Ans. This is not an overt assertion (unless DL said it in response to a question, "Who are you looking for?"). Whether it is an implied assertion that DL is looking for John Henry depends on your professor's position on implied assertions.

Q. 3. Police officers are searching X's apartment for drugs. The phone rings, and PO1 answers.

Caller: Is X there?

PO1: He's busy. What's up?

Caller: This is Freddy Big Hat. Tell X I want two ounces for tonight.

PO1: You got em.

Is Freddy's directive, "Tell X I want two ounces for tonight," hearsay, if offered to suggest that X in fact sold drugs from his apartment?

Ans. Most courts classify a call like this as a non-assertion and therefore not hearsay. Freddy's main purpose in making the call was to place an order, not to assert anything, so if we take the "declarant's intent" approach to implied assertions, Freddy's call is not an assertion that X sells drugs. But if we take a "hearsay risk" approach, X's lawyer can argue that the evidence is relevant only if we rely on Freddy's memory (i.e. that he accurately remembered who he could buy cocaine from, and what that person's phone number was, and that he correctly dialed that number).

[5] The Written Word

Return to the collision between the bus and the auto in § 2.01. It just so happened that 25 out-of-town clergy were at the intersection that afternoon with their host, Rev. A. All except Rev. A saw the accident. Each immediately wrote down a description of what he or she saw (i.e. that the bus had run the light and collided with the car), signed it, and handed it to Rev. A. Unfortunately, by the time the case comes to trial, only Rev. A is still in New York.

Questions

Q. 4. Rather than incur the expense of bringing clergypersons B–Z back from the states and countries to which they have returned, P's attorney decides to offer the written accident descriptions into evidence.

a. What must P's attorney do before offering the descriptions in evidence? How should he go about doing so?

Ans. P's attorney has to authenticate the descriptions. See Article IX of the Federal Rules of Evidence.

b. Are the written descriptions statements?

Ans. The witnesses wrote the accident descriptions with the intent of asserting what they saw. Therefore, they are "statements."

c. Re-examine Fed. R. Evid. 801(c). Are the statements hearsay?

Ans. The statements were made (written) out-of-court. P's attorney is offering them in evidence in the hopes that the jury will accept them as true (i.e. "to prove the truth of the matter asserted"). Yes, they are hearsay.

Note that these statements don't present significant hearsay risks. It's highly unlikely that all 25 witnesses would misperceive, misremember or misdescribe who had the red light; it's even less likely that they would deliberately lie about what they saw. Nevertheless the statements are hearsay, because they fit the definition.

This does *not* necessarily mean they will be excluded; it *does* mean that to secure their admission over a hearsay objection, P will have to find a provision within Fed. R. Evid. 801(d) (exceptions to the hearsay definition) or Rules 803, 804 or 807 (exceptions to the hearsay rule) in order to overcome a hearsay objection.

Written words may be assertive or non-assertive just as spoken words may be assertive or non-assertive. "Has anyone seen John Henry?" is presumptively non-assertive whether it is spoken or written.

[6]   Assertive and Non-assertive Conduct

Recall the bus-auto collision. A minute after the collision, a police officer rushes to the scene. He calls out to the bystanders, "What happened?" Six or eight people immediately respond, "We saw it all. The bus ran the light!" At trial, P's lawyer calls the officer to the stand, and seeks to have him testify as to what the bystanders said. Is this hearsay?

Of course. The bystanders made out-of-court "statements"—assertions of fact. P is now offering those statements into evidence, through the police officer, to prove that what the bystanders asserted was true (i.e. to prove the bus ran the light). Hence, hearsay.

Change the facts slightly. By coincidence, the bystanders are all law students who have just begun to study hearsay. They don't want to get involved but they want to see that justice is done.

Q. Tell us, officer, what happened when you arrived on the scene?

A. There was a bunch of people standing there, and I asked them, "Did any of you see what happened?" Nobody said a word, but they all nodded their heads. Then I asked, "Did one of them run the light?" They all nodded again, and then they all walked over and pointed to the bus.

Defense counsel objects to this testimony as hearsay. P's lawyer responds that it can't be hearsay, because none of the bystanders said anything. Ruling?

Rule 801(a)(2) provides: "A statement is . . . (2) nonverbal conduct of a person, if it is intended by the person as an assertion." The corresponding Advisory Committee Note comments, "The key to the definition is that nothing is an assertion *unless intended to be one.*" Why (with what intent) did the bystanders nod their heads and, a few seconds later, point to the bus? To answer the officer's questions (i.e. to assert that they saw the bus run a red light and collide with the car). Nodding and pointing, in these circumstances, constituted *assertive conduct*, because the actors intended that conduct to be an assertion of fact. Thus, their conduct constituted out-of-court statements, which plaintiff is offering in evidence to prove the truth of the matter asserted. Hence, the nodding and pointing are hearsay.

In deciding whether conduct was intended to be assertive, the key factor is common sense. What's the *most probable* reason the actor did what he or she did? If the answer is, "To communicate or assert information," then the conduct is considered assertive and, therefore, a statement. If the answer is anything else, the conduct is considered nonassertive and, therefore, not hearsay. In doubtful and ambiguous situations, the law assumes that no intent to assert existed.

Questions

Q. 5. An important issue in a lawsuit is whether it was raining at 1 p.m. on a particular afternoon. W1 testifies that she looked out of her office window on the seventh floor at that time and noticed that many pedestrians on the sidewalk below were holding open umbrellas over their heads.

a. How is this relevant?

Ans. When people hold open umbrellas over their heads, they generally do it to keep from getting wet. Therefore, we can logically conclude that it was raining.

b. The adversely affected party objects, on the ground that the pedestrians' behavior constituted assertive conduct (i.e., hearsay). How should the judge rule?

Ans. When people hold open umbrellas over their heads, they generally do it to keep from getting wet in the rain. They are not trying to communicate anything; they're just trying to stay dry. Since they did not intend to assert anything, there's no "statement," and therefore, no hearsay.

c. In the same lawsuit, W2 takes the stand, and testifies: "A friend and I were on our way out of the office building at one o'clock. He got to the door first and I asked him whether it was raining. He turned to me, pointed to his umbrella, and opened it." Objection: hearsay, on the ground that W2's friend's behavior constituted assertive conduct. Ruling?

Ans. W2's friend opened the umbrella and pointed as a dramatic way of telling W2 about the weather. This was an "assertion." Objection sustained.

Q. 6. Return to the bus-auto collision suit. Plaintiffs call W3, who testifies, "I was standing near the intersection of Broadway and 48th at about 1 p.m., and noticed a young woman pushing a baby carriage on the sidewalk by the curb. She glanced in the direction of the light and started to push the carriage into the intersection. Suddenly I saw this bus barreling right at her—if P's car hadn't pulled into the intersection going the same direction as the woman, the bus would've knocked her all the way to Times Square.[5] Instead, the bus broadsided the car."

a. How is this relevant?

Ans. We don't *know*, for certain, why this woman was pushing a baby carriage at the intersection of Broadway and 48th that afternoon. Maybe her ex-boyfriend's suits were in the carriage, and she was wheeling them to the nearest trash bin. And maybe she was so spaced out on drugs that she couldn't even *see* the traffic light, let alone tell whether it was red or green. Or maybe she deliberately crossed against the light because she was attempting to kill herself. Anything is possible (particularly within a few blocks of Times Square).

Common sense and experience tell us, though, that the most likely explanation for her conduct is that she had a baby in the carriage. If so, it's unlikely she would expose the baby to unnecessary danger. She didn't step into the street until after she glanced at the light. Logically, therefore, she must have been satisfied that the light was in her favor. If all this is true, then since she was going in the same direction that P was, if she had the green light, so did P.

b. Defendant objects on the ground that the woman's conduct was hearsay. Ruling?

Ans. What was her intent when she (and the carriage) left the sidewalk? Why did the woman cross the road? The most likely reason is, "to get to the other side." She didn't intend to assert anything, she just wanted to cross 48th Street. Hence, no assertion; no hearsay.

Q. 7. During a murder investigation, Detective W went to S's home and asked Mrs. S to give him the clothing her husband, the prime suspect, had been wearing on the day of the homicide. She handed the officer a knit shirt. At trial, the prosecutor seeks to have W testify about this event and then offer the shirt into evidence. (Once it is admitted, she will call T, a lab technician, who will testify that the shirt contained a blood stain matching the victim's blood type.)

---

5 Times Square is located at Broadway and 42nd Street, six blocks south of Broadway and 48th.

a. D objects that W's testimony consists of hearsay. Ruling?

Ans. Objection sustained in part. When Mrs. S handed the shirt to W, she was answering W's question, asserting, in essence, "This is the shirt my husband wore that day." This assertive conduct occurred out of court and is offered to prove the truth of the matter asserted.

b. What should the prosecutor do at this point?

Ans. She has two options. First, she can call Mrs. S as a witness, and ask her if she recognizes the knit shirt as the one her husband had worn the day of the crime. This may not work, though. Mrs. S may assert a spouse's privilege not to testify against her husband (*see* Fed. R. Evid. Art. V); or she may no longer remember which shirt her husband had worn.

The second option is to have Detective W testify, "On such and such a date I went to S's home and obtained this shirt from the premises." This involves no hearsay, because it contains no assertion, by Mrs. S or anyone else, that S had been wearing the shirt on the day of the homicide. Ultimately, after T testifies, the prosecutor will argue that W's and T's testimony, taken together, constitute circumstantial evidence that S committed the murder (while wearing that shirt); still, in this sanitized version, no hearsay problems arise.

To repeat: to determine whether a person's conduct was assertive, so as to constitute a "statement" within Fed. R. Evid. 801(a)(2), we must discern the intent with which she acted, keeping in mind (as the Advisory Committee emphasizes) that "[t]he rule is so worded as to place the burden upon the party claiming that the intention existed; ambiguous and doubtful cases will be resolved against him and in favor of [classifying the conduct as non-assertive and therefore non-hearsay]."

[7] Photographs, Films, Videotape

X lives in a third-story apartment across the street from the bank on 10th Street and Metropolitan Avenue. At 2:00 on February 1, he sees a man wearing a three-piece blue suit and a ski mask run out of the bank, glance quickly up and down the street, remove the mask, stuff it quickly into a black leather doctor's bag, and walk hurriedly away. D is later charged with the robbery. If X testifies as to what he saw, describes the man's facial features, and identifies D as the man he saw that afternoon, no hearsay is involved, because all of his statements about the event are being made in court, on the witness stand.

Now suppose instead X happened to be holding a 35mm camera with a telephoto lens that day, and managed to snap several shots of the man before and after he removed the mask. At trial, X testifies as to when and how he took the photographs, which are then offered into evidence. Just as in the previous paragraph, none of this involves hearsay. When X took the photographs, he wasn't "stating" anything; he merely preserved on film what he saw when he looked through the camera. As far as the law of evidence is concerned, the photos are simply another way for X to say, "Here's what I saw that day."

As a rule, therefore, a photograph, movie, videotape, etc. is not a "statement" (except perhaps in an artistic sense). It's simply the end-product of a series of chemical processes that begin when film is exposed to light through a camera. If it would not be hearsay for a witness to take the stand and describe a certain scene or certain events, it would not be hearsay for that witness to take the stand and testify, "This is a photograph (movie, videotape) of what I saw that day."

If, on the other hand, the actions or scene portrayed in the photo, videotape, etc. were posed or staged with the primary purpose of demonstrating or communicating something, then we have a film of assertive conduct. Testimony describing assertive conduct raises hearsay problems; a film of that same conduct raises the exact same hearsay problems.

Questions

Q. 8. The day after he took the photographs, X read in the newspaper about the bank robbery, notified the police, gave the photographs to Detective Y, and explained when and how he took them.

A trial, the prosecutor calls Y to the stand. If permitted, Y will testify, "X told me he took these photographs at 2 p.m. on February 1 from his apartment across the street from the bank." D objects: hearsay. Ruling?

Ans. Objection sustained. The photographs aren't hearsay, but X's statement to Y is hearsay.

Q. 9. The bank had an automatic camera that videotaped the robbery. At trial the prosecutor calls a bank official who testifies how the camera works, then offers the videotape in evidence. D objects: hearsay. Ruling?

Ans. Objection overruled. In deciding whether the videotape is hearsay, we *don't* ask, "why was the videotape made"; we ask, "why did the people whose actions were captured on film do what they were doing at the time?" When the robber pointed a gun at a teller and demanded money, his purpose wasn't to make assertions, it was to commit robbery. Thus, the videotape is not hearsay even though it was *made* for the sole purpose of using it as evidence at a trial.

Q. 10. P claims she was injured in an industrial accident, and sues for damages, claiming that as a result of nerve damage, there is a constant tremor in her hands. At trial, to help illustrate the extent of her injuries, she testifies that her attorney hired C, a photographer, to come to her house and videotape her as she went through her normal daily routine. P testifies that nothing was pre-arranged or rehearsed; when C arrived, she simply began filming P's activities. C testifies likewise.

The videotape shows P washing her face, brushing her teeth, pouring cereal and milk into a bowl, eating it. Because of the constant shaking in her hands, she has considerable difficulty doing each of these things. Then she turns to the camera and says, "Let me show you what happens when I try to put on lipstick." She walks to the bathroom and does so; the result is a garish smear. She wipes the lipstick off, walks into the living room, and, with difficulty, manages to put a compact disk into the player and push the play button.

Defendant objects that the videotape is hearsay. Ruling?

Ans. Objection sustained in part. The key question is not why the videotape was made; rather, we have to consider why P did the things she did that were captured on film. Presumably she washed her face, brushed her teeth, ate breakfast and listened to music for their own sakes: to be clean, to prevent tooth decay, to provide the body with sustenance and to sooth the soul (or to annoy her parents, depending on her age and the kind of music). As to these acts, therefore, the objection should be overruled.

But the objection should be sustained with regard to the lipstick, because that episode was a conscious "performance": "let me show you. . . ."

You may be wondering: how do we know that P wasn't faking, or exaggerating, the extent of her disability when she did the other things? We don't; but the jury will be able to view the videotape (except the lipstick episode) and watch P on the stand, and will be able to form a judgment about whether she was exaggerating.

[8] Silence

Courts must occasionally determine whether silence should be considered hearsay. The situation most often arises when, in defending against an allegation that plaintiff's injury was caused by a defect or unsafe condition in defendant's product or premises, defendant seeks to testify that no previous customers had complained about that product or premises. For such testimony to be relevant, the fact finder must infer that because no previous customers complained, they must have perceived nothing about which to complain, and that therefore the product or premises was indeed safe. Because these inferences depend upon the perception of the previous customers and their perception cannot be tested at trial by cross-examination, prior to enactment of the Federal Rules of Evidence some courts categorized such testimony about an absence of complaints as hearsay.

(Matthew Bender & Co., Inc.)

Fed. R. Evid. 801 rejects this approach. Silence is usually ambiguous at best; and, as we have already seen, "ambiguous and doubtful cases will be resolved against [inferring an intent to assert.]"[6] Thus, testimony that prior to P's injury no one had complained about unsafe conditions on D's premises is not hearsay. A trial judge nevertheless has discretion to exclude such evidence, because a lack of complaints may be so ambiguous that it is not very probative as to whether D's premises was safe.

Under Fed. R. Evid. 801, a person's silence cannot be considered hearsay unless we can conclude that by remaining silent, she intended to assert something. Suppose, for example, M asks F to join him that night for dinner. F responds, "Thank you, but I may have to ask for a rain check; I may have to go out of town this afternoon on business. If you don't hear from me by 4 p.m., you'll know I had to catch a flight for Cleveland." In this unusual situation, F has in effect told M that he should interpret her silence as communicating a particular fact.

[9] Non-Human "Declarants"

Fed. R. Evid. 801(b) defines "declarant" as "a person who makes a statement." Thus, animals and inanimate objects (radar guns, thermometers, etc.) cannot be "declarants," and the things they "tell" us cannot be hearsay. Similarly, a computer is not a "declarant,"[7] and information produced by the internal operations of a computer program, such as long distance telephone records, is not hearsay. (But assertions written by human beings and stored in a computer are, of course, statements.)

§ 2.06 "Offered to Prove the Truth of the Matter Asserted"

The third element of the definition of hearsay is that the statement is "offered in evidence to prove the truth of the matter asserted." To determine whether an out-of-court statement is hearsay requires a two-step process.

1. Determine what the declarant intended to assert, and whether, if at all, we should apply the "implied assertion" doctrine beyond what the declarant intended to assert.

2. Determine why the lawyer who is offering the evidence wants the judge or jury to hear it (i.e. why the statement is relevant to the lawsuit being tried).

1. What the declarant intended to assert.

As we saw in § 2.05[4], sometimes it is necessary to look behind the words that DL spoke to discern what she really meant. Obviously there are limits: an attorney cannot simply "rewrite" a declarant's words whenever it suits her. But in applying the term "the matter asserted," we are not required to ignore the way people actually speak. If L says Leonardo DiCaprio is good looking and R responds, "You ain't just whistling Dixie," everyone understands that R isn't really commenting on L's taste in music; she is agreeing with L's assessment of Mr. DiCaprio's physiognomy. Similarly, if a key issue at trial is whether a car driven by X was speeding, consider declarant's statement, "X just about broke the sound barrier." This statement is not being offered to prove that X was driving at roughly 750 miles per hour, the approximate speed of sound;[1] it is being offered as evidence that X was driving dangerously fast given traffic and road conditions. To categorize the statement as non-hearsay is absurd. It is perfectly consistent with the definition of hearsay to categorize the declarant's statement as such; we need only realize that the declarant was merely choosing a somewhat exaggerated and colorful way of saying "X was driving much too fast."

---

[6] Fed. R. Evid. 801(a) (advisory committee's note).

[7] I leave for future generations of evidence scholars how this rule might apply to advanced androids such as Star Trek's Commander Data (*see*, perhaps, the 23d edition of this Student Guide).

[1] Sound travels at 1,090 feet per second, give or take a few feet depending upon atmospheric pressure, air temperature, and a few other variables. This translates to roughly 750 mph.

2. Why the statement is being offered.

If the out-of-court statement is relevant only if the trier of fact accepts that statement as both truthful and accurate, then it is hearsay. On the other hand, if the out-of-court statement is relevant regardless of whether the trier of fact believes that the out-of-court declarant spoke truthfully and accurately, then the out-of-court statement is *not* hearsay.

Another way of putting it, which has proven helpful to some students, is the following: an out-of-court statement is hearsay if it is offered in evidence to prove that *the words inside the quotation marks are true*. In the blizzard case (*see* § 2.01), an important issue is what time of year a man and woman first met. The woman is asked to describe when and how she first met the man. She testifies:

It was in the middle of January. I had just gotten off a bus on my way home from work. It was a miserable day—snowing, windy. This man got off right behind me and said, "I enjoy these sunny summer days." I laughed and we struck up an acquaintance.

Is the man's statement, "I enjoy these sunny summer days," relevant only if the fact-finder believes that the man (the declarant) was telling the truth? In other words, is the attorney offering this evidence to prove that what's inside the quotation marks is true? Obviously not. Hence, the man's statement to the woman is not hearsay.[2]

Questions

Q. 11. In the bus-auto collision case, the key issue is which vehicle ran the light. Plaintiff has called Winston Smith as a witness, and Smith has testified that he was on the corner of Broadway and 48th Street at 1 p.m. on the day in question. Direct examination continues:

Q. Did anything unusual occur at that time and place?

A. Yes. I was looking at a movie poster when I heard a woman shout, "Oh my gosh, the bus is running the red light!"

Is the woman's statement relevant only if the fact-finder believes that she (the declarant) was telling the truth? Is plaintiffs' attorney offering this evidence to prove that what's inside the quotation marks is true?

Ans. Yes. Unless the judge or jury believes the woman's statement, what she said is irrelevant. Her statement is being offered to prove the truth of the matter asserted; hence, it is hearsay.

Q. 12. A witness reported to police that two men robbed him at gunpoint. A few days later, police arrested D1 and charged him with being one of the perpetrators. Now D2 is on trial for being the other robber. At D2's trial, W will testify that a few days after D1 made bail, D1 came upon D2 and W and that D1 said to D2, "Don't worry, I didn't tell the police about you."

D2 objects that this is hearsay. The prosecutor responds that it's not hearsay because she is not offering it to prove "the truth of the matter asserted" (i.e. she is not offering it to prove that D1 did not tell the police about D2). Ruling?

Ans. To decide whether D1's statement is hearsay, apply the two-step analysis:

First, what did D1 mean when he told D2, "I didn't tell the police about you?"

D1 could have meant lots of things. He could have meant, "I didn't tell the police that you were the guy who hacked into the Defense Department's computer and inserted obscene cartoons on all their web sites." He could have meant, "I didn't tell the police you were the guy who put crazy

---

[2] But wait a minute, you might be thinking. When the man said to the woman, "I love these sunny summer days," wasn't he really asserting, "I hate this lousy weather"? Well, maybe. Or maybe he was asserting, "I am powerfully attracted to you and I hope this remark will impress you with what a clever, witty guy I am, so you'll say something back, and we'll introduce ourselves, and go have a cup of coffee and one thing will lead to another and who knows where it all might end?" But most likely he just felt like saying something he thought was mildly amusing, without any particular assertive intent in mind.

glue on Mrs. McIntyre's chair in third grade." He could have meant, "I didn't tell the police that you were the other guy who pulled the robbery with me." He could have meant any number of things.

Second, why is the prosecutor offering D1's statement at D2's trial? Why is D1's statement relevant at D2's trial?

D1's statement is relevant to prove that D2 was the other robber only if D1 meant, "I didn't tell the police that you were the other guy who pulled the robbery with me." And the prosecutor is offering D1's statement to prove that D2 was the other robber. Therefore, D1's statement is hearsay. Objection sustained.

Sometimes, of course, a witness will not be so considerate as to offset the declarant's out-of-court statement in formal quotation marks. In the bus-car collision case, for example, Smith might have testified: "Yes. I was looking at a movie poster when a woman shouted that a bus had just entered the intersection against the light." To analyze whether the out-of-court statement in this testimony is hearsay, we must mentally reconstruct the testimony and put quotation marks around what the woman said. That makes it is easier to determine why her statement is being offered. Having done so, we can determine whether it is hearsay.

§ 2.07 Categories of Non-Hearsay

[1] In General

Courts often overrule a hearsay objection by "explaining" that "the statement was not hearsay because it was not being offered to prove the truth of the matter asserted, but merely to prove that the words were spoken." Unfortunately, this doesn't really explain why the mere *making* of the statement (regardless of its truth) is relevant. Each out-of-court statement must be analyzed in the context of the particular case being tried, to determine whether it is being offered to prove the truth of the matter asserted in the statement, or for some other purpose.

Some situations involving non-hearsay use of out-of-court statements recur often enough that it is comparatively easy to categorize the statement as non-hearsay. Widely recognized categories of non-hearsay include statements probative of a person's mental state; verbal acts; and verbal parts of acts.

[2] Mental State

[a] Mental State Can Arise in Either of Two Contexts

The mental state with which a person acted is often a crucial issue in a lawsuit. The issue can arise in either of two contexts: mental state as an element of a crime, claim or defense; or relevant facts inferable from someone's state of mind.

[b] Mental State as Element of Crime, Claim, or Defense

Mental state (sometimes referred to in criminal cases as "mens rea" or "scienter") is an element of nearly all crimes, many civil claims, and some defenses. A prosecutor will have to prove, for example, that a defendant acted "willfully," "with malice aforethought," "knowingly," "intentionally," or the like. Similarly, in many civil actions, in order to prevail, a litigant must show that a particular person acted "negligently" or "recklessly" or "with intent to defraud." Quite often a defendant will attempt to prove that she did *not* act with the mental state the prosecutor or plaintiff is attempting to prove; or she might assert an affirmative defense which has its own mental element, such as insanity, duress, or justification (*see* Questions, 17, 18). A statement made by or to someone often provides important evidence from which the fact finder can infer the mental state of the person who made, or who heard, the statement.

Such statements therefore often have evidentiary significance regardless of whether the statement was true.

Thus, applying the third element of the hearsay definition to a statement offered as evidence of someone's mental state requires several preliminary steps.

1. Examine the court opinion, relevant statutes, or evidence problem, to determine:

(a) Whether mental state is a contested element of the crime, cause of action or defense, and if so,

(b) *Whose* mental state, and

(c) How (if at all) the law defines the particular mental state in question.

2. An out-of-court statement made *by or to* that person ("X") must be examined to determine whether it casts light on X's mental state.

3. Analyze whether the statement is relevant even if it was inaccurate or a lie.

If the answer to the final question is yes, then the statement is not hearsay. But if the answer to the final question is no (i.e. if the statement is relevant only if it is accurate), then the statement is being offered for a hearsay purpose, and cannot be admitted unless it fits within some provision of Rule 801(d), 803, 804, or 807, which set out the exceptions to the hearsay definition and hearsay rule.

[c] Relevant Facts Inferable From Someone's State of Mind

Even when mental state is not a contested issue, important facts sometimes can be inferred from a person's state of mind. In this situation, too, words said by or to that person may be relevant even though the statement is not offered to prove the truth of the matter asserted. Assume, for example, that V is found dead—shot, poisoned *and* drowned—circumstances leaving no doubt that this was an intentional killing; the only question is, who did it. Evidence that shortly before V's death, D said, "V is a no-good, lying, scurvy louse. He ruined my business, he convinced my fiancee to dump me, he seduced my daughter and he roots for the Yankees!" Whether or not any of this is true, it is highly relevant to suggest that (in D's mind, at any rate) D had several powerful motives to want to kill V, which makes it more probable than it would be without the evidence that D in fact is the killer.

[3] Declarant's State of Mind

The least complicated situation arises when we need to know the *declarant's* state of mind. Simply look at what DL (declarant) said. A direct statement by DL as to his or her state of mind is hearsay; it is relevant to prove DL's state of mind only if we accept that DL is communicating accurately and sincerely. Generally, such statements contain phrases such as "I like," "I'm bored by," "I understand," "I'm confused by," etc. If, on the other hand, the declarant's state of mind may be inferred indirectly, regardless of whether the statement is true and accurate, then the statement is not hearsay.

Questions

Q. 13. Assume that a key issue in a trial is the extent of F's emotional attachment toward M. W will, if permitted, testify that F said to her: "I'm in love with M." Is this hearsay?

Ans. Yes. It is a direct statement by F about her attitude toward M. It is relevant only if we assume that F was accurately and sincerely describing her feelings.

Q. 14. Suppose instead *W1* will testify that on one occasion, during a discussion among several women about the men they work with, *F* commented that *M* has "a great sense of humor." *W2* will testify that on another occasion, while watching a video of *The Empire Strikes Back*, F commented, "There's a guy at work, *M*, who looks a little like Harrison Ford." *W3* will testify that on a different occasion, when several friends were discussing their bosses, *F* described *M* as "very considerate and supportive." Is this hearsay, if offered to prove F's romantic interest in M?

Ans. None of this testimony would be hearsay, because it would be offered, not to prove that M in fact had these admirable qualities, but that F, correctly or not, *believed* that M had them—from which we can infer that she was very attracted to him. (Indeed, the evidence would be relevant even if, in fact, M could see the point of a joke only by appointment, was a dead ringer for the "human bug" in *Men in Black*, and was totally self-centered.)

And none of these statements would qualify as an "implied assertion" of F's romantic interest in M, because on each occasion, F apparently intended only a casual comment about a man she happened to know.

Q. 15. But now comes W4, who will testify that on another occasion, F, with a dreamy look in her eyes, said, "There's this guy at work, M—he's my boss, actually. He's a dead ringer for Harrison Ford in *Star Wars*, and he's got a great sense of humor, and he's so considerate and supportive. . . ." Is this hearsay, if offered to show her romantic interest in M?

Ans. If we apply the phrase "the matter asserted" in the definition of hearsay literally, this statement still is not hearsay. But this result is silly, because presumably F knew, when she described M in these terms, that W4 would understand that F was really (or also) saying, "This is a guy I could see myself spending the rest of my life with."[1]

[4] To Show Declarant's Knowledge

It is often important to prove, first, that a certain fact is true; and second, that a particular person ("X") had knowledge of that fact. In such a case, if a party can prove the existence of the fact independent of the statement in question, a statement by X demonstrating that X had knowledge of the fact is not hearsay.

Questions

Q. 16. D arranged for his mother to obtain a $25,000 loan, which D co-signed, to purchase a new car, but although bank officials asked about other indebtedness, D did not tell the bank that he and his mother owed $56,000 on a loan from another bank to purchase a motor home. Since D's mother was the primary obligor on the car loan, D was able to arrange an insurance policy on her life at no charge. Less than a month later, D's mother died of cancer; the insurance policy paid for the car, which D inherited free and clear from his mother's estate. D was subsequently indicted for misrepresenting his, and his mother's, indebtedness on the car loan with intent to defraud; the government's theory was that the loan was obtained to cash in on the fact that his mother was dying. As evidence of his knowledge of her condition, the Government called the admitting nurse at the hospital to which D brought his mother only three days after applying for the auto loan. If permitted, the nurse will testify, "D said his mother was kept at home with the family, but apparently she had been doing worse and D felt that she was probably pre-terminal, so we admitted her." D objects that this is hearsay. Ruling?

Ans. Overruled. D's statements to the nurse were not offered to prove the truth of the matter asserted (i.e. were not admitted to prove that his mother *was* pre-terminal). (That had already been proven by evidence that she died less than a month after she obtained the car loan.) The statement was relevant to prove that defendant *knew* his mother would die long before she, or he as co-signer, would have to pay off the auto loan. (Moreover, even if she had *not* been pre-terminal, his statement would be relevant to show that he *believed* she was, which is all the government needs to show intent to defraud.)

---

[1] Or, sadly, the contemporary equivalent: "This is a guy I could see my kids spending every other weekend with."

(Matthew Bender & Co., Inc.)

[5] To Show the Effect on the Hearer

In this situation, the focus is not on the declarant's mental state, but on someone else's ("X"). What DL said to X is not hearsay, if that statement is being offered *solely* to show what effect the statement had on X's mental state, regardless of its truth. (Obviously, before DL's out-of-court statement is admissible to show the effect it had on X, sufficient evidence must establish that X heard or read the statement.)

Questions

Q. 17. D is being tried on an indictment charging that he intentionally and unlawfully shot and killed V on March 1. In her opening statement, D's lawyer told the jury, "The evidence will show that D was legally justified in killing V, because D acted in the reasonable belief that if he didn't use deadly force to defend himself, V would have killed or badly injured D."

a. What must the prosecutor prove to obtain a conviction?

Ans. That D shot V; that he did so intentionally; and that he did so unlawfully.

b. W1, a government witness, testifies that he, D and V all worked in a warehouse for XYZ Co. His testimony continues:

On February 27, just as our shift was ending, V walked up to D and said, "Gimme $500." D said, "Why should I give you $500?" V said, "Cause if you don't, I'm gonna turn you in to the boss for stealin' stuff off the shelves." I walked away real quick, so I didn't hear any more.

Why is V's statement—"Cause if you don't [give me $500], I'm gonna turn you in to the boss for stealin' stuff off the shelves," relevant?

Ans. It suggests that, once D heard V threaten him, D had a *motive* to kill V, to keep V from reporting him to their boss. Showing that D had a motive to kill V makes it more likely that D did so intentionally and without legal justification.

c. Is V's statement hearsay?

Ans. No. The relevance of V's statement depends on the impact it had on D when D heard V say it. So long as D heard it and believed it, it is relevant *even if V never really intended* to report D to their boss. Therefore, V's statement to D is not being offered to prove the truth of what V said to D; the mere fact that it was said is relevant to show D had a motive to kill V.

Q. 18. After the state rests, D takes the stand. First, he denies that the incident W1 testified about ever took place. Next, D testifies that late in February he attended a dance, met a very nice young woman, and danced several times with her:

Q. And then what happened?

A. W2 walked over to me and said, "Don't you know that she is V's girlfriend?" I asked him, "Who is V?" W2 said, "V is a guy it's a good idea to stay away from," and then W2 told me that once he parked his car in front of V's house, and V came running out and told W2 to move the car, that was "his" parking space. W2 said, "I don't see your name on it," and then V said "Yeah, well I got my name on this," and whacked W2 with a baseball bat and broke W2's collarbone.

a. What is the mental element in D's defense?

Ans. That D acted in the *reasonable belief* that he had to use deadly force to protect himself from death or serious injury at V's hands.

b. What is the relevance of D's testimony about what W2 said to him? What does D hope to prove by this testimony?

Ans. What W2 told D about V is relevant on two different theories.

1. If W2's story to D is true, it shows that V was a violent, assaultive person, which supports D's claim (about which he will soon testify) that V in fact would have injured or killed D if D hadn't shot V first.

2. Whether W2's story is true or not, the fact that W2 told it to D is relevant to show that, when D and V had their fatal encounter, D *believed* that V was violent, assaultive, irrational—and angry at D. (Remember, to assert a valid justification defense, all D has to prove is that D acted in the *reasonable belief* that he had to use deadly force to protect his life or health from V (*see* answer to Q. 18a).

   c. The prosecutor objects that what W2 told D is hearsay. Ruling?

Ans. What W2 told D is certainly a statement, and the conversation between W2 and D occurred out of court. Whether it's hearsay depends on why the evidence is offered:

1. If it is offered to prove that V in fact broke W2's collarbone, W2's statement *is* hearsay, because it is offered to prove the truth of the matter asserted by W2 to D.

2. But if it is offered for the *limited* purpose of casting light on D's state of mind (his reasonable fear of V) when he and V encountered each other on March 1, W2's statement to D is *not* hearsay, because even if the collarbone incident never really happened (even if W2 lied to D when he told him the story), a person in D's position, having heard that story, might reasonably fear that V was out to "get" him.

   d. The evidence therefore has a valid nonhearsay purpose, and a tainted, hearsay purpose. How should the judge rule?

Ans. Overrule the objection and admit the evidence; but, if the prosecutor requests, the judge should deliver a limiting instruction (Fed. R. Evid. 105), telling the jury they may consider the evidence in assessing D's state of mind about V on March 1, but may not accept the collarbone story as true, or as evidence of what kind of person V really was.

[6] Verbal Acts

Certain legal acts can be performed only by uttering words. In such situations, even though the words might seem to fit the hearsay definition, the law considers the words to be "verbal acts," and therefore not hearsay.

Forming a contract is a verbal act, because the *only* way two parties can form a contract is with words (i.e. by saying, orally or in writing, "We agree to the following terms . . ."). If a dispute later arises as to whether there was a contract, or as to its terms, the words spelling out the terms of the contract, and the words signifying that the parties agreed, comprise a verbal act, and are not hearsay.[2]

Questions

Q. 19. B files a suit claiming that S contracted to sell him 100,000 midget widgets at $1.00 each, that S failed to deliver, that B had to purchase them at the last minute from someone else at $1.50 each, and that S should therefore be required to compensate B for the $50,000 loss he suffered as a result of S's breach of contract. B takes the stand, testifies to these events, and then identifies

---

[2] You may ask: When L and M sign a contract in which L says "I agree to undertake a particular project for M" and M says "If L performs as per this contract, I will pay L 'X' thousand dollars a year," aren't those *both* assertions? In a sense, they are; but the law treats them differently, because these words have legal significance regardless of whether they are "true." Suppose, for example, after L completes the project, M refuses to pay, saying, "We never really had a contract, because I never intended to pay him; I always intended to stiff L for his fee." Would the law recognize that defense? Of course not. When a person signs his name to a contract (or states his verbal agreement), this creates a binding legal rights and obligations, regardless of whether the signer "intended" to agree.

a piece of paper as the contract that he and S had signed. His attorney offers it in evidence; S's attorney objects that the contract is hearsay. Ruling?

Ans. Objection overruled. The contract is a verbal act; therefore it is not hearsay.

Q. 20. X, a motorist, was insured by the D Insurance Co. On October 1, X went to W, his insurance company's representative, and said, "I want to cancel the policy and receive a refund for the rest of the policy I've paid for." W secured X's signature on the appropriate form and promised X that the check would be in the mail shortly. On October 2, X, driving negligently, caused an accident in which he was killed and P was injured.

P sues X's estate; X's estate impleads D Company, alleging that as X's insurer, D Company is liable. At trial, D Company calls W, who will, if permitted, testify that on October 1, X came to him and said, "I want to cancel," and filled out the appropriate form. Is what X told W hearsay?

Ans. No. Forming a contract is a verbal act; so is canceling a contract. The words X and W uttered canceling the contract therefore are not hearsay.

Other examples of verbal acts include:

1. *Defamation.* To establish a cause of action for defamation, a plaintiff must prove: (1) that the defendant uttered the words in question and communicated them to others; and (2) that defendant's defamatory words damaged plaintiff's reputation.[3] Plaintiff therefore must offer evidence that defendant committed the verbal act of uttering the defamatory words, or suffer a directed verdict. Assume, for example, that P is suing D, alleging that D told X: "P is an ambulance chaser who suborns perjury in every case he tries." When P calls X as a witness to testify that D made that statement, D's statement is not hearsay; obviously, P is not offering D's statement to prove the truth of the matter asserted, but rather, to prove that D committed the verbal act of defaming him.

2. *Oath.* In a prosecution for perjury, the prosecutor must prove: (1) that on some prior occasion X testified under oath; (2) that X gave the testimony in question; (3) that X knew at the time that her testimony was untrue; and (4) that the testimony was "material" (i.e. had some relevance or significance) to the issues that were the subject of the proceeding. To prove the first element of the crime, the prosecutor will probably introduce a transcript of the prior proceeding, in which X was asked, "Do you solemnly swear that the testimony you about to give is the truth," and answered, "I do." This looks like an assertion, but the law treats it differently: once a person takes the oath at a formal proceeding, she takes on a legal obligation to tell the truth, and subjects herself to legal penalties if she breaches that obligation, regardless of whether she "meant it" or not. We are not relying on X's accuracy or sincerity when she said "I do"; as long as she said those words, she performed the verbal act of being under oath.

3. *Fraud.* Where a prosecutor or plaintiff alleges that D committed fraud, uttering the fraudulent words may be considered to be a verbal act.

This does not exhaust the list of situations in which statements constitute verbal acts, but it should be enough to give you the idea.

[7] Verbal Parts of Acts

Litigation sometimes focuses on the legal significance of a physical act. In such cases, a statement made before or during the act, which was intended by the participants to define the act, is considered a verbal part of the act. Even though a statement that is the verbal part of an act may seem to fit the hearsay definition, a verbal part of an act is not considered hearsay because, technically, it is not being offered to prove the truth of the matter asserted; rather, it is offered to prove the legal significance of the act of which it was a verbal part.

---

[3] As a rule, defendant has the burden of pleading and proving the truth of the allegedly defamatory utterance as an affirmative defense.

(Matthew Bender & Co., Inc.)

Questions

Q. 21. Two well-dressed men, X and Y, are sitting in a hotel room. X opens an attache case, removes 50 bundles of currency, and places them on a desk. Each bundle contains 20 $50.00 bills, so the total amount of money is $50,000. After X finishes putting the money on the desk, Y just as methodically takes the money and puts it into his own attache case. Then Y leaves, taking the money with him.

A year or so later, X sues Y for $50,000 plus interest, claiming the money was a loan and that Y failed to repay it. X takes the stand at trial, and testifies:

A few weeks earlier, Y had asked me to lend him $50,000. On the day in question, Y came into my hotel room. I put the money on the desk and said, "I am lending this money to you, as you requested."

Y objects that what X had said to Y is hearsay: it was an of-court statement now being offered in evidence to prove the truth of what was asserted. Ruling?

Ans. Objection overruled. Handing over $50,000 is an act, but unless we know the words which accompanied or shortly preceded the act, we have no way of knowing the legal or factual significance of that act. Was X making a loan to Y, as X now claims; or was it a bribe; or was X paying a gambling debt; or . . . ? The point is, we don't know, unless we know the underlying circumstances including what was said before and during the act, because the words *define* the act.

What X and Y said to one another prior to or at the time of the act, therefore, are "verbal parts of the act." If the meaning or significance of the act becomes a fact of consequence in a lawsuit, the words which were a verbal part of the act are not hearsay.

Q. 22. In the same lawsuit, X calls W1, his accountant, as a witness. W1 testifies: "On the afternoon in question, X called me on the phone and said, 'I just loaned $50,000 to Y.' " Objection: hearsay. Ruling?

Ans. Sustained. By the time X made *this* statement to W1, the act was over. Moreover, W1 was not a participant in the act. X's statement therefore was not "part" of the act; it fits the hearsay definition; hence, it is hearsay.

Q. 23. Later in the trial Y takes the stand. He testifies:

I remember exactly what happened. X invited me to his room and said to me, "I enjoyed your last novel so much that I am giving you this money as a gift, as a token of my esteem for you."

X objects that Y is testifying to an out-of-court statement which is now offered in evidence to prove the truth of what was asserted, and is therefore hearsay. Ruling?

Ans. Overruled. This statement was part of the act, and therefore is not hearsay. (X, of course, will deny ever having said this; but that's a factual issue for the jury to decide. Whichever version of X's statement the jury accepts—Y's version, given in this problem, or X's version, given in Q. 21—the statement was a verbal part of the act of giving Y the money.)

CHAPTER

3

EXCEPTIONS TO THE HEARSAY DEFINITION, EXCEPTIONS TO THE HEARSAY RULE: AN INTRODUCTION

§ 3.01 Introduction

As explained in Chapter 1, the hearsay rule is simply one of several hurdles an attorney must overcome to secure the admissibility of an item of evidence. Whenever an offer of evidence consists of spoken or written words or arguably assertive conduct, you must analyze that evidence against the definition of hearsay set out in Fed. R. Evid. 801(c). If the evidence fits that definition, as spelled out in Chapter 2, it *is* hearsay, and if counsel for the adverse party interposes a hearsay objection, the evidence must be excluded—unless, of course, the evidence fits within any of the provisions of Fed. R. Evid. 801(d), 803, or 804, in which case the hearsay objection must be overruled.

§ 3.02 Exceptions to the Rule; Exceptions to the Definition

[1] Rules 803 and 804

Fed. R. Evid. 803 and 804 contain a total of 28 more-or-less specific separate *exceptions to the hearsay rule*, each with its own requirements, peculiarities, and procedural wrinkles. They have a common underlying theme: each describes a situation in which a statement fits the definition of hearsay set out in Fed. R. Evid. 801(c), but is nonetheless considered sufficiently *trustworthy* to overcome the hearsay hurdle.

[2] Rule 807

Fed. R. Evid. 807 is a catch-all (or "residual") exception, a central requirement of which is that the statement must be shown to be *trustworthy* enough to overcome the law's bias against hearsay.

[3] Rule 801(d)

In addition, Fed. R. Evid. 801(d) contains eight separate provisions that are classified as *exceptions to the hearsay definition*. A statement that fits within the 801(c) definition but also fits within a provision of Fed. R. Evid. 801(d) is categorized as *non*-hearsay. While the theoretical justifications for the Rule 801(d) provisions differ from those in Rules 803, 804 and 807, the practical effect is the same: a statement that satisfies the requirements of any provision of Rule 801(d), 803, 804 or 807 overcomes a hearsay objection.

In other words, to resolve the hearsay issue, first determine whether the evidence is hearsay, as defined in Fed. R. Evid. 801(c). If it is, determine whether it fits within any of the 37 provisions of Fed. R.

Evid. 801(d), 803, 804 or 807. If it does, the hearsay objection must be overruled. The only practical difference between an "exception to the definition" and an "exception to the rule" is the label. Whether a statement satisfies an exception to the definition or an exception to the rule, the impact is the same: the hearsay objection is overruled.

§ 3.03 Applying the 37 Exceptions

At this point, students often are troubled by several questions.

Questions

Q. 1. Do they really expect me to learn 37 more separate technical little rules, just to handle the hearsay issue?

Ans. Yes. (That's why you bought this book, isn't it?)

Q. 2. How will I know which of the 37 provisions to apply in any given situation?

Ans. Until you develop a feel for how these 37 provisions work, you *won't* know which of them to apply. The only safe way to assure that you don't overlook important issues, therefore, is to apply *each* of them, to determine which are worth detailed analysis. (That overstates it a bit, of course. If the statement consists of a person shouting, "Look out, look out, the bus is running the red light," for example, you can fairly quickly eliminate the exceptions dealing with ancient documents, records of religious organizations, dying declarations, learned treatises, and a few others besides.)

Q. 3. Suppose a statement violates the requirements of one exception, but satisfies the requirements of a second exception. Which one "controls"?

Ans. The second one. To overcome a hearsay objection, it is only necessary to satisfy any *one* of the 37 exceptions in Fed. R. Evid. 801(d), 803, 804 or 807. The party offering the evidence gets to "choose" whichever exception (or exceptions) she thinks will provide the best chances for admissibility.[1] But she had better choose the right exception, and do so quickly. When a hearsay objection is made, a judge will expect a prompt and specific response. A lawyer can meet these expectations only if she is familiar with each of the hearsay exceptions.

§ 3.04 Burden of Proof

When one party offers what appears to be hearsay evidence, to raise the issue of its admissibility, the adverse party must object. If the evidence falls within the definition of Fed. R. Evid. 801(c), the judge must exclude it unless the offering party persuades the judge by a preponderance of the evidence[1] that the statement satisfies the requirements of an exception to the hearsay definition (Fed. R. Evid. 801(d)) or of an exception to the hearsay rule (Fed. R. Evid. 803, 804 or 807).

§ 3.05 Hearsay and the Grand Jury

A witness testifies before a grand jury. Months or years later, a party (usually, the prosecutor; occasionally, the defendant; rarely, a litigant in a civil case) offers that grand jury testimony in evidence at a trial. The adverse party objects: hearsay. The offering party cites one or several hearsay exceptions.

To understand whether an exception will overcome the objection, it is important to understand what a grand jury is and the procedures it follows.

What it is. A grand jury consists of a group of civilians (usually 23 in number), empaneled by a court much in the same way a trial jury is empaneled. Generally a grand jury will sit for a specified term—one month, six months, or whatever.

---

[1] Thus, "all exceptions are created equal." The only exceptions to *this* general rule relate to Fed. R. Evid. 803(8)(B) and 803(8)(C) (*see* §§ 8.59, 8.60).

[1] The Supreme Court established this as the burden of persuasion in United States v. Bourjaily, 483 U.S. 171, 176 (1987).

During its term, a grand jury has two basic roles. The first is to screen the prosecutor's evidence in the cases presented to it. In the federal system and in some state systems, almost every felony charge must be presented to a grand jury if the prosecutor hopes to take the defendant to trial on that charge. The prosecutor's burden of proof is comparatively light: she need only establish "probable cause" to believe that X committed a particular crime. If the grand jury finds probable cause, it will vote an indictment (a formal accusation) of X for the crime or crimes. If the grand jury concludes that probable cause is lacking, the charges are dismissed.

The second role of a grand jury is to be the prosecutor's investigative partner. A grand jury can subpoena witnesses and physical evidence. It can force people to testify against their will, and can even overcome a witness's assertion of his Fifth Amendment privilege, by granting immunity from any use of his testimony against him. Grand jury investigations play a crucial role in investigating organized crime, white collar crime and political corruption.

Procedure. Picture what you know about the typical criminal *trial*. The judge presides. The defendant is always present, as is his attorney. Trials are open to the public, including the media. The defendant gets to see and hear every witness who testifies and to examine every shred of physical evidence that is offered. Defense counsel is entitled to make an opening statement to the jury, to object to alleged mistakes or misconduct by the prosecutor, to cross-examine every government witness, to call witnesses on behalf of his client, and to make a closing argument to the jury, urging it to acquit. Before the judge instructs the jury on relevant points of law, defense counsel has the right to suggest issues about which the judge should instruct, and to object if he believes that the judge has given an erroneous instruction.

Do you have that picture firmly in your mind? Good. Now take that picture and crumple it up. Tear it into pieces. Gather the pieces into a loose pile, and burn the pile. Because *none of the procedures I described in the previous paragraph apply to the grand jury.*

The grand jury meets, hears evidence, and deliberates in secret.[1] The judge does not enter the grand jury room or participate any in way in its proceedings. Neither does the defendant or his or her attorney.[2] Because no defense attorney can enter the grand jury room, he or she cannot make an opening statement, cross-examine government witnesses, call defense witnesses, or make a closing argument.[3]

The prosecutor decides what cases to bring, what witnesses to call, what questions to ask, what evidence to subpoena, and what charges to recommend to the jury against each potential defendant. (A grand jury has the power to do these things on its own or against the prosecutor's wishes, but this rarely happens.) The prosecutor, not the judge, is the grand jury's legal advisor. That means she, not the judge, instructs the grand jury on the law.

Does this sound a little one-sided? Well, yes, it is; the system is designed that way. The Supreme Court has consistently refused to impose procedural safeguards on the grand jury that would interfere with its efficiency as an investigative body.

There are those of course who bemoan the one-sided nature of the grand jury system. "A grand jury," the famous complaint goes, "would indict a ham sandwich if the prosecutor asked it to." Personally,

---

[1] Occasionally information about a grand jury investigation is leaked to the press. The investigation of President Clinton's relationship with Monica Lewinsky was so plagued with leaks and posturing and spin-doctoring that it might as well have been conducted on a daytime soap. In fact it *was* a daytime soap, in more ways than one. But such disgraces are happily the exception, not the rule.

[2] This is because, in a grand jury proceeding, technically there *is* no defendant unless and until the grand jury has voted to indict someone, at which point its job is done. Often, of course, the particular suspect or target has already been arrested and charged with the crime. Often it is a foregone conclusion that that person will be indicted. Still, until the indictment, this suspect is not a "defendant," and therefore enjoys none of the constitutional rights granted to a criminal defendant.

[3] Also, the prosecutor is allowed to use illegally seized evidence in the grand jury, and to use evidence that if offered at trial would be inadmissible hearsay.

(Matthew Bender & Co., Inc.)

I believe this criticism is a broad exaggeration. In my eight years as a prosecutor, I only once asked a grand jury to indict a ham sandwich, and that was because it had claimed to be kosher.[4]

Whenever you come upon references to grand jury testimony in subsequent discussions or problems, reread this section.

---

[4] The technical meaning of "Kosher" is, "in accordance with Jewish dietary laws." (The opposite of "kosher" is "trayf," the technical definition of which is . . . "not kosher.") Pork products (including ham) can never be kosher because . . . well, it has to do with how many stomachs an animal has, and, and how it digests its food, and how its feet are shaped; for purposes of this book, just take my word for it. My point (yes, I had a point) is that a ham sandwich that claims to be kosher is guilty of fraud, and *deserves* to be indicted. Don't you agree? Of course you do. (This will not be on the exam.)

CHAPTER

4

EXCEPTIONS TO THE HEARSAY DEFINITION: PRIOR STATEMENTS BY WITNESSES, RULE 801(d)(1)

§ 4.01 In General

In Chapter 2, we learned that a declarant's out-of-court statement is hearsay even if the declarant testifies at the trial (*see* § 2.04). Fed. R. Evid. 801(d)(1) creates three narrow exceptions to this rule, by defining three situations in which a prior statement by a declarant who is now a witness at the trial is *not* considered hearsay. Offering such statements poses issues relating to procedure and trial strategy, as well as evidentiary issues.

§ 4.02 "Witness; Subject to Cross-Examination"

[1] Introduction

Fed. R. Evid. 801(d)(1)(A), 801(d)(1)(B), and 801(d)(1)(C) have a requirement in common: for a statement to be admissible under any of these provisions, it is necessary that "[t]he declarant testifies at the trial and is subject to cross-examination concerning the statement." In other words, the declarant whose prior statement is being offered in evidence must now be a witness, in the courtroom, on the witness stand, in the ongoing trial, so that if the attorney for one party elicits testimony about a prior statement, the declarant can be cross-examined about the statement by any attorney in the case.

Don't be confused by the phrase, "is subject to cross-examination." The Rule 801(d)(1) provisions do *not* require that the declarant was subject to cross-examination when she made the *prior* statement. Fed. R. Evid. 801(d)(1)(A), 801(d)(1)(B), and 801(d)(1)(C) only require that all the attorneys in the current trial have an opportunity *now* during the present proceeding, to cross-examine the declarant about the statement.

[2] "Meaningful Cross-Examination"

Suppose the witness claims she cannot remember making the prior statement, or even worse, claims she cannot remember the events discussed in her statement. If the witness answers every question with "I don't remember," some state courts, and many professors, have argued that because she cannot really be cross-examined, the "subject to cross-examination concerning the statement" requirement of Fed. R. Evid. 801(d)(1) is not satisfied. In *United States v. Owens*, 484 U.S. 554, 559 (1988), however, the Supreme Court concluded otherwise. The Court held that the Rule 801(d)(1) "subject to cross-examination" requirement is satisfied even if a witness claims he can no longer remember anything about his prior statement or the underlying facts.

In dictum, the Court suggested that the result would be different if a declarant refused to testify at all by asserting the Fifth Amendment privilege against self-incrimination.

[3] Proving That the Declarant Made the Statement

Before an attorney can introduce a prior statement by the witness, she must prove that the witness made the statement. This presents some interesting procedural and tactical wrinkles that are discussed in §§ 4.03[6], 4.04[7], and 4.05[4].

§ 4.03 Rule 801(d)(1)(A): Prior Inconsistent Sworn Statements

[1] Prior Inconsistent Statements: Rule 613

P was injured when a bus collided with his car at the intersection of Broadway and 48th Street. At trial, the bus company calls W1 as a witness. Direct examination proceeds as follows:

Q. Did you see what happened that day?

A. Absolutely. I was standing right there. The light turned red for the eastbound traffic on 48th Street and green for the north-south traffic on Broadway. Suddenly this car on 48th went through the red light into the intersection and got hit by the bus heading south on Broadway.

Q. The bus had the green light?

A. The bus had the green light. Absolutely. I saw it all.

This may sound pretty convincing to the jury; but on cross examination by P's attorney, the following exchange occurs:

Q. I believe you testified on direct that you saw the entire accident?

A. Absolutely.

Q. No question about that in your mind?

A. Like I said, I saw it all.

Q. Do you remember speaking to Police Officer Renko shortly after the collision?

A. Yeah, there was cops there.

Q. And you spoke to Officer Renko about the collision?

A. Absolutely.

Q. Did you tell Officer Renko, quote, "The bus went barreling through the red light and hit the car like a tank," unquote?

(D's lawyer): Objection! Hearsay.

D has a valid objection, because if P offers W1's out-of-court statement to Officer Renko to prove that the bus ran the red light, the statement is hearsay. But W1's statement to Renko has another, more limited use. Even if the jury cannot consider it as evidence that the bus ran the *red* light, it is relevant in helping the jury assess how much weight or credibility it should give to W1's in-court testimony that the bus had the *green* light. The inconsistency between the two statements impeaches the credibility of W1's sworn testimony.

The law has long permitted a party to use a witness' prior inconsistent statement to impeach that witness' testimony, even when, as here, the statement is inadmissible hearsay if offered as substantive evidence. Fed. R. Evid. 613 codifies this common law principle. Fed. R. Evid. 613 provides:

Rule 613. Prior Statements of Witnesses

(a) Examining witness concerning prior statement. In examining a witness concerning a prior statement made by the witness, whether written or not, the statement need not be shown nor its contents disclosed to the witness at that time, but on request the same shall be shown or disclosed to opposing counsel.

(b) Extrinsic evidence of prior inconsistent statement of witness. Extrinsic evidence of a prior inconsistent statement by a witness is not admissible unless the witness is afforded an opportunity to explain or deny the same and the opposite party is afforded an opportunity to interrogate the witness thereon, or the interests of justice otherwise require. This provision does not apply to admissions of a party-opponent as defined in Rule 801(d)(2).

An attorney can use a witness' prior inconsistent statement at two different stages of the trial. First, she can cross-examine the witness about the statement, as P's attorney did to W1 in the Q-and-A set forth above (*see* Fed. R. Evid. 613(a), *above*). Second, under some circumstances, Fed. R. Evid. 613(b) permits the attorney to wait until it is her turn to call witnesses, then call a second witness to testify that the first witness made the prior inconsistent statement. Under this second option, instead of cross-examining W1 about his statement to Officer Renko, P could have waited until D rested, and then, in rebuttal, called Renko to testify that W1 told him that the bus ran the red light.

Sometimes an attorney can employ both options. For example, if P's attorney cross-examines W1 about the statement and W1 *denies* he said it, in rebuttal P could call Renko to testify that W1 in fact made the statement.

A statement is admissible under Fed. R. Evid. 613 if three conditions are satisfied:

1. The declarant is testifying (or has already testified) at the trial or hearing about events that are relevant to the trial.

2. The prior statement is *inconsistent* with what declarant has testified to.

3. Except in unusual circumstances, at some point in the trial (usually, during cross-examination of the declarant), the declarant must be given an opportunity to deny or explain why he made the inconsistent statement and each party's attorney must have an opportunity to question the declarant about the inconsistent statement.[1]

Thus, the cross-examination set forth above is likely to continue as follows:

(D's lawyer): Objection! Hearsay!

(P's lawyer): Prior inconsistent statement, your honor.

(Court): Overruled.

Q. Did you say that to Officer Renko?

A. Uhhh . . .

Q. Well, did you?

A. Uh, I may have.

Q. You "*may* have"? Did you say that, or not?

A. I guess so.

Q. You "guess so"?

---

[1] Fed. R. Evid. 613 raises tactical and procedural issues that will not be covered in this book.

(Matthew Bender & Co., Inc.)

A. I gue—yeah. I did say that.

Q. "Absolutely"?

A. Yeah.

Q. So now you're telling us that it was the *bus* that ran the light?

A. No, no. It happened just like I said before: the bus had the *green* light.

Q. Let me make sure I have this straight. Today you say the bus had the green light, even though back then, five minutes after the collision, you told Officer Renko that the bus ran the red light?

A. Yeah.

Question

Q. 1. What should D's attorney do at this point?

Ans. Request, per Fed. R. Evid. 105, that the judge instruct the jury that they can consider W1's statement to Renko ("red light") only in assessing how much weight to give to W1's testimony that the bus had the green light; they cannot consider W1's statement as substantive evidence that the bus ran the red light.

[2] Rule 801(d)(1)(A)

Fed. R. Evid. 801(d)(1)(A) provides:

Rule 801(d). A statement is not hearsay if—

(1) The declarant testifies at the trial or hearing and is subject to cross-examination concerning the statement, and the statement is

(A) inconsistent with the declarant's testimony, and was given under oath subject to the penalty of perjury at a trial, hearing, or other proceeding, or in a deposition, . . .

To satisfy Fed. R. Evid. 801(d)(1)(A), the party offering the statement has to persuade the judge that four conditions are satisfied:

1. The declarant is testifying (or has testified) at the trial or hearing about events that are relevant to the trial.

2. The prior statement is inconsistent with what declarant has just testified to.

3. At some point in the trial, each party's attorney must have an opportunity to cross-examine the declarant concerning the prior statement.

4. The prior statement was made while the declarant was "under oath subject to the penalty of perjury at a trial, hearing or other proceeding, or in a deposition."

Note that to satisfy Fed. R. Evid. 801(d)(1)(A), a statement must meet the requirements for Fed. R. Evid. 613, and must also satisfy a fourth requirement: it must have been made while the declarant was "under oath subject to the penalty of perjury at a trial, hearing or other proceeding, or in a deposition." If the prior statement satisfies Rule 801(d)(1)(A), then, unlike a statement that satisfies only Rule 613, it is admissible over a hearsay objection as *substantive* evidence, to prove the truth of the matter asserted in the statement. If W1's statement in [1], *above*, had been made, for example, not to Officer Renko on the street, but at a pretrial deposition, then the statement would be admissible, not only to impeach W1's in-court testimony that the bus had the green light, but also as substantive evidence that the bus ran the red light. Moreover, D's attorney would not be entitled to a limiting instruction. Instead, the judge might instruct the jury:

(Matthew Bender & Co., Inc.)

W1 has told two conflicting versions of what happened. At a deposition a few months ago, he testified that the bus ran the red light. Today he testified the bus had the green light. You can believe whichever one you choose; or, if you think they cancel each other out, you can ignore W1's testimony on this point altogether.

Rationale. Congress excepted Fed. R. Evid. 801(d)(1)(A) statements from the hearsay definition for several reasons. First, that the prior statement was made under oath at a somewhat formal proceeding increases the likelihood that declarant spoke truthfully; a person is less likely to lie in such a setting. Second, because testimony at trials, hearings, depositions and other formal proceedings is recorded stenographically or electronically, the "proceeding" requirement makes it unlikely that a dispute will arise as to what the declarant actually said. Third, because declarant must testify at trial and be subject to cross-examination, the circumstances underlying the prior statement and the reasons for the inconsistencies between the trial testimony and the prior statement can be explored by all the attorneys in the case.

[3] "Witness"; "Subject to Cross-Examination"

See § 4.02 for discussion.

[4] "Inconsistent"

The prior statement must be inconsistent with the testimony the declarant has just given at trial. Several decisions have pondered how the term "inconsistent" should be defined. If the two statements directly contradict each other, they are clearly inconsistent. But courts do not restrict application of Fed. R. Evid. 801(d)(1)(A) so narrowly. Judges have found sufficient inconsistency in evasive answers, silence, changes in memory as to some important details, and in claims of forgetfulness, particularly if the judge is convinced that the "forgetfulness" is really only a reluctance to testify.

Questions

Q. 2. In the trial of the bus-auto collision, D called W1, who testified on direct:

. . . this car on 48th went through the red light and went into the intersection and got hit by the bus heading south on Broadway. . . . The bus had the green light. Absolutely. I saw it all.

During a deposition a few months earlier W1 had testified that "The bus ran the red light and smashed into the car."

On cross-examination, P's attorney brings out W1's deposition testimony. D objects: hearsay. Ruling?

Ans. Overruled. The "declarant testifies" and "oath-proceeding" requirements of Fed. R. Evid. 801(d)(1)(A) are satisfied, and W1's deposition testimony clearly contradicts, and therefore is inconsistent with, his trial testimony.

Q. 3. Suppose, instead, W1's pretrial deposition testimony had been: "I wasn't paying that much attention at first. I think the bus had the green light, but it happened so fast I'm not sure." Is this "inconsistent" with his trial testimony?

Ans. Yes. Even though W1's conclusion was the same (both times, he said the bus had the green light), his lack of certainty at the deposition is inconsistent with his "absolute" insistence at trial that he "saw it all." Therefore the deposition statement is sufficiently inconsistent with his trial testimony to be admissible under Fed. R. Evid. 801(d)(1)(A).

The trickiest situation arises when, at trial, the witness claims to no longer remember the event in question.

(Matthew Bender & Co., Inc.)

(Pub.748)

Q. 4. Police arrested X and Y on June 1 for a bank robbery committed on May 15, charging that Y went into the bank and took money from a teller at gunpoint while X drove the getaway car. (As you know from your criminal law course, if the charge is true, X was legally Y's accomplice, and therefore can be convicted of the robbery.)

The prosecutor worked out a deal with X and his lawyer: X would admit his guilt and testify against Y in the grand jury and at trial. In exchange, the prosecutor promised to recommend a lenient sentence for X.

As agreed, X pleaded guilty. In the grand jury, X testified:

> Y told me it would be easy. He cased the bank, he stole the getaway car, all I had to do was drive. He picked me up that morning. I drove around for half an hour to get used to the car, then double-parked in front of the bank. Y went in, then came running out a few minute later, jumped in, and said, "Let's get the hell out of here." When we got back to his place he gave me $400 and said I done real good.

At trial, though, when the prosecutor begins to question X about Y's plans to rob the bank, X responds, "I don't remember nothin' about Y and some bank." Moreover, he insists he doesn't remember driving the car, or getting arrested, or pleading guilty, or testifying in the grand jury, either.

The prosecutor therefore seeks to offer X's grand jury testimony into evidence. (We will talk about procedure in [6], *below*.) Y's attorney interposes a hearsay objection. The prosecutor responds by citing Fed. R. Evid. 801(d)(1)(A).[2] Ruling?

Ans. X's grand jury testimony is admissible under Fed. R. Evid. 801(d)(1)(A) only if, among other things, it is considered "inconsistent" with his trial testimony. There are two very different approaches to this issue.

One approach reasons that for all practical purposes, X *has not testified* at the trial. It is as if he wasn't called at all, because he has added not one iota of relevant evidence to the key issue, which is whether Y is the man who robbed the bank on May 15. Since X has said nothing, his prior statement is not "inconsistent" with his (non)testimony at trial. Moreover, how can Y's attorney "cross-examine" a witness who answers every question, "I don't remember"? Therefore the prosecutor should not be permitted to use Rule 801(d)(1)(A).

The second approach focuses on the likelihood that X's supposed forgetfulness is really an attempt to avoid testifying. (It is easy to guess why X is likely to be reluctant to testify. Perhaps Y threatened him, or maybe X simply knows how unpopular he'll be, in prison and on the street, if he testifies against Y at trial.) When a confessed criminal suddenly develops "amnesia" to avoid testifying against a co-defendant, advocates of the second approach argue, the judge should have discretion to declare such convenient memory loss "inconsistent" with the detailed factual testimony X gave in the grand jury just a few months earlier. Otherwise, we'd often be giving double-turncoat criminals like X the power to control the outcome of criminal prosecutions.

Most courts have taken the second approach, holding that if the trial judge is convinced that X's claim of forgetfulness at trial is feigned, the judge can classify such trial testimony as inconsistent with X's grand jury testimony, and admit the latter under Fed. R. Evid. 801(d)(1)(A).

[5] "Proceeding"

The prior inconsistent sworn statement must have been made at a "trial, hearing, deposition or other proceeding." Courts have accepted testimony given at prior trials, depositions, preliminary hearings, grand jury proceedings, and legislative hearings, as falling within Fed. R. Evid. 801(d)(1)(A). Somewhat less

---

[2] The defendant might object that he never had the opportunity to cross-examine X in the grand jury (*see* § 3.05). But Rule 801(d)(1)(A) does not require that the *prior sworn statement* was subject to cross-examination; it only requires that the declarant-witness can be cross-examined during the *current proceeding*.

formal "proceedings" have also been accepted. In one case, an immigration officer at a Border Patrol Station gave *Miranda* warnings to two illegal immigrants, then placed them under oath and tape recorded his interrogation of them, during which they made statements incriminating D, the man who had brought them across the border from Mexico. At D's trial, however, the immigrants denied D had helped them enter the United States. Over D's hearsay objection, relying on Rule 801(d)(1)(A), the trial judge admitted their tape recorded statements as substantive evidence against D. On appeal, the Circuit Court affirmed. *United States v. Castro-Ayon*, 537 F.2d 1055, 1058 (9th Cir.), *cert. denied*, 429 U.S. 983 (1976). But station house interrogations are *not* 801(d)(1)(A) proceedings; neither are affidavits, except perhaps where special legislation so provides.

[6] "Procedure"

The most direct way of proving that W1 made a prior inconsistent sworn statement is to ask him. Assume W1 testifies for D on direct. P's cross-examination would proceed as follows:

Q. Do you recall testifying at a deposition in this case on September 17, 199X?

A. Yes.

Q. Do you recall being asked these questions and giving these answers?

P's attorney turns to her opponent, tells him where in the deposition transcript she'll be reading from, and then reads the relevant questions and answers that constitute the prior inconsistent statement. After reading the questions and answers, she again asks W1: "Do you recall being asked those questions and giving those answers?" If W1 answers "Yes," P's attorney has proved that W1 made the statements.

If W1 says "No, I don't remember saying that," then to prove that W1 made the statement the attorney must authenticate the transcript as accurate, per Article IX of the Federal Rules of Evidence. The most direct way is to call the stenographer to testify: "I took the transcript of that deposition, I took it accurately, I typed it accurately. W1 said precisely what I typed." Even if W1 denied having made those statements, the stenographer's testimony is sufficient "proof" of the transcript's accuracy (*see* Fed. R. Evid. 901(b)(1)) to get the issue to the jury. The difficulty with calling the stenographer is that it is inconvenient (the stenographer might be unavailable) and cumbersome. After all, W1 is D's witness. P won't be able to call witnesses of her own until after D rests. Then, after the stenographer testifies, P or D may want to recall W1 to question him further about the prior statement.

There are two ways around this awkwardness. When the stenographer prepared the transcript, he included a paragraph at the end, attesting: "I hereby certify that the foregoing is a correct and accurate transcript of [the deposition, preliminary hearing, or whatever]." If the stenographer was an official court reporter, this certification will suffice to authenticate the transcript under Fed. R. Evid. 902(4). If the stenographer was a free-lancer, in all likelihood D will stipulate that if the stenographer were called as a witness, he would testify that the transcript accurately reflects W1's testimony. This, too, is sufficient proof of the transcript's accuracy to get the question to the jury.

§ 4.04 Rule 801(d)(1)(B): Prior Consistent Statements to Rebut Charges of Witness Misconduct

[1] Prior Consistent Statements Generally

The mere fact that W1, prior to trial, made a statement consistent with what W1 testifies to during the trial is no reason to admit the prior statement. The fact that W1 has told the same basic story for several months is not particularly relevant. Moreover, the prior statements usually are hearsay. There is no general exception to the hearsay definition or hearsay rule covering prior consistent statements. Thus, if a proper objection is made, such statements generally are excluded.

Questions

Q. 5. In the bus-automobile collision litigation, W2 told Officer Renko at the scene that the bus had the green light when it entered the intersection. That night he told his cousin about it. The next day he said the same thing to several colleagues at work. A month or so later, he told the same story to investigators for the lawyers in the case. Several months later, at a deposition, he said the same thing again.

At trial, W2 is asked:

Q. Did you see what happened?

A. Yes. The light changed, so traffic going north and south on Broadway had the green. The bus pulled into the intersection. Then this car sped eastbound into the intersection along 48th Street, right into the path of the bus.

Q. a. Is there anything objectionable about this testimony?

Ans. No. W2 is testifying as to what he saw.

Q. b. Counsel for D Bus Co. asks, "Before testifying here today, did you ever tell anyone else that the bus had the green light?" P objects: hearsay. Ruling?

Ans. Sustained. There is no general "prior consistent statement" provision in Article VIII of the Federal Rules of Evidence. Nor (as you will know by the end of the book) are any of W2's prior statements in this case likely to qualify under other exceptions to the hearsay definition or rule. They are all inadmissible.

[2] Rule 801(d)(1)(B): Text, Rationale, and Requirements

Fed. R. Evid. 801(d)(1)(B) provides:

Rule 801(d). A statement is not hearsay if —

(1) The declarant testifies at the trial or hearing and is subject to cross-examination concerning the statement, and the statement is . . .

(B) consistent with the declarant's testimony and is offered to rebut an express or implied charge against the declarant of recent fabrication or improper influence or motive, . . .

Rationale. A prior consistent statement that rebuts an accusation of recent fabrication or improper motivation is relevant in helping the fact-finder decide whether, despite the accusation, to believe the testimony.

To satisfy Fed. R. Evid. 801(d)(1)(B), the party offering the statement must persuade the judge that four conditions are satisfied:

1. "The declarant testifies at the trial or hearing and is subject to cross-examination concerning the statement."

2. The prior statement is *consistent* with what the declarant has just testified to at trial.

3. At some point in the trial, an attorney impeaches the declarant by explicitly or implicitly accusing the declarant of having recently fabricated his testimony, or of allowing his testimony to be improperly influenced or motivated.

4. The prior statement is relevant to rebut the accusation.

[3] "Witness"; "Subject to Cross-Examination"

The declarant must testify at the trial or hearing being conducted, and the party against whom the prior statement is being offered must have an opportunity to cross-examine the declarant/witness about the prior statement (*see* § 4.02).

[4] "Consistent"

The only requirement Fed. R. Evid. 801(d)(1)(B) imposes with regard to the prior statement itself is that it be consistent with what W has now testified to at trial.

Absolute consistency is not required; nobody tells a story exactly the same way twice, unless he or she is reciting from a memorized script. It suffices if the prior version is consistent enough with the current testimony to rebut the accusation of improper motive or recent fabrication.

Unlike Rule 801(d)(1)(A), an 801(d)(1)(B) statement need *not* have been made while under oath and need *not* have been made in a formal setting. A statement to a police officer, private investigator, attorney, bartender, barber, radio talk show host, or anyone else can qualify.

[5] "Recent Fabrication, Improper Influence or Motive"

P sues D; D calls W2 as a witness. After W2 testifies on direct, P cross-examines, seeking to impeach W2's testimony. Later in the trial, P might also call W3 as a witness to further impeach W2's testimony. D, seeking to persuade the jury to believe W2 despite P's efforts at impeachment, wants to bring out the fact that W2 made one or more statements prior to trial consistent with what W2 testified to on direct.

D may do so under Fed. R. Evid. 801(d)(1)(B) only if, in addition to the other requirements discussed in [2]–[4], *above*, P's impeachment of W2 explicitly or implicitly accused W2 of recent fabrication, or accused W2 of allowing his testimony to be improperly influenced or motivated (e.g. by friendship, a bribe, or bias or prejudice). If, instead, P's impeachment of W2 merely tries to show that W2's testimony is simply inaccurate, or that the jury shouldn't believe W2 because he is not a truthful person, D will *not* be able to use Rule 801(d)(1)(B) to introduce W2's prior statements.

A question sometimes arises about the term "recent fabrication": is it part of "improper influence or motive," or a separate and distinct ground for admitting a prior consistent statement?

Questions

Q. 6. In the bus-auto collision suit (Q. 4, *above*), after W2 testifies that the bus had the green light, P's attorney cross-examines W2 as follows.

Q. How did you happen to be at that intersection at one o'clock when the collision occurred?

A. I had just finished having lunch at a place up the block.

Q. Do you remember the name of the restaurant?

A. Uhhhh . . .

Q. It was the "Bar None," wasn't it?

A. Yeah.

Q. And you'd been there that morning since they opened, hadn't you?

A. Yeah.

Q. You'd been drinking all morning and afternoon?

A. I guess. Yes, I was.

Q. So that by 1 p.m. you were quite intoxicated?

A. I was feelin' pretty good, but I wasn't drunk or nothin'.

On redirect, D's attorney wants to bring out the fact that at about 1:20 that afternoon W2 told Officer Renko that the bus had the green light. P objects: hearsay. D responds: Rule 801(d)(1)(B). Ruling?

Ans. Objection sustained. P's cross-examination accused W2 of being drunk (and therefore, presumably, in no shape to accurately perceive how the collision occurred); but that is *not* an expressed or implied accusation of recent fabrication or improper influence or motive. ("Under the influence of alcohol" is not the kind of "improper influence" the Rule is concerned with.)

Q. 7. Suppose instead P's cross-examination of W2 is as follows.

Q. You just testified that you saw the car enter the intersection against the red light?

A. That's right.

Q. Do you recall being interviewed by PI, an investigator for my law firm, about a month after the collision?

A. Yes.

Q. Didn't you tell PI that you didn't really see what caused the collision?

Does this constitute accusing W2 of "recent fabrication"?

Ans. Perhaps. P's cross reveals that W2 made a prior inconsistent statement. Whether this implicitly accuses W2 of "recently fabricating" his current testimony is a judgment call.

Q. 8. Suppose instead P's cross-examination of W2 is as follows.

Q. You testified on direct that the bus had the green light.

A. That's right.

Q. Why did you testify that way?

A. 'Cause that's the way it happened.

Q. That's the only reason?

A. Yes.

Q. I see.—Oh, by the way, do you happen to be personally acquainted with the woman who was driving that bus?

A. Yes—

Q. And that acquaintanceship is more than just casual, I believe.

A. We're engaged to be married.

Q. The driver of the bus is your fiancee?

A. That's right.

Q. No further questions.

D later attempts to bring out the fact that approximately 20 minutes after the collision, W2 told Officer Renko that the bus had the green light. P objects: hearsay. D responds: Rule 801(d)(1)(B). Ruling?

Ans. P's cross-examination of W2 implicitly accused W2 of testifying the way he did to protect his fiancee. (Even love is an "improper influence or motive" if it motivates someone to lie under oath.) There is nothing improper with this cross-examination, but it does open the door to any prior consistent statements by W2 that rebut the implicit accusation.

Does this cross-examination open the door to W2's on-the-scene statement to Officer Renko? Not automatically; it depends on the circumstances (*see* [6], *below*).

[6]   Rebutting the Accusation

A prior consistent statement qualifies as an exception to the hearsay definition only if it rebuts an accusation of recent fabrication or improper motive or influence. Thus, we must analyze the statement, when and to whom it was made, and how those circumstances relate to the impeaching attorney's accusation.

In *Tome v. United States*, 513 U.S. 150 (1995), the Supreme Court held that a prior consistent statement is admissible to rebut an accusation of improper influence or motive only if the prior statement was made before the improper influence or motive arose.

Questions

Q. 9. In the bus-auto trial, on redirect, W2 testifies that he met the bus driver for the first time at a party several months after the collision. Then D's attorney calls Officer Renko as a witness:

Q. On the day of the collision, did you interview a witness named W2?

A. I did.

Q. Did W2 tell you what he saw?

Q. Yes. He said —

(P's attorney): Objection! Hearsay!

(D's attorney): 801(1)(B), Your Honor.

If permitted, Renko will testify that W2 said, "The bus had the green light and the car zipped right into its path." How should the judge rule?

Ans. Objection overruled. The statement to Renko satisfies each of the Rule 801(d)(1)(B) requirements:

(1) W2 has testified at the trial and can be recalled for more cross-examination about the statement.

(2) W2's statement to Renko is consistent with his trial testimony.

(3) The cross-examination in Q. 7 suggests that W2 testified as he did because he wants to protect his fiancee from possible loss of her job. W2's statement to Renko rebuts this implicit accusation, because W2 made the statement before he even met, let alone became engaged to, the bus driver.

Because the statement to Renko was made before W2 was interviewed by P's investigator (Q. 7), that statement also rebuts the accusation in Q. 7 that W2's testimony is a "recent" fabrication.

Q. 10. Suppose instead W2 had already been engaged to the bus driver at the time of the collision. Would his statement to Renko still have adequate "rebuttal value"?

Ans. According to Supreme Court's reading of Rule 801(d)(1)(A) in *Tome*, the answer is "no," because W2 would have had the same "improper motive" the day of the accident as he did at trial (unless, at the time he made the statement to Renko, he did not yet know that his fiancee was driving that particular bus).

The statement to Renko would, however, still rebut the "recent fabrication" accusation made in Q. 7.

[7]   Procedure and Tactics

The simplest way to prove that W2 made a prior consistent statement is to ask him: "Do you recall telling Officer Renko, about 20 minutes after the collision, that the bus had the green light?" But if the jury thinks W2's testimony is influenced by his desire to protect the bus driver, they may not believe his claim that he made the statement to Renko. Tactically, therefore, it might be better for D to wait until she can call Officer Renko and have Renko testify about W2's statement.

If testimony about the prior consistent statement is admissible under Fed. R. Evid. 801(d)(1)(B), D's attorney can choose either method of proving that W2 made the statement to Renko; however, the jury is much more likely to believe the testimony of a police officer with no stake in the case, than the fiancee of one of the motorists.

§ 4.05   Rule 801(d)(1)(C): Statements of Prior Identification of a Person

[1]   In General

Fed. R. Evid. 801(d)(1)(C) provides:

Rule 801(d). A statement is not hearsay if —

(1) The declarant testifies at the trial or hearing and is subject to cross-examination concerning the statement, and the statement is

(C) one of identification of a person made after perceiving the person. . . .

The rationale underlying the Rule is demonstrated by the following example. On June 1, V is knocked down by two men, and his wallet is taken. A few minutes later he flags down a passing police car and describes the perpetrators. He gets into the car, cruises the area with Sergeant Lucy Bates, and points excitedly: "That's one of them!" The sergeant hops out of her car and arrests D1.

On June 2, V goes to the police station and looks through several dozen pages of mugshots. Finally he sees D2's picture. "This looks like the other one," V tells Sergeant Bates.

On June 3, Sergeant Bates phones V: "Can you come back to the station house at four o'clock tomorrow? We've arranged for a lineup." At the lineup the next day, V selects D1 and D2 out of the ten men in the array. "They're the ones," he tells Sergeant Bates.

V doesn't see D1 or D2 again until the following March, when the case comes to trial. On direct examination, the Assistant D.A. takes V through his carefully rehearsed recitation of what happened to him the prior June 1st. Then comes the dramatic moment when the A.D.A. asks:

Q. And do you see the men who knocked you down and kicked you and stole your wallet—do you see those men in court today?

A. Yes, I do.

Q. Point them out for the judge and jury.

A. (Pointing) That's them. The guy with the silver shirt and the one sitting next to him with the shaved head.

A.D.A.: Your Honor, let the record reflect the witness has identified the defendants.

Judge: The record will so reflect.

This may be high drama, but as evidence of defendants' guilt, it is vulnerable to attack on at least two counts. First, it has been ten months between the crime and the trial; a jury might well question whether V can remember his attackers after so long a time. Second, the setting of the courtroom identification is far too suggestive to resolve such doubts: anyone familiar with the layout of an American courtroom could pick out the defendant even if he'd never before laid eyes on him.[1]

---

[1] On the other hand, someone who is *not* familiar with an American courtroom can make life quite interesting for a prosecutor. When I was in the New York County District Attorney's Office, a colleague tried a robbery case in which the victim, a foreigner, identified the *foreman of the jury* as the perpetrator. What is truly astonishing is that the jury convicted the defendant anyway. Of course it helped that: (a) the foreman and the defendant looked somewhat alike; (b) the defendant had been arrested with the victim's wallet in his pocket; and (c) the foreman apparently had a good sense of humor and, presumably, a solid alibi as well.

V's identification of D1 on the street shortly after the crime, his selection of D2's mug shot the next day, and his identification of both defendants at the June 3 lineup are all far more probative, and far more persuasive, evidence of the defendants' guilt than is the courtroom identification. Each occurred while the crime, and the perpetrators, were fresh in V's mind, and the circumstances of each were far less suggestive than the courtroom identification.

Fed. R. Evid. 801(d)(1)(C) excepts such out-of-court identifications from the hearsay definition on grounds of reliability and necessity. First, they are usually much more reliable than in-court identifications, for the reasons just discussed. Second, admitting evidence of the out-of-court identifications is necessary to permit the jury to fairly evaluate a defendant's guilt or innocence, particularly if (as sometimes happens) the witness at trial cannot any longer identify the perpetrators, or may be too frightened to do so.

To invoke Rule 801(d)(1)(C), a prosecutor[2] must elicit testimony satisfying the following requirements:

1. Sometime prior to trial, declarant perceived a person, and made a statement to someone (usually, but not necessarily, a police officer or prosecutor) identifying that person.

2. The declarant testifies at trial and is subject to cross-examination about the statement.

[2] "Perceived" and "Identified"

The prosecutor must show that at some time after the crime, the declarant perceived the defendant. This may have happened in person, on the street or in the station house; or declarant may have picked out D's photograph. The "perceiving" might have been with a sense other than sight. Suppose, for example, D is accused of making extortionate phones calls to V. W1, V's receptionist, never met D, but answered some of the calls. The police thereafter arrange for W1 to hear D's voice (in person, over the phone or on tape); if W1 is able to identify that voice as the one who made the threatening phone calls, evidence of W1's identification of the voice satisfies the 801(d)(1)(C) "perception" requirement.

It is worth noting that while Fed. R. Evid. 801(d)(1)(C) can resolve the *hearsay* objection to evidence of the prior identification, other objections might still require its exclusion. The Supreme Court has held that if the police employ an unnecessarily suggestive identification procedure, this may in some cases "taint" both the out-of-court identification and the in-court identification, too.

[3] Declarant Testifies, Is Subject to Cross-Examination

See § 4.02 for discussion.

In *United States v. Owens*, 484 U.S. 554, 559 (1988), the Supreme Court held that so long as declarant testifies and can be cross-examined about his or her out-of-court identification of D, this requirement is satisfied, *even if, at trial, declarant can no longer identify D as the perpetrator.* All that is required is that declarant testify and can be cross-examined about the out-of-court identification.

[4] Procedure

Evidence of an out-of-court identification will follow one of two sequences:

1. *If declarant is able to make an in-court identification:*

a. Declarant testifies, describes what he saw or heard the perpetrator do or say, and makes an in-court identification of D as the perpetrator.

b. Declarant also testifies that at some point after the crime but before the trial, he participated in an identification procedure of some kind (lineup, photograph or whatever) and made a statement to the police identifying D as the perpetrator.

---

[2] So far as I know, Rule 801(d)(1)(C) has been used only in criminal cases, and only by prosecutors. In appropriate circumstances, however, a defendant, or a civil litigant, could also use the Rule.

(Matthew Bender & Co., Inc.)

c. Declarant testifies, "The person I identified at the lineup (photo array, etc.) is the defendant, sitting over there in the gold and green pants."

d. Declarant is cross-examined by D's attorney.

e. (Optional:) The prosecutor calls the police officer, who testifies: "When Declarant attended the lineup, he identified D as the perpetrator."

f. The officer is cross-examined (assuming the prosecutor has called her as a witness).

g. D may recall declarant for further cross-examination.

2. *If declarant cannot make an in-court identification:*

a. Declarant testifies, describes what he saw or heard the perpetrator do or say, and is asked:

Q. Do you see that man in the courtroom today?

A. I don't know. It's been so long, I really don't remember anymore.

b. Declarant also testifies that at some point after the crime but before the trial, he participated in an identification procedure of some kind (lineup, photograph or whatever) and made a statement (to a police officer, most likely) identifying the perpetrator.

Q. Can you tell us now who you identified on that occasion?

A. No, I can't. I'm sorry; like I said, I just don't remember anymore.

Q. But at the time you attended the lineup, you made a statement to Sergeant Bates identifying the perpetrator?

A. Yes, I did.

c. (Optional, if the prosecutor is confident of a helpful answer.)

Q. When you identified the perpetrator at the lineup, were you sure you had the right man?

A. Oh, yes. I was quite sure at the time. I'm sure I picked out the right man.

d. Declarant is cross-examined by D's attorney.

e. The prosecutor calls Sergeant Bates, who testifies: "When declarant attended the lineup, he identified D as the perpetrator."

f. Sergeant Bates is cross-examined.

g. Thereafter D may recall declarant for further cross-examination.

CHAPTER

5

EXCEPTIONS TO THE HEARSAY DEFINITION: ADMISSIONS BY PARTY-OPPONENT, RULE 801(d)(2)

A. "ADMISSIONS BY PARTY OPPONENT"

§ 5.01 Overview of Rule 801(d)(2)

Fed. R. Evid. 801(d)(2) contains five exceptions to the hearsay definition. The common theme is that the declarant who made the statement must be a *party* to the lawsuit (or a spokesperson, agent, or coconspirator of a party); and the litigant who is offering the statement must be the "party opponent" of the declarant.

Rationale. Most Article VIII provisions are based at least in part on the belief that statements made under certain circumstances are trustworthy enough to escape the hearsay ban. The Fed. R. Evid. 801(d)(2) provisions, by contrast, are based on two very different theories:

- First, there is the common sense conviction that a party should not be permitted to exclude his own statement on hearsay grounds; to allow such an objection would amount to allowing a party to claim, "My own statement should not be admissible against me, because what I said was untrustworthy."

- Second, if a party is unhappy that his own statement is being offered against him, the antidote is simple: he can take the stand and attempt to explain what he said, what he meant, or why the jury should not hold what he said against him.

The Fed. R. Evid. 801(d)(2) provisions can be summarized as follows. In a lawsuit P v. D, P and D are "party-opponents," because they are on opposite sides of the "v". Therefore:

- Any statement D made or adopted is not hearsay, if it is offered in evidence by P. (Fed. R. Evid. 801(d)(2)(A), (B)).

- Any statement made by D's spokesperson, agent, servant, employee or coconspirator, which satisfies the requirements of Fed. R. Evid. 801(d)(2)(C), (D) or (E) is not hearsay—if offered in evidence by P.

- Similarly, any statement P made or adopted, and any qualifying statement made by P's spokesperson, agent, servant, employee or coconspirator, is not hearsay—if offered in evidence by D.

(Matthew Bender & Co., Inc.)

(Pub.748)

B. RULE 801(d)(2)(A): "THE PARTY'S OWN STATEMENT"

§ 5.02 In General

Fed. R. Evid. 801(d)(2)(A) provides:

> **Rule 801(d). Statements which are not hearsay. A statement is not hearsay if—**
>
> **(2) Admission by party-opponent. The statement is offered by the opponent of a party and is**
>
> **(A) the party's own statement, in either an individual or a representative capacity . . .**

This is the simplest rule in the entire Federal Rules of Evidence—so simple that even law professors have a hard time complicating it. It can be summarized in a single sentence:

Fed. R. Evid. 801(d)(2)(A) provides that in lawsuit P v. D, if P can prove that D made a statement, D's hearsay objection to the admission of that statement must be overruled.

So long as P and D are on opposite sides of the "v," anything D said that P offers into evidence will be admissible over a hearsay objection (and vice versa, of course).

It doesn't matter who D was speaking to at the time. If P can call a witness who heard D make the statement, D's hearsay objection will be overruled.

It doesn't matter who the witness is. W (the witness) can be P, he can be D's bartender, she can be a tinker, a tailor, a soldier, a sailor; if W heard D say it, and P, D's party-opponent in the lawsuit, calls W as a witness to testify about it, D's hearsay objection will be overruled.

It doesn't matter *why* D said it. If W heard D say it, and P, D's party-opponent in the lawsuit, calls W as a witness to testify about it, D's hearsay objection will be overruled.

It doesn't matter whether D was talking about past events, current conditions, or future expectations; in fact, it doesn't matter *what* D said!

So long as

- W heard D say it, and
- P, D's party-opponent in the lawsuit, calls W as a witness to testify about it,

D's hearsay objection will be overruled.

And, of course, the rule applies in exactly the same way if the roles of P and D are reversed.

The rationale underlying Fed. R. Evid. 801(d)(2)(A) is that a party should not be permitted to exclude his own statement on the ground that what he said was untrustworthy. The only remedy is for the party to take the stand and deny he said it, or explain what he meant, or try to persuade the jury not to rely on it.

Questions

Q. 1. D contracted to supply P with left-handed gromleys, which P needed to manufacture midget widgets. D delivered, but subsequently P brought a breach of contract action against D, claiming the gromleys D delivered were defective and that, as a result, P had to scrap an entire production run of widgets. D answered that its gromleys complied with contract specifications, and that P's troubles must have been caused by mistakes in P's own production process.

At trial, after P presents his case, D calls W1, who will testify that he was present on March 1 when P inspected several ruined widgets.

Q. And what, if anything, did P say?

A. I heard P say, "I can't understand what went wrong. D's gromleys matched the contract specifications to a 'T'!"

P objects that W1's answer is hearsay.

a. Would this be hearsay under Fed. R. Evid. 801(c)?

Ans. Yes. P's statement was made out-of-court; D is offering it in evidence, through W1's testimony, to prove the truth of what P asserted in his statement, i.e. to prove that D's gromleys fulfilled the specifications of D's contract with P.

b. Is it hearsay under Fed. R. Evid. 801(d)(2)(A)?

Ans. No. W1 heard P say it, and D, P's party-opponent in the lawsuit, has called W1 as a witness to testify about it. Therefore, P's hearsay objection will be overruled.

c. Suppose P denies ever having said it. Does this change how the judge should rule on P's hearsay objection?

Ans. No. In ruling on admissibility, the judge must assume that W1's testimony is truthful. Later on, if P wants to take the stand to testify and deny he made the statement, he can do so; then it will be for the jury to decide whether P actually made the statement, as W1 claims, and if so, what use they should make of the statement.

Q. 2. Suppose, instead, after D rests, P, in rebuttal, calls W2, who testifies:

Q. Were you present on March 1 when P inspected the production run of midget widgets?

A. Yes.

Q. What, if anything, did you hear P say?

A. I heard P say, "I was afraid it would come out all wrong. D's gromleys missed the contract specifications by a mile!"

a. Is this evidence admissible, if D objects that it is hearsay?

Ans. No; and yes.

(1) It *is* hearsay, if P is offering it to prove that D's gromleys failed to comply with contract specifications. Fed. R. Evid. 801(d)(2)(A) does not overcome the hearsay objection, because this time P's statement is not being offered by D, P's party-opponent in the lawsuit. Instead, P, the declarant, is offering his *own* statement; Fed. R. Evid. 801(d)(2)(A) never applies in that situation. Objection sustained.

(2) But W2's testimony is also relevant on a second, subsidiary issue: did P in fact say on March 1 what *W1* claims P said? Because W1's testimony is potentially quite important, P is permitted to offer evidence contradicting that testimony. W2's testimony is relevant to help the jury assess whether W1 testified accurately. If offered for this limited purpose, D's hearsay objection should be overruled, and the evidence admitted.

b. What should D do at this point?

Ans. Request a limiting instruction per Fed. R. Evid. 105. The judge should tell the jury, "You may not consider W2's testimony as proof that D's gromleys were defective. You may consider W2's testimony, however, in deciding whether to credit W1's testimony."

Q. 3. Someone hit a golf ball through P's window, shattering it and causing P substantial injuries. An hour or so later, W1 told D, P's neighbor, what had happened. "It was probably my no good son," D exclaimed. "If I told him once I told him a thousand times, not to hit golf balls in the back yard!"

Because this occurred in a jurisdiction that makes parents liable for the torts of their minor children, P sued D, alleging that D's son hit the ball. At trial, P calls W1 to testify as to D's statement.

a. D's attorney interposes a hearsay objection. Ruling?

Ans. Overruled: Fed. R. Evid. 801(d)(2)(A). D, the declarant, is the party-opponent of P, who is offering the statement.

b. D's attorney further objects that because D lacked first-hand knowledge whether his son hit the golf ball, the evidence should be excluded on that ground. Ruling?

Ans. Overruled! First-hand knowledge by the declarant is almost always a requirement for admissibility, but *not* if the statement fits one of the Fed. R. Evid. 801(d)(2) provisions.

§ 5.03 "Party-opponent"

As I've already mentioned, you can determine whether the declarant and the party offering the statement are "party-opponents" simply by looking at who is suing whom. If they are on opposite sides of the "v," they are party-opponents.

Questions

Q. 4. P purchased a Rockchecker electric saw at X's local Rockchecker hardware store. A year later, he brought it back for servicing. One week afterwards, the blade flew off the saw and badly injured P. P brought suit against Rockchecker, alleging negligent manufacture, and against X, alleging faulty and negligent servicing. Rockchecker and X filed a joint defense, asserting that the saw was well-manufactured and had been properly serviced, and that P must have abused the saw by using it in a reckless manner.

If permitted, W1 will testify that she heard X say, "I never should have let P's saw leave my store in that condition."

a. If W1 so testifies on behalf of P, is X's statement hearsay?

Ans. No. X, the declarant, is a party-opponent of P; hence, Fed. R. Evid. 801(d)(2)(A) overcomes the hearsay objection.

b. If W1 so testifies on behalf of Rockchecker, is X's statement hearsay?

Ans. Yes. Rockchecker and X are codefendants, not party-opponents. Therefore X has a valid hearsay objection if Rockchecker (rather than P) offers the statement.

c. Suppose when P filed suit against Rockchecker and X, Rockchecker had filed an affirmative defense and cross claim against X, asserting that X's faulty servicing, not the saw itself, caused the malfunction. Would X's statement be hearsay if Rockchecker called W1?

Ans. No. Now the suit isn't just P v. Rockchecker and X, with Rockchecker and X on the same side of the "v"; rather, it is:

P v. Rockchecker;
P v. X;
Rockchecker v. X.

Now Rockchecker is a party-opponent of X; X's hearsay objection therefore is overruled.

Party-opponents in criminal cases.

Suppose D is accused of assaulting L. If L sues D for damages, they are party opponents, and if D offers a statement made by L into evidence, D can use Fed. R. Evid. 801(d)(2)(A) to overcome L's hearsay objection. But if D is prosecuted by the state or federal government, the case is no longer, L v. D; it is State v. D or United States v. D. L is no longer a party in the case (even though he's the alleged victim, complainant and key witness). In the criminal prosecution, therefore, D cannot use Fed. R. Evid. 801(d)(2)(A) to secure admissibility of statements by L.

If L's testimony at trial is inconsistent with any prior statements he made, however, D *will* be able to use those prior inconsistent statements pursuant to Fed. R. Evid 613 for the limited purpose of impeaching L's trial testimony. *See* § 4.03.

§ 5.04 Proving the Party Made the Statement

The usual way to prove that a party made a statement is to call a witness who heard him or her say it, but that is not the only way. If D's statement was in writing, for example, P can call a witness who can authenticate the document as being in D's handwriting. A litigant can prove that her party-opponent made a statement by playing a tape recording of it[1] and having a witness identify D's voice. And so on.

§ 5.05 "Representative Capacity"

A leading treatise summarizes this aspect of Fed. R. Evid. 801(d)(2)(A):

For purposes of Fed. R. Evid. 801(d)(2)(A), it matters not whether a statement was made in the declarant's "individual" or his "representative" capacity. Thus where an executor, administrator, trustee, or guardian either sues or is sued, his own statement qualifies as an admission within the meaning of the Rule regardless of whether made in his "official" or his individual capacity, and inquiry into the surrounding circumstances is irrelevant for purposes of deciding admissibility.

Mueller & Kirkpatrick, 4 *Federal Evidence* § 411 at 220 (2d ed. 1994).

§ 5.06 Other Objections

Just a reminder: all Fed. R. Evid. 801(2)(A) does (all *any* Article VIII provision can do, for that matter) is overcome a hearsay objection. Other objections still have to be met before the evidence is admissible.

Questions

Q. 5. D sold P some photography chemicals; when P used them, the chemicals ruined the film on a lengthy shoot P had done for her biggest client. P made an irate call to D, who promised to check into it. "You'd better," P said, "because it's going to cost me thousands of dollars to do the shoot again—if I don't lose the account altogether."

A few days later D called P back. "Look," he said, "the last thing I want is to get tied up in a lawsuit. You're right; the chemicals were defective. Let's see if we can work out an agreement on damages."

P's worst fears were realized: she lost the client, and suffered substantial harm to her professional reputation. She demanded $250,000 in damages, which D was unwilling to pay. P sued. At trial, P sought to testify to D's acknowledgment that the chemicals were defective.

a. D objects that what he said to P was hearsay. Ruling?

Ans. Overruled. Fed. R. Evid. 801(d)(2)(A).

b. What other objection should D assert? How should the judge rule?

Ans. If you've studied Fed. R. Evid. 408, you recognized (I hope) that, because D's remarks clearly were in the context of an attempt to compromise potential litigation ("the last thing I want is to get tied up in a lawsuit"), the entire statement should be excluded.

The point is that while Fed. R. Evid. 801(d)(2)(A) answers the hearsay objection, you still must analyze any other issues that exist, before you can determine admissibility.

Remember, too, that other issues (aside from evidence law) may have to be addressed. For example, in a criminal case, if a prosecutor offers a defendant's confession in evidence at trial, Fed. R. Evid.

---

[1] Assuming the conversation was taped legally.

801(d)(2)(A) overcomes the defendant's hearsay objection; but the prosecutor must still convince the judge that the police officers had given the defendant adequate *Miranda* warnings and that D made a knowing and intelligent waiver of her privilege against self-incrimination.

C. RULE 801(d)(2)(B): ADOPTED STATEMENTS

§ 5.07 In General

Fed. R. Evid. 801(d)(2)(B) provides:

> **Rule 801(d). Statements which are not hearsay. A statement is not hearsay if—**
>
> **(2) Admission by party-opponent. The statement is offered by the opponent of a party and is**
>
> **(B) a statement of which the party has manifested an adoption or belief in its truth . . .**

Two cars collide; a few minutes later a police officer arrives on the scene. X, a bystander, calls out: "I saw it all, officer! The red car ran the red light!" D, the driver of the red car, nods and says "That's right, officer." At trial P seeks to offer evidence of this exchange, either through his own testimony, or the officer's, or through anyone else who heard what X and D said. D objects, arguing that X's statement is hearsay. Ruling?

By itself, X's out-of-court statement, offered by P to prove the truth of the matter asserted (that D ran the light), is hearsay. But D's adoption of X's statement ("That's right, officer") in essence makes it his (D's) own statement, which P can now offer against D, P's party-opponent.

Fed. R. Evid. 801(d)(2)(B) covers two somewhat different situations: expressed or explicit adoptive admissions, and implicit or tacit admissions.

§ 5.08 Expressed Adoptive Admissions

In the example in the previous section, D expressly adopted the bystander's statement when he said, "That's right, officer." So long as D adopted or endorsed someone else's statement clearly and unambiguously, then D's opponent in the case being tried (P) can offer the declarant's statement and D's adoption of it as an admission by D under Fed. R. Evid. 801(d)(2)(B), and D's hearsay objection will be overruled.

Fed. R. Evid. 801(d)(2)(B) applies to written as well as oral statements, so long as the party's adoption of it is clear and unambiguous. Signing a document prepared by someone else, for example, is often considered to be an adoption of what is stated in the document.

According to the Advisory Committee, Fed. R. Evid. 801(d)(2)(B) can apply even if the party does not know what the declarant actually said. Suppose W comes up to P and says, "I've been talking to X about your dispute with D." P responds, "X is a reliable person and knows what he is talking about." P thereby "adopts" whatever X said on the subject. If it turns out that what X said to W is helpful to D, D can call W to testify to what X said *and* to P's adoption of it.

§ 5.09 Implicit or Tacit Admissions

X says something in Y's presence. Y remains silent. In a subsequent lawsuit in which Y is a party, may Y's silence be offered as a tacit admission that what X said was true?

The answer depends on circumstances. To secure admissibility under this theory, the party offering X's statement as an admission by Y must show, at a minimum, the following:

1. The party (Y) heard and understood the statement and its significance.

2. Y had first-hand knowledge of the event, condition or situation X was speaking about.

3. X's statement, and the circumstances in which X made the statement, were such that Y likely would have responded to or denied the statement if he did not mean to accept what X said. (Or, as the Advisory Committee Note to Fed. R. Evid. 801(d)(2)(B) puts it, "When silence is relied upon, the theory is that the person would, under the circumstances, protest the statement made in his presence, if untrue.")

The first requirement is self-explanatory. Concerning the second, note that, unlike all the other Fed. R. Evid. 801(d)(2) statements (including expressed adoptive admissions), there *is* a first-hand knowledge requirement for implicit adoptive admissions.

The third requirement is the most important, and the most difficult to resolve. As the Advisory Committee comments, "The decision . . . calls for an evaluation in terms of probable human behavior." Almost any fact can be relevant in making this determination:

*   Who was X? If she was someone Y respected, Y's silence strongly suggests that he acquiesced in the truth of Y's statement. On the other hand, Y might have respected X too much to disagree publicly, even if Y was convinced that X was incorrect. If X was someone Y was likely to ignore, by contrast (an obviously intoxicated person, for example), Y's silence suggests nothing of the kind.

*   Did some social, physical or psychological distraction prevent Y from responding? If X said something to Y about a business deal as Y's beloved grandmother was being lowered into her grave, Y's refusal to respond was probably prompted by grief or a sense of propriety, and therefor was not a tacit acknowledgment that what X said was true.

Criminal cases.

A defendant's nonresponse to an accusation in a noncustodial setting should be analyzed on the same basis as in a civil case. When D is in custody, however, relying on her silence presents both evidentiary and constitutional difficulties. In particular, once a defendant has been given *Miranda* warnings ("You have a right to remain silent; anything you say can be used against you in court . . ."), to use a defendant's silence against her violates the Fifth Amendment.

Questions

Q. 6. On January 2, two men rob a bank. A week later, S is arrested and charged with being one of the robbers. In May, D is arrested and charged with being the other robber. At D's trial, the prosecutor calls W.

Q. Do you recall an incident involving D and S that took place in mid-January?

A. Yeah. I was hangin' out with D when S walked up to us. D said "Hey, I heard you got busted for that bank robbery." S said, "That's right. But don't worry, I haven't told nobody about you, so you're still in the clear."

Q. And what did D say?

A. D didn't say nothing.

D objects that all of this is inadmissible hearsay. Ruling?

Ans. Overruled. The clear implication of S's remark ("you're in the clear, I haven't told nobody about you") is that D was the other robber. We would expect an innocent man to vigorously deny this implication—("What d'you mean, you haven't told nobody about me—there's nothin' *to* tell!" or words to that effect). D's silence therefore may reasonably be interpreted as a tacit admission that he was the other robber.

(Matthew Bender & Co., Inc.)

Q. 7. D1 and D2 were arrested for breaking into an apartment. As they were being driven to the police station, D1 said to D2, "I can't believe we got caught. And there wasn't even anything much in the apartment worth taking!" D2 remained silent. At trial the prosecutor plans to call a police officer to testify to this exchange.

a. Both defendants bring a pretrial motion *in limine*, objecting that the testimony will be inadmissible hearsay. Ruling?

Ans. As to D1, overruled: Fed. R. Evid. 801(d)(2)(A).

As to D2, the prosecutor's theory is that his silence is a tacit admission under Fed. R. Evid. 801(d)(2)(B), but this is a weak argument. First, if the defendants had been given *Miranda* warnings, the fact that D2 exercised his right to remain silent cannot be used against him. Even if no warnings had been given, an innocent person in D2's situation might well decide that the smartest thing to do is keep his mouth shut. D2's objection should be sustained.

b. Thus, the evidence is admissible against D1 but inadmissible against D2. Nevertheless the jury is likely to consider D1's statement against D2 even if the judge gives a limiting instruction (Fed. R. Evid. 105). How should the judge handle the resulting problem?

Ans. In essence, there are three options. (1) Try D1 and D2 separately; the prosecutor can use the statement in D1's trial, not in D2's. (2) Exclude the statement altogether in a joint trial of D1 and D2 because a limiting instruction is inadequate to protect D2's right to a fair trial. (3) Redact (edit) D1's statement, if possible, so the jury will not infer that it incriminates D2 as well. In essence, the judge tells the officer: when you testify about this in front of the jury, say that D1 said "I can't believe *I* got caught" not ". . . *we* got caught." This gives the prosecutor what she is entitled to against D1, while protecting D2 from the risk that the jury will improperly use D1's statement against D2 as well.

D. RULE 801(d)(2)(C): STATEMENTS BY A PARTY'S AUTHORIZED SPOKESPERSON

§ 5.10 In General

Fed. R. Evid. 801(d)(2)(C) provides as follows:

> **Rule 801(d). Statements which are not hearsay. A statement is not hearsay if—**
>
> **(2) Admission by party-opponent. The statement is offered by the opponent of a party and is . . .**
>
> > **(C) a statement by a person authorized to make a statement concerning the subject, . . . The contents of the statement shall be considered but are not alone sufficient to establish the declarant's authority under subparagraph (C) . . .**

It is simple common sense that if X authorized S to speak for him on a subject, whatever S said on that subject while acting as X's spokesperson should be admissible against X. Fed. R. Evid. 801(d)(2)(C) provides that such statements, when offered at trial against X, are not hearsay. Under this provision, in a lawsuit (X v. Y or Y v. X), to overcome a hearsay objection by X, Y does *not* have to show that X authorized S to make the *specific* statement in question. It is enough for Y to show that X authorized S to speak for X on the subject.

When an attorney represents a client, for example, she is that client's authorized spokesperson on all matters relating to the subject of the representation. (It's not for nothing that lawyers are sometimes called "mouthpieces.") Thus, anything the attorney says on the client's behalf, whether in pleadings, in comments to the media, during interviews of potential witnesses, etc., if offered against the client, is excluded from the definition of hearsay by Fed. R. Evid. 801(d)(2)(C).[1] It is important to remember, once you are practicing law, that "anything you say may be used against your client."

Two issues sometimes arise regarding Fed. R. Evid. 801(d)(2)(C).

1.   To use Fed. R. Evid. 801(d)(2)(C), Y must first show that S was in fact authorized by X to speak for X on the subject; S's statement, by itself, cannot satisfy this requirement.

2.   The rule covers statements made "in-house" by one agent to another or by the agent to the principal, as well as statements made by an agent to someone unaffiliated with his principal.

The first issue is discussed in § 5.11. As to the second issue, because the same question arises with regard to Fed. R. Evid. 801(d)(2)(D), discussion is reserved to § 5.14.

§ 5.11 Proving Declarant Was an Authorized Spokesperson

The party seeking to admit the statement has the burden of convincing the judge by a preponderance of the evidence that the declarant was his party-opponent's authorized spokesperson. The trick here is to realize that S's out-of-court statement, "I am authorized to speak for X," if offered to prove that S is authorized to speak for X, is hearsay. In assessing admissibility, the final sentence of Fed. R. Evid. 801(d)(2) directs, the judge should consider "[t]he contents of the statement," but those contents "are not alone sufficient to establish the declarant's authority under subparagraph (C)."

Questions

Q. 8. On March 1, Y receives a letter from S:

Dear Ms Y:

I represent the X Widget Company. I know that you utilize widgets in your factory, and X wants to be your sole supplier.

To persuade you to purchase your widgets from us, we will sell you 1,000 widgets a month at the incredibly low price of $2 per widget, satisfaction guaranteed! Not only that; we'll deliver them to you at no extra charge!

Please call me at your earliest convenience.

Sincerely,

S

Sales Representative,

X Widget Company, Inc.

Y, who is familiar with the excellent reputation of the X Widget Company and is delighted with the low price, calls S and orders 1,000 widgets to be delivered to her factory on April 1. At the same time, she cancels her existing contract to purchase widgets from another supplier at $3 each.

April 1 comes, but the widgets don't. Y calls S back, only to learn that the number is disconnected. Next, she calls X Co.'s main headquarters, and is connected with M, the company's sales manager. M tells her, "I'm sorry, ma'am, but S was never a representative of ours. We'll be happy to sell you widgets at $4.50 each, plus a delivery charge." Holding her temper with difficulty, Y says a cold "No thank you!" and hangs up. Eventually she finds another supplier at $4 per widget. Now she sues X Co., alleging that the extra expense and production delays caused by its breach of contract cost her $15,000.

---

[1] Remember, though, that Fed. R. Evid. 801(d)(2)(C) does not automatically assure that such statements are admissible against the client. Article VIII provisions don't guarantee admissibility; they only overcome a hearsay objection. Fed. R. Evid. 801(d)(2)(C) statements might be excluded on a variety of other grounds (e.g. Fed. R. Evid. 401–403, 408–411).

a. On the merits, should Y be able to recover damages from X?

Ans. It depends. If S in fact had been a salesperson for X on March 1, X should be found liable, even if S was not supposed to go below $4 per widget, because, according to the law of agency, an employer is responsible for the acts, promises, etc. of its agent. But if S had *falsely* represented himself to be an X salesperson, then X cannot be held liable, because neither X nor any of its agents had anything to do with Y's dilemma.

b. If Y seeks to testify about S's statements, are S's statements admissible over X's hearsay objection?

Ans. The law of evidence takes the same basic approach to whether S's statements should be *admissible* against X. *If* S was in fact a salesman for X, Fed. R. Evid. 801(d)(2)(C) overcomes X's hearsay objection, because a salesman is (in the language of Fed. R. Evid. 801(d)(2)(C)) "authorized by the party [for whom he is a salesman] to make a statement [to a potential customer] concerning the subject [of what the company sells and for how much]." But *before* Y can use the statement against X, Y must show, by evidence independent of the statement as well as the statement itself, that S was X's agent at the time S made the statement.

Q. 9. How can Y attempt to show this?

In a variety of ways. Y can subpoena X's personnel records; Y can subpoena other employees of X, to elicit testimony that S was a salesman there; Y can subpoena S (if he can be found) and have him testify; and so on. But Y *cannot* attempt to prove that S was X's agent simply by taking the stand herself and testifying, "S told me he was X's agent."

Once Y has offered evidence independent of S's statement showing that S, the declarant, was X's agent, S's statement ("X will sell you all the widgets you want at $2 each") will be admitted over X's hearsay objection.

E. RULE 801(d)(2)(D):
STATEMENTS BY A PARTY'S AGENT, EMPLOYEE, OR SERVANT

§ 5.12 In General

Fed. R. Evid. 801(d)(2)(D) provides as follows:

> **Rule 801(d). Statements which are not hearsay. A statement is not hearsay if—**
>
> **(2) Admission by party-opponent. The statement is offered by the opponent of a party and is . . .**
>
> **(D) a statement by the party's agent or servant concerning a matter within the scope of the agency or employment, made during the existence of the relationship. . . . The contents of the statement shall be considered but are not alone sufficient to establish . . . the agency or employment relationship and scope thereof under subparagraph (D), . . .**

At common law, a statement by an agent was admissible against his principal or employer as an "admission" only if the agent had been specifically authorized by the principal to make statements on that particular subject. (The common law rule is restated without significant change in Fed. R. Evid. 801(d)(2)(C). *See* §§ 5.10 and 5.11.)

Courts gradually became dissatisfied with this approach, however, because it often resulted in the loss of valuable, reliable evidence. In response to this dissatisfaction, Fed. R. Evid. 801(d)(2)(D) greatly expands the common law rule governing admissibility of agents' and employees' statements. The party offering the statement need only show that:

1. The declarant was his opponent's agent or employee;

2. The statement "concerned a matter within the scope of the [declarant's] agency or employment"; and

3. The statement was made "during the relationship," i.e. while the declarant was working for the party-opponent, not before she was hired or after she quit or was fired.

Two additional issues sometimes arise that are worth mentioning here:

4. The party offering the statement need *not* show that the declarant had first-hand knowledge of the particular event or situation that was the subject of her statement.

5. The rule covers statements made "in-house" by one agent of the party to another or by the agent to the party, as well as statements made by an agent to someone unaffiliated with that party.

The rationale underlying the rule is that an employee would not make statements detrimental to his employer about a subject within the employee's responsibilities, unless the employee had good reason to believe the statement to be true.

§ 5.13 Satisfying the Requirements

As a rule, the party offering the statement has the burden of satisfying the three requirements set forth in § 5.12 by a preponderance of the evidence. Prior to enactment of the Federal Rules, this burden had to be satisfied by evidence independent of the statement itself. Although for a time under the FRE it was uncertain whether a judge could consider the statement itself in deciding whether the requirements have been satisfied, the rule as amended now explicitly directs that "The contents of the statement shall be considered but are not alone sufficient to establish . . . the agency or employment relationship and scope thereof under subparagraph (D) . . ."

Question

Q. 10. P, while driving in his brand new Decatur Daredevil, suffers serious injury in a collision. While P is recovering from his injuries, X comes to visit him. "Sorry to hear what happened," X tells P. "I'm an engineer for Decatur, and I worked on the brakes of the Daredevil. I tried to tell my boss they were designed badly, but he wouldn't listen. If the company knew I was telling you this, they'd fire me, but I think you have a right to know."

P sues the Decatur Auto Company, alleging that defective brakes caused the collision. At trial, P wants to testify about X's statement; Decatur objects that it is hearsay. Ruling?

Ans. At this point, the objection should be sustained. P has offered no evidence other than X's statement to show that X *was* in fact an employee of Decatur, or that he helped design the brakes of the Daredevil, or that he was still a Decatur employee at the time he made the statement. Unless he can do so, the statement cannot satisfy the Fed. R. Evid. 801(d)(2)(D) requirements.

In this respect, Fed. R. Evid. 801(d)(2)(D) is identical to Fed. R. Evid. 801(d)(2)(C) (*see* § 5.11).

§ 5.14 Applying the Five-Issue Checklist

Assess whether each of the following satisfies the three requirements for admissibility, and discuss the two additional issues as well (*see* § 5.12).

Questions

Q. 11. On March 1, P, a farmer, orally contracted with D for D to spray P's fields. Subsequently insects infest P's fields, and the crops are ruined. On September 1, P files suit, claiming that D failed to spray his fields with insecticide as D had agreed to do. In his answering papers, D replies that the contract called for D to spray a weed killer, not insecticide, and that D's employee X in fact sprayed weed killer over P's fields. Consider the relevance, and the admissibility as an admission, of the following evidence.

In November at a pre-trial deposition of Y, D's secretary, P elicited the following testimony.

Q. Did D and X have a conversation on September 5, shortly after P filed his lawsuit?

A. Yes. D called X into the office, and asked: "What did you spray on P's fields?" X responded: "I must have goofed. I think you told me insecticide, but I sprayed weed killer by mistake. Sorry about that! Incidentally, today's my last day on the job—I start my new job next month with the Environmental Protection Administration."

At trial, P calls Y as a witness, and asks her the same question. D objects that X's remarks constitute hearsay; P responds by citing Fed. R. Evid. 801(d)(2)(D). How should the judge rule, and why?

Ans. X's out-of-court statement to D, which was overheard by Y, is admissible under Fed. R. Evid. 801(d)(2)(D) when offered by P against D. Applying the checklist of requirements and issues, we see that the statement passes all the tests.

1. X, the declarant, was D's agent or employee.

2. The statement "concerned a matter within the scope of X's employment."

3. X made this statement to D made while X was still an employee of D.

4. X had first-hand knowledge of the subject-matter of the statement (what X sprayed), not that this is a requirement.

5. Although this is an "in-house," employee-to-employer statement, the rule covers such statements; hence this is no reason to exclude it.

Q. 12. Two weeks after deposing Y, P's attorney deposed X, as follows:

Q. What did D tell you to spray on P's fields?

A. He told me to spray insecticide, but I sprayed weed killer by mistake.

a. At trial, instead of calling X as a witness, P offers a transcript of X's deposition testimony in evidence. D objects that the testimony is hearsay. P responds that X's pretrial deposition testimony is admissible under Fed. R. Evid. 801(d)(2)(D). How should the judge rule, and why?

Ans. Objection sustained. X's statement in his deposition fails to satisfy the first requirement of Fed. R. Evid. 801(d)(2)(D), because by the time X was deposed, he was no longer an employee of D. (We know from Y's testimony in Question 11 that X left D's company to take a position with EPA early in September; X wasn't deposed by P until November.)

b. How could P introduce the equivalent evidence?

Ans. Call X as a witness! If X testifies at trial that he was told to spray insecticide but sprayed weed killer by mistake, hearsay is an issue only with regard to D's statement to X, "Spray insecticide"; but since D, the declarant, is a party, and this statement is offered by P (through the testimony of X), D's statement to X survives a hearsay objection per Fed. R. Evid. 801(d)(2)(A). X's trial testimony as to what he sprayed does not constitute hearsay because we are not dealing with any "out-of-court" statements by X; he is in court on the witness stand.

Q. 13. P next calls B, a barber, as a witness. B will, if permitted, testify that in December, while Z, D's warehouse foreman, was having his hair cut, he told B: "Poor P! He hired us to spray insecticide on his fields, and we sprayed weed killer by mistake, and his crops were ruined." D objects that Z's remark is hearsay. If P cites Fed. R. Evid. 801(d)(2)(D), how should the judge rule, and why?

Ans. It's unclear, but P probably has not satisfied the rule. Again applying the issue-requirement checklist:

1. Z, the declarant, was an employee of D when he made the statement. (Note that *B*, the barber, to whom the statement was made, was not D's employee, but that doesn't matter. To satisfy the first Fed. R. Evid. 801(d)(2)(D) requirement, P only has to show that the *declarant* was an employee of D.)

2. Did the statement "concern a matter within the scope of [Z's] employment"? Z isn't a pilot; perhaps his job for X has nothing to do with who sprayed what, and when. If this is the case, the statement does not satisfy Fed. R. Evid. 801(d)(2)(D), and the hearsay objection should be sustained.

On the other hand, if Z's job as warehouse foreman included responsibility for making sure the proper chemicals are loaded into the appropriate airplanes, then the statement *did* "concern a matter within the scope of his employment."

Because P is offering the statement, he has the burden of persuading the judge that the statement satisfies this (and all other) requirements for admissibility. Unless he can do so, the judge should exclude the statement.

P can attempt to satisfy this requirement in a variety of ways, e.g. by calling Z or some other employee of D as a witness and asking him to describe Z's duties.

3. Z's statement to B satisfies the third requirement, because Z was still an employee of D when he made the statement.

D may object that Z was "off-duty" when he made the statement: he was at the barber shop, not at the warehouse. But this is no reason to exclude the statement. Fed. R. Evid. 801(d)(2)(D) does not require that the declarant be "on duty" at the time he made the statement, but only that the declarant was an agent, servant or employee at the time he made the statement, and that the statement concerned a matter "within the scope of the agency or employment."

Q. 14. Subsequent to this lawsuit, the state brings a civil action against D for spraying weed killer without a permit. The state offers D's pleadings in the P v. D suit, as evidence that D sprayed weed killer. D objects: hearsay. Admissible?

Ans. Yes. If D himself signed the pleadings, they are not hearsay because they satisfy Fed. R. Evid. 801(d)(2)(A): D's own statement, offered by his party-opponent in the current lawsuit. The fact that D originally made the statement in a different lawsuit against a different opponent is irrelevant.

If D's pleading in the P v. D lawsuit were signed by D's attorney, instead of by D, then the pleadings still are not hearsay in the new litigation because they satisfy Fed. R. Evid. 801(d)(2)(C) and 801(d)(2)(D): the attorney was D's spokesperson and agent with regard to that litigation. Even if that attorney no longer represents D, the pleading still qualifies under Fed. R. Evid. 801(d)(2)(C) and 801(d)(2)(D), because the attorney was D's "agent" or "spokesperson" when the attorney filed the pleading.

§ 5.15 Statements by Government Agents

Prior to adoption of the Federal Rules of Evidence, statements by government officials were not admissible against the government as admissions by agents in either civil or criminal litigation. Since enactment of the Federal Rules, many courts that have considered the issue have concluded that a statement made by a government agent, when offered against the government in civil *or* criminal litigation, will be admissible over a hearsay objection so long as it satisfies the requirements of either Fed. R. Evid. 801(d)(2)(C) or 801(d)(2)(D).

F. RULE 801(d)(2)(E): STATEMENTS BY A PARTY'S COCONSPIRATORS

§ 5.16 In General

Fed. R. Evid. 801(d)(2)(E) provides as follows:

> **Rule 801(d). Statements which are not hearsay. A statement is not hearsay if—**
>
> **(2) Admission by party-opponent. The statement is offered by the opponent of a party and is . . .**
>
> > **(E) a statement by a coconspirator of a party during the course and in furtherance of the conspiracy. . . . The contents of the statement shall be considered but are not alone sufficient to establish . . . the existence of the conspiracy and the participation therein of the declarant and the party against whom the statement is offered under subdivision (E).**

A conspiracy is a combination of two or more people for the purpose of committing one or more unlawful acts. To convict a person of the crime of conspiracy, the prosecutor need only show that he *agreed* with at least one other person to commit a crime.[1]

The primary purpose of the law of conspiracy is to permit the authorities to apprehend, prosecute and convict would-be wrongdoers before they have had an opportunity to achieve their unlawful goal. Even where some defendants may be prosecuted for completed crimes, however, prosecutors frequently add a conspiracy count to those other charges. This permits the prosecution of individuals who might not be convictable for any of the completed crimes. Furthermore, the law of conspiracy affords the prosecution several additional tactical and procedural advantages.

Fed. R. Evid. 801(d)(2)(E) deals with the admissibility of out-of-court statements made by one member of the conspiracy that are offered in evidence against other conspirators.

It is worth noting that although the rule is most frequently invoked in criminal prosecutions when defendants are charged with the crime of conspiracy, if the rule's prerequisites are satisfied, statements by one conspirator are admissible against other conspirators in criminal and even in civil cases in which no specific conspiracy count has been alleged.

§ 5.17 Prerequisites to Admissibility

Fed. R. Evid. 801(d)(2)(E) provides that a statement made by a co-conspirator of a party is not hearsay if it was made during the course and in furtherance of the conspiracy. To qualify for admissibility under the rule, the offering party must satisfy the judge that five conditions existed when the statement was made:

1. A conspiracy in fact existed.

2. The declarant was a member of the conspiracy.

---

[1] In some jurisdictions, the prosecutor must also show that at least one member of the conspiracy committed an overt act that was intended to bring the crime the conspirators agreed to commit closer to fruition. The overt act need not itself be unlawful, so long as it was performed by a member of the conspiracy with the requisite intent.

3. The non-declarant defendant, against whom the statement is being offered, was a member of the conspiracy.

4. The statement was made "during the course" of the conspiracy.

5. The statement was made "in furtherance" of the conspiracy.

These issues are illustrated by the following example. X, Y and Z have been indicted for conspiring to distribute heroin. The indictment alleges that on three separate occasions, Y and Z sold heroin to an undercover agent, and that X supplied the heroin to Y and Z. A key issue at trial is the admissibility, against Z and X, of statements made by Y to the undercover agent.

At trial, the agent testifies that in January he met Y and negotiated a heroin purchase with him. After Y and the agent agreed as to price, quantity and quality, Y took the agent to Z, who accepted the money and gave him the heroin. Two weeks later the agent made a second purchase, which followed the same pattern. After the second purchase, the agent met with Y and complained that the purity of the heroin wasn't what Y and Z promised. Hoping to retain the agent as a customer, Y assured the agent, "Listen, Z and I work for X, and X insists that we keep our customers happy. X will make sure that the next package is pure."

Before the agent can testify about the third sale, X and Z each object that Y's statement is inadmissible hearsay. To determine admissibility against either X or Z, we have to assess whether the prosecutor has satisfied the five prerequisites outlined above as to that particular defendant.

Admissibility against Z.

1. Because Y and Z acted together to sell drugs to the agent, it is obvious that the two of them agreed to do so; hence, a conspiracy existed.

2. It is equally obvious that Y, the declarant, was a member of the conspiracy: he negotiated the terms of each sale, and brought the agent to Z to complete the transactions.

3. Z, the non-declarant defendant, clearly was a member of the conspiracy: after all, Z actually delivered the heroin to the undercover agent.

4. Y's statement to the agent was made between the second and third sales; hence, "during the course" of the conspiracy.

5. It is reasonable to conclude that Y's statement was made in the hope of retaining the agent as a customer; hence, his statement appears to have been "in furtherance" of the conspiracy. (Had Y made the same remark in an idle boast to his girlfriend, however, it would not have been "in furtherance.")

Thus, Y's statement is admissible against Z; and this is so even though Z was not present at the time it was made.

Admissibility against X.

Y's statement, if accepted as true, clearly establishes that X was a member of the conspiracy. X, of course, denies any involvement with Y and Z, and objects that Y's statement about him his hearsay.

The same evidence that satisfies requirements (1), (2), (4), and (5) with regard to admissibility against Z likewise satisfies those requirements with regard to admissibility against X: the government's evidence clearly establishes (1) that a conspiracy existed, (2) that the declarant, Y, was a member of it, and that the statement was made (4) during the course and (5) in furtherance of the conspiracy. The third requirement presents the crucial issue in this problem: was X, the non-declarant defendant against whom Y's statement is being offered, a member of the conspiracy? To resolve this question, we must address several procedural issues.

§ 5.18 Procedural Issues

To assess whether the prosecutor has adequately satisfied the five requirements (such as, in our example, that X, the nondeclarant defendant, was a member of the conspiracy), we must first consider the following questions.

1. What evidence should the judge consider in deciding whether the prosecutor has satisfied the requirements?

2. Against what evidentiary standard should the judge measure the prosecutor's showing (in our example, connecting X to the conspiracy)?

3. What is the appropriate order of proof? Should the prosecutor be permitted to offer Y's statement against X *before* satisfying the requirements of Fed. R. Evid. 801(d)(2)(E), or only after?

In *United States v. Bourjaily*, 483 U.S. 171, 175 (1987), the Supreme Court resolved some of these issues; subsequently Fed. R. Evid. 801(d)(2) was amended to answer some of the remaining questions.

1. Evidence to be considered; "bootstrapping."

Prior to the enactment of the Federal Rules, courts had held that the prosecutor could not use Y's statement as evidence that X was a member of the conspiracy unless other evidence, *independent* of Y's otherwise inadmissible hearsay, connected X to Y-Z heroin conspiracy. In other words, the contested statement could not "lift itself up by its own bootstraps"; in assessing admissibility, the judge was obliged to *ignore* the contested statement itself, and consider *only* other nonhearsay evidence.

In *Bourjaily* the Supreme Court, per Chief Justice Rehnquist, concluded that the FRE abrogated this approach. Fed. R. Evid. 104(a), the Court emphasized, provides that when deciding questions of admissibility of evidence, the trial judge "is not bound by the rules of evidence except those with respect to privileges." Thus, a court can and should consider the contested statement itself, *together with* any other relevant evidence, in deciding whether the requirements for admissibility have been satisfied.

The "independent evidence" requirement.

Bourjaily did *not* decide whether the trial judge could rely *solely* on the statement itself to determine whether the prosecutor had satisfied the rule's requirements. The subsequent amendment to Fed. R. Evid. 801(d)(2), directing that "[t]he contents of the statement shall be considered but are not alone sufficient to establish . . . the existence of the conspiracy and the participation therein of the declarant and the party against whom the statement is offered under subdivision (E)," provides the answer.

2. Prosecutor's burden of proof.

Against what evidentiary standard should the judge measure the prosecutor's attempt to satisfy the five requirements? Both before and after enactment of the Federal Rules, courts used a variety of verbal formulas, from "clear and convincing evidence" (a comparatively heavy burden) to "a preponderance of the evidence" (the same burden of proof as in civil cases) to merely "prima facie case" or "substantial independent evidence" (levels of proof somewhat less than a preponderance). In *Bourjaily*, the Court opted for the "preponderance of the evidence" test.

Thus, in our example, when the prosecutor offers a statement by hearsay declarant (Y) against a nondeclarant defendant (X) and argues that Fed. R. Evid. 801(d)(2)(E) overcomes X's hearsay objection, the judge must decide whether all of the evidence (including Y's contested statement) establishes, by a preponderance of the evidence, the existence of the conspiracy, Y's participation in it, and X's participation in it, and that the statement was made during the conspiracy and in furtherance of it. If so, then Y's statement is admissible, and the jury may consider it in determining whether X's participation in the conspiracy has been proven beyond a reasonable doubt.

3. Order of proof.

A statement made by an alleged coconspirator is not admissible against a nondeclarant defendant unless the prosecutor has satisfied the Fed. R. Evid. 801(d)(2)(E) requirements. Suppose, though, the prosecutor wants a witness to testify about such a statement early in the trial, and the judge concludes that those requirements have not yet been met. Assuming the defendant interposes an objection, should the judge allow the jury to hear Y's statement about X before the prosecutor has offered enough evidence to satisfy the judge that the evidence is properly admissible against X?

The judge has three options. She can:

1. admit the statement "subject to connection," as per Fed. R. Evid. 104(b);

2. reject the statement until the prosecutor has offered enough evidence (including the statement itself) to satisfy the rule; or

3. admit the statement when the prosecutor first offers it, subject to later connection, but only if the prosecutor makes an offer of proof (out of the jury's hearing, of course) of the evidence he expects to offer later that will satisfy the requirements of admissibility.

Appellate courts have often expressed a preference for the second or third approach, while acknowledging that taking the first approach is within the trial judge's discretion.

§ 5.19   Conditional Admissibility: Procedure

By admitting the evidence "subject to connection," the judge in essence tells the prosecutor, "You haven't satisfied the rule yet, but I'll admit the evidence now on condition that you will satisfy the rule's requirements by the time you rest your case." When the government does rest, therefore, each non-declarant defendant against whom such statements were conditionally admitted should move to strike the statements. This motion requires the judge to determine whether, as to each defendant and as to each statement, the requirements for admissibility have been satisfied. If the judge concludes that, as to any particular statement and as to any particular defendant, the requirements have not been satisfied, the judge should instruct the jury to disregard the statement as to that defendant. If the statement is too prejudicial to be dealt with in that fashion, then any defendant adversely affected by the statement should move for and be granted a mistrial.

As in every criminal case, when the government rests, each defendant should also move for a judgment of acquittal on the ground that the government has failed to make out a prima facie case against her. The judge should grant the motion only if he concludes that, viewing all of the evidence (including any properly admitted coconspirator statements) in the light most favorable to the prosecutor, no rational jury could find the defendant guilty beyond a reasonable doubt. If these motions are denied, the defendant presents her case; after both sides rest, each defendant again moves for a directed verdict.[1]

§ 5.20   Miscellaneous Coconspirator Statement Issues

Coconspirator statements are admissible even if no conspiracy has been charged, so long as the prosecutor offers sufficient evidence that a conspiracy in fact existed, and the other prerequisites for admissibility have been met.

The same is true in civil litigation. The issue arises with some frequency in antitrust actions, where plaintiff must allege and prove that defendants entered into a "contract, combination or conspiracy" in restraint of trade or commerce. The issue may also arise, however, where no conspiracy is alleged in the pleadings. In a suit by P against D1 and D2 for fraud, for example, if P can satisfy the five foundational

---

[1] The procedures discussed in this section apply, incidentally, not just with regard to Fed. R. Evid. 801(d)(2)(E), but to *all* evidence a judge admits conditionally pursuant to Fed. R. Evid. 104(b), in civil as well as criminal litigation. If evidence has been admitted conditionally, when the party who offered that evidence rests, the other party should move to strike. Once such a motion is made, the judge must determine whether the requirements for admission have been satisfied. After the judge has ruled on the motion to strike, the appropriate litigant(s) should move for a directed verdict. (In a civil case, a judge should grant defendant's motion for a directed verdict only if no rational jury could find for plaintiff by a preponderance. Similarly, a judge should grant plaintiff's motion for a directed verdict only if no rational jury could find for defendant by a preponderance of the evidence.)

requirements of Fed. R. Evid. 801(d)(2)(E), statements made by one of the defendants would be admissible over a hearsay objection against the other defendant as well.

§ 5.21 Questions

Q. 15. Borachio (D1) and Conrade (D2) are charged with assault and robbery. The indictment alleges that on March 1, 1999, they shot and seriously wounded Leonato and stole $5,000 from him.

As her first witness at trial, the prosecutor calls Don John, who will testify that before he was convicted in July, 1999 on narcotics charges, he was a crack dealer. Don John testifies that in late February of 1999 (as best as he can remember, the 25th), Conrade told him, "Me and Borachio will be lookin' to score an eighth of a key soon. We been scopin' out a bad dude, and we're gonna take him off in just a couple of days." What substantive and procedural issues are presented by this testimony?

Ans. First, Conrade and Borachio can both interpose a Fed. R. Evid. 404(b) objection, arguing that they are charged with assault and robbery, not a drug offense. Those of you who have already covered Fed. R. Evid. 404(b) will have to analyze those issues on your own, unless Matthew Bender offers me a contract to write a "Student Guide to Character Evidence and Related Phenomena." If you haven't covered Fed. R. Evid. 404(b) yet, don't worry about having missed this issue.

Next, both defendants will object that Conrade's statement is hearsay, and also violates the Sixth Amendment Confrontation Clause, which is covered in Chapter 6.

As to Conrade, the prosecutor is offering Conrade's own statement against him. The hearsay objection is overruled, per Fed. R. Evid. 801(d)(2)(A).

As to Borachio, the prosecutor will cite Fed. R. Evid. 801(d)(2)(E). Fed. R. Evid. 801(d)(2)(E) can apply even though no conspiracy is charged. The DA's theory is that the defendants conspired to rob Leonato to raise the money to purchase crack from Don John.

Because the prosecutor hasn't offered any other evidence yet, the state cannot possibly have satisfied the five prerequisites for admissibility (*see* § 5.17). Thus, the judge must decide the third procedural issue discussed in § 5.18:

a. admit the evidence subject to connection, per Fed. R. Evid. 104(b); or

b. admit it now if the prosecutor can make an offer of proof out of the hearing of the jury, outlining how she expects to satisfy the prerequisites of Fed. R. Evid. 801(d)(2)(E); or

c. sustain the objection until the prosecutor offers sufficient evidence at the trial to satisfy the prerequisites.

Q. 16. Assume that the judge grants the prosecutor's request to allow Don John to testify, subject to connection, per Fed. R. Evid. 104(b). The following evidence is thereafter admitted at trial.

a. Don John also testifies that on March 2, Conrade purchased an eighth of a kilogram of crack cocaine from him for $ 4,400.

b. The state next calls Claudia Benedict. She testifies that she was the bartender at the Arragon Bar on West 42nd Street on February 28, 1999 from 6 p.m. to midnight. She identifies Conrade and Borachio as customers. "I remember them. They kept asking me to go party with them after I got off duty. I tried to brush'em off polite-like, but they just kept comin' on. I was afraid these guys were gonna follow me out the door when my shift ended, and I said to myself, this is no life for a nice girl from Brooklyn! So I tell my boss, 'Charlie, I'm quittin'! I can't take it no more, I'm gettin' outa here. You call me a cab, or I'm callin' me a cop!' Charlie called a cab for me, and I ain't been back there since. Anyhow, that's how come I remember them so good."

c. The prosecutor calls Leonato. On direct examination, after Leonato is sworn and identifies himself as a "personal services broker," the following exchange takes place:

Q. Where were you at about 2 a.m. on March 1?

A. I had just come out of a client's apartment, 3rd floor, 12 West 34th Street, when I heard two guys on the stairs. I turned toward them, when, BOOM! BOOM! I heard these shots. I go down and two guys go through my pockets. I had $5,000 on me; they got it all. Then I passed out; next thing I knew I'm in the hospital.

Q. Do you see those men here today?

A. I recognize one of them—him, the one in the purple jacket and green tie (pointing at Conrade). He's one of the guys that held me up. I never got a good enough look at the other one.

d. The prosecutor calls Detective Dogberry as her next witness. Dogberry testifies that on March 6, he executed a search warrant at Borachio's apartment, and seized an ounce of crack cocaine and a .22 caliber revolver.

e. The government's final witness, Detective Verges, testifies that he is a ballistics expert, and that the two bullets that wounded Leonato were .22 caliber rounds.

The government rests. What are the substantive and procedural issues that should be addressed at this point?

Ans. Borachio should bring a motion to strike Don John's testimony about Conrade's statement (Q. 15). Issue: has the prosecutor satisfied the Fed. R. Evid. 801(d)(2)(E) requirements by a preponderance (including at least some "independent" evidence)?

a. *Existence of conspiracy.* We know from Leonato's testimony that two men, acting together, committed the robbery. Their concerted action establishes that they acted pursuant to a prior agreement—i.e., a conspiracy to commit the robbery.

b. *Declarant's involvement in the conspiracy.* Leonato's in-court identification of Conrade establishes that Conrade (the declarant) was a member.

c. *Borachio's (the non-declarant defendant's) participation.* As "independent evidence" the prosecutor has offered Claudia Benedict's testimony and the crack and pistol Dogberry found in Borachio's home.

Ms. Benedict's testimony is significant because it puts Conrade (whom we know from Leonato's testimony was one of the robbers) together with Borachio only two hours before the crime was committed.

The quantity of crack seized from Borachio is roughly 1/4 what Borachio and Conrade allegedly bought from Don John a few days earlier. This amount is reasonably consistent with the government's theory: it's half of what Borachio's share would have been.

The revolver is also circumstantial corroboration, because it was a .22 and Leonato was shot with a .22.

In addition to Ms. Benedict, the cocaine and the pistol, the judge can consider Conrade's statement itself (*Bourjaily*). (*See* § 5.18.) Viewed in the context of that statement, Borachio's possession of crack is evidence of the conspiracy to rob Leonato to obtain the money needed to purchase the drugs.

It's a close call, but I think a judge could find this evidence (including Conrade's statement) sufficient to establish Borachio's participation by a preponderance of the evidence.

d. *During the conspiracy.* The statement (late February) was during the conspiracy (robbery: early March).

e. *In furtherance of the conspiracy.* The statement arguably furthers the conspiracy (to buy drugs) by encouraging Don John to have crack available for Borachio and Conrade after they robbed Leonato.

In sum, if I were the judge, I'd deny Borachio's motion to strike.

Q. 17. After the judge rules on Borachio's motion, what should defense counsel do next? What is the proper outcome?

Ans. Each attorney should move for a directed verdict (or for a judgment of acquittal, which is the same thing). This requires the judge to assess whether a rational juror, viewing the evidence in the light most favorable to the prosecution, could find each defendant guilty beyond a reasonable doubt.

Clearly, Conrade's motion should be denied. Leonato's testimony alone is enough to convict, if the jury finds it truthful and accurate.

If the judge denied Borachio's motion to strike in the prior question, he should also deny Borachio's motion for a directed verdict. Conrade's statement to Don John, together with the circumstantial corroboration discussed in the previous question, makes out a strong enough case to allow a jury to decide whether Borachio was one of the robbers. On the other hand, if the judge granted Borachio's motion to strike in Question 16, he must also grant Borachio's directed verdict motion, because without that statement, there is not enough evidence against Borachio to allow a rational juror to find him guilty.

CHAPTER

6

HEARSAY AND THE SIXTH AMENDMENT CONFRONTATION CLAUSE

§ 6.01 Introduction

As we have seen, some out-of-court utterances are not hearsay, because (for one reason or another) they do not fit within the definition of hearsay provided in Fed. R. Evid. 801(c). Rule 801(d), moreover, contains several exceptions to the hearsay definition. Rules 803, 804 and 807, covered in chapters 8–10, contain numerous exceptions to the hearsay rule; statements fitting within those provisions are admissible over a hearsay objection even though they are hearsay.

When a *prosecutor* seeks to use an out-of-court statement as evidence in a *criminal case*, in addition to satisfying the hearsay objection, the evidence must also satisfy the Sixth Amendment Confrontation Clause of the U.S. Constitution.[1] That clause reads:

In all criminal prosecutions, the accused shall enjoy the right . . . to be confronted with the witnesses against him.

To be "confronted with" a witness means the witness must come to court, testify in the presence of the defendant, and be available for cross-examination by defense counsel. The primary purpose of the Confrontation Clause, the Supreme Court has said, is to assure that a criminal conviction is based on evidence the reliability of which has been tested by the traditional safeguards: oath, demeanor, and cross-examination.

If the Clause was applied literally, it would require, on objection, the exclusion of any out-of-court statement offered by a prosecutor unless the declarant who had made the statement testifies at the trial. This result, however, the Supreme Court has "long rejected as unintended and too extreme." *Ohio v. Roberts*, 448 U.S. 56, 63 (1980). Thus, some otherwise admissible hearsay will survive a Confrontation Clause objection even if the declarant does not testify.

This chapter outlines the principles governing the Confrontation Clause and hearsay that have emerged from the Supreme Court's decisions, and also tells you now how the Confrontation Clause interacts with Fed. R. Evid. 801(d)(1)(A)–(C), which were covered in Chapter 4, and Fed. R. Evid. 801(d)(2)(A)–(E), which were covered in Chapter 5. The discussion of each exception to the hearsay rule found in Fed. R. Evid. 803 (Chapter 8), 804 (Chapter 9) and 807 (Chapter 10) will include an application of the Confrontation Clause to that exception.

---

[1] Some professors don't cover the Confrontation Clause. If yours is one such professor, ignore the rest of this chapter, and the discussions of the Confrontation Clause in the rest of the book. If you go on to become a defense attorney or prosecutor, however, carefully frame this chapter and hang it on your office wall.

(Matthew Bender & Co., Inc.)

(Pub.748)

§ 6.02 Statements Offered for Non-Hearsay Purposes

In *Tennessee v. Street*, 471 U.S. 409, 414 (1985), the Supreme Court unanimously held that no Confrontation Clause violation occurs when a declarant's out-of-court statement is admitted for a non-hearsay purpose. Street, Peele, and others were charged with murder. At Street's trial, after his own confession was admitted in evidence, Street testified that the confession had been coerced: that the officers interrogating him had forced him to repeat the statements contained in a confession made earlier by Peele. In rebuttal, the prosecutor was permitted to offer Peele's confession in evidence, not to prove the truth of the statements contained therein, but to show that there were factual inconsistencies between the two confessions, inconsistencies that contradicted Street's claim that he had been forced to repeat what Peele had told the police. The Court held that the trial judge's instructions to the jury, to consider Peele's confession only for rebuttal purposes and not to consider the truthfulness of the statement itself, was consistent with, and satisfied, Street's Confrontation Clause rights.

§ 6.03 Statements Offered for Hearsay Purposes: Basic Principles

The basic principles governing the Confrontation Clause are as follows.

a. The Confrontation Clause issue need be addressed *only in a criminal case*, and only when the *prosecutor* offers an out-of-court statement in evidence. If the case on trial is civil, or if the statement is offered by a defendant, there is no Confrontation Clause issue, and the rest of this outline can be ignored.

b. If the hearsay objection is sustained, the evidence is excluded as inadmissible hearsay, and the constitutional issue need not be considered (i.e. the rest of this outline can be ignored).

c. If the hearsay objection is overruled because the statement was offered for a nonhearsay purpose, its admission does not violate the Confrontation Clause, and the rest of this outline can be ignored.

d. If the *declarant testifies and is cross-examined, the Clause has been satisfied*, and the rest of this outline can be ignored. Thus, statements falling within Fed. R. Evid. 801(d)(1)(A)–(C) *automatically satisfy the Confrontation Clause.*[1] And if the prosecutor calls the declarant to testify, statements falling within Fed. R. Evid. 801(d)(2)(C)–(E), any of the Rule 803 exceptions, or Rule 807, also survive a Confrontation Clause challenge without further analysis.

e. *If the statement falls within either Fed. R. Evid. 801(d)(2)(A) or (B), it automatically satisfies the Confrontation Clause*, because in each case the declarant is the defendant himself. If the defendant wants to deny that he made or adopted the statement, or wants to explain why it should not be used against him the way the prosecutor claims it should, the defendant can do so by taking the witness stand.

f. *If the declarant does not testify* and the statement falls within *Fed. R. Evid. 801(d)(2)(C)–(E)* or within one of the exceptions to the hearsay rule codified in *Fed. R. Evid. 803, 804 or 807*, however, it is necessary to analyze the issue further.

g. The Confrontation Clause issue has two prongs: the "declarant" prong and the "reliability" prong. The "declarant" prong requires the prosecutor to call the declarant as a witness, or find a legal excuse for not doing so. The "reliability" prong dictates that, if the prosecutor has not called the declarant as a witness, she must demonstrate that the hearsay statement being offered in evidence is reliable enough to satisfy the underlying purpose of the Confrontation Clause.

h. The "*declarant prong*" can be addressed in either of two ways. In *United States v. Inadi*, 475 U.S. 387, 390–392 (1986), the Supreme Court held that if a hearsay statement falls within a hearsay exception that describes statements having "*independent evidentiary significance,*" this automatically satisfies the declarant prong, and the prosecutor need not call the declarant as a witness or explain away her failure

---

[1] Stop here for a moment: *why* do statements falling within Fed. R. Evid. 801(d)(1)(A)–(C) automatically satisfy the Confrontation Clause? Re-read those Rules until you understand the answer.

to do so. A statement has "independent evidentiary significance" if the out-of-court statement would be significant evidence even if the declarant also testified at trial. See the discussion of *United States v. Inadi* in § 6.05. If the hearsay exception does not describe statements having "independent evidentiary significance" (i.e. if the hearsay statement is only a "weaker substitute" for live testimony), then the state must either call the declarant as a witness, or demonstrate that it made a good-faith effort to find the declarant and call him to the stand.

i. The "*reliability*" prong has to be addressed *only* if the prosecutor has not called the declarant as a witness. It can be addressed in either of two ways. If the hearsay statement falls within a "*firmly rooted*" exception, this automatically satisfies the reliability prong.[2] If the hearsay exception is not "firmly rooted," then the prosecutor must satisfy the "reliability" prong by making what the Supreme Court, in *Ohio v. Roberts*, called a "particularized showing of trustworthiness." Concerning the "particularized showing," see § 6.04.

j. Thus, it is necessary to determine the "Confrontation Clause status" of the hearsay exception in question.

k. If the exception is both "firmly rooted" and describes statements made under circumstances having "independent evidentiary significance" (i.e. if it is a "FRIES" exception), the statement automatically satisfies both the declarant prong and the reliability prong, and the Confrontation Clause is overruled.

l. If the exception is not a "FRIES" exception,[3] the prosecutor must satisfy whichever prong or prongs of the Confrontation Clause the hearsay exception fails to satisfy automatically.

§ 6.04 "Particularized Showing of Trustworthiness"

If the statement does not satisfy a hearsay exception that is "firmly rooted" (i.e. if the applicable exception is "unfirmly rooted") and the prosecutor has demonstrated that the state cannot call the declarant as a witness despite a good-faith effort to do so, to secure admissibility of the statement the prosecutor must demonstrate that the statement is sufficiently reliable to fulfill the underlying objectives of the Confrontation Clause by making a "*particularized showing of trustworthiness.*" In assessing the statement's trustworthiness, the Supreme Court said in *Idaho v. Wright*, 497 U.S. 805, 819 (1990), the judge is to examine statement itself and "the . . . circumstances . . . that surround the making of the statement and that render the declarant particularly worthy of belief." The judge may not, however, consider external corroboration.[1]

Thus, in assessing trustworthiness, the judge can consider:

(1) The declarant. Who was he? What was his connection to the events or conditions he spoke about? What was his mental capacity, character for truthfulness or untruthfulness, profession, criminal record if any, etc.?

(2) His "audience." Who he was speaking to, and under what circumstances?

(3) The circumstances. Did the declarant had a strong motive to tell the truth or to lie? Was the statement self-serving or disserving? Would the declarant have risked getting into trouble if he had lied?

(4) The statement itself. Does it make sense? Does it sound plausible, given the underlying circumstances?

---

[2] "Admission under a *firmly rooted hearsay exception* satisfies the constitutional requirement of reliability because of the weight accorded longstanding judicial and legislative experience in assessing the trustworthiness of certain types of out-of-court statements." *Idaho v. Wright*, 497 U.S. 805, 815 (1990).

[3] If a hearsay statement satisfies two hearsay exceptions only one of which is a FRIES exception: the FRIES exception "controls" the situation, and the Confrontation Clause objection must be overruled.

[1] *Id.*

But the judge is not permitted to consider that other people made similar statements, or that independent evidence confirms some of the facts contained in the declarant's statement.

To repeat: the Confrontation Clause requires a judge to undertake this kind of "particularized" examination of a hearsay statement's trustworthiness only if the hearsay does not fall within a "firmly rooted" exception.

§ 6.05 The Provisions Covered Thus Far

[1] Rules 801(d)(1)(A), 801(d)(1)(B), 801(d)(1)(C)

A statement that satisfies any of these provisions automatically satisfies the Confrontation Clause as well, because to satisfy any of the Fed. R. Evid. 801(d)(1) provisions, the declarant must testify at the current trial and be subject to cross-examination about the statement. This guarantees the defendant the right to confront and cross-examine.

[2] Rules 801(d)(2)(A), 801(d)(2)(B)

Statements satisfying Fed. R. Evid. 801(d)(2)(A) or (B) satisfy both the declarant prong and the reliability prong, and therefore satisfy the Confrontation Clause. These provisions cover statements that the defendant himself has made or adopted. A defendant cannot complain that he is being denied the right to "confront" himself.

[3] Rule 801(d)(2)(E)

In *United States v. Inadi*, 475 U.S. 387, 395 (1986), the Supreme Court held that statements that fall within the coconspirator exception, Fed. R. Evid. 801(d)(2)(E), have "independent evidentiary significance." Because "they are made while the conspiracy is in progress," the Court held, "such statements provide evidence of the conspiracy's context that cannot be replicated, even if the declarant testifies to the same matters in court." The declarant's *testimony* would not have the same evidentiary value for several reasons. First, "[c]onspirators are likely to speak differently when talking to each other in furtherance of their illegal aims than when testifying on the witness stand." Second, "the relative positions of the parties will have changed substantially between the time of the statements and the trial." Instead of partners in a conspiracy, the declarant and other members of the conspiracy may now be in conflict with one another. The declarant may himself be a defendant, in which case he is unlikely to testify in a way that aids the prosecutor, and yet may also be "wary of coming to the aid of his former partners in crime." Thus, coconspirator statements "derive much of their value from the fact that they are made in a context very different from trial, and therefore are usually irreplaceable as substantive evidence."

Thus, if a statement falls within *Fed. R. Evid. 801(d)(2)(E)*, it automatically satisfies the Confrontation Clause as well, and the prosecutor need do nothing further to overcome a Sixth Amendment objection.

[4] Rules 801(d)(2)(C), 801(d)(2)(D)

Statements that satisfy these two provisions probably also automatically satisfy the Confrontation Clause, for much the same reasons as apply to *Fed. R. Evid. 801(d)(2)(E) (see [3], above). But this is not entirely certain.*

CHAPTER

7

EXCEPTIONS TO THE HEARSAY RULE: PRELIMINARY MATTERS

§ 7.01 Introduction

As we saw in Chapter 1, hearsay is considered unreliable for three basic reasons. The typical out-of-court statement is not made under oath. The fact-finder had no opportunity to observe the declarant's demeanor when the statement was made. Most important, the adversely affected party is unable to test the declarant's credibility by cross-examination. Despite this distrust of hearsay, however, the law recognizes numerous exceptions to the hearsay rule, based on the assumption that utterances made in certain more-or-less specific situations are trustworthy enough to overcome the absence of an oath and the inability to observe demeanor or to cross-examine. The Federal Rules of Evidence codify 28 specific exceptions (Rules 803(1)–803(23) and 804(b)(1)–804(b)(4)), most of which were recognized at common law (although several of the Federal Rules of Evidence exceptions are broader than their common law antecedents). In addition, Rule 807 permits a judge, under certain circumstances, to admit hearsay that does not fall within any of the specific exceptions. Chapters 8–10 analyze when these provisions apply, when they do not, and the factual and legal issues that have arisen in the application of each. First, however, it is worthwhile to note certain requirements and issues that are common to almost all of the exceptions.

§ 7.02 The Requirement of First-Hand Knowledge

In general, a witness is not permitted to testify unless he or she has first-hand knowledge of the facts to which he will testify (*see* Fed. R. Evid. 602). In a hearsay situation, this usually imposes a dual requirement. First, the *witness* who is to testify to the declarant's statement must have first-hand knowledge of the statement (i.e. *must have heard the declarant make the statement*); it would not suffice for the witness to have heard about the declarant's statement from someone else.[1] Second, as the Advisory Committee's Note to Fed. R. Evid. 803 specifies, before hearsay can qualify under most exceptions to the rule, it must appear that the *declarant must have seen, heard or experienced the event or condition that is the subject matter of the statement.*[2]

The fact that declarant had first-hand knowledge may be proved, the Advisory Committee's Note to Rule 803 observes, by direct evidence, or "[i]t may appear from [the declarant's] statement or be inferable from the circumstances." The following examples illustrate each of the possible methods.

---

[1] If the statement was written rather than oral, the witness must have personally read the statement; if the statement was in the form of assertive conduct, the witness must have seen the declarant engage in the conduct.

[2] The only significant exceptions to this requirement arise when a party offers "diagnoses or opinions" under Fed. R. Evid. 803(6) or "factual findings" under Fed. R. Evid. 803(8)(C). Several rarely used exceptions also relax the first-hand knowledge requirement: Rules 803(9), (11)–(13), (19)–(23), and 804(b)(4).

1. Direct evidence that declarant had first-hand knowledge.

Assume it is important to prove the temperature of the water in a hotel swimming pool. W testifies, "I saw declarant dive into the pool. As soon as he surfaced he exclaimed, 'Good grief, this is cold!'" W's testimony is direct evidence that he heard DL make the statement, and also is direct evidence that DL had first-hand knowledge of the water temperature.

2. Declarant's first-hand knowledge inferable from declarant's statement.

Recall the bus and auto collision case discussed in Chapter 1. Winston Smith takes the stand and testifies:

Q. Did anything unusual occur?

A. Yes, I was looking at a movie poster when I heard a woman shout, "Oh, look, the bus is running the red light!" A second later I heard a crash.

The woman's very words—"Oh, look"—provided convincing evidence that she had first-hand knowledge of the subject of her out-of-court statement (i.e. that she saw the bus run the red light).

3. Declarant's first-hand knowledge inferable from circumstances.

In the same lawsuit, a police officer testifies:

Q. What happened?

A. I heard a crash; then, a few seconds later, a man rushed up to me and said, "Come quickly! A bus just ran the light and collided with a car!"

Here we are less sure that the declarant actually saw (had first-hand knowledge of) the fact he asserted. He didn't say he saw the collision. Perhaps he was only repeating what someone else had said, or was assuming the bus driver was at fault because of some previous experience with (or bias against) bus drivers. On the other hand, we can *infer* first-hand knowledge from the brief time between the crash and the statement, and the declarant's apparent lack of doubt as to the cause of the collision, etc.

Question

Q. 1. Who makes the preliminary determination as to whether the declarant had first-hand knowledge? What rule provides the answer?

Ans. Fed. R. Evid. 104(a) provides, in pertinent part: "Preliminary questions concerning . . . the admissibility of evidence shall be determined by the court. . . ."

§ 7.03 Assessing Credibility

Hearsay evidence usually involves the credibility of two people: the declarant who made the statement and the witness who is to testify to it at trial. Did the declarant correctly perceive, remember and narrate what he saw, and is there any reason to doubt his sincerity? Did the witness accurately hear what the declarant said? Has he remembered and is he narrating accurately the declarant's words, emphasis, and meaning? Is there any reason to doubt the witness' sincerity?

As a rule, of course, the issue of *witness* credibility is exclusively within the province of the jury; a judge may not normally exclude a witness' testimony simply because she does not believe that the witness is telling the truth, or fears that the witness would testify inaccurately. The same is generally true with regard to *declarant* credibility; a judge is not permitted to exclude a statement which appears to satisfy a hearsay exception, simply because she has doubts as to the declarant's truthfulness or accuracy.

There are, however, exceptions to these general rules. As will be seen below, under *some* circumstances the judge may be permitted or required to assess the *declarant's* credibility before ruling on the admissibility of hearsay statements offered under Fed. R. Evid. 803(6), 803(8), 804(b)(3) and 807. Further, some courts have concluded that, at least in *some* circumstances, the judge is also obliged to assess the *witness'* credibility before ruling on the admissibility of hearsay statements offered under Fed. R. Evid. 804(b)(3) and 807.

§ 7.04 Hearsay Within Hearsay

When a declarant's statement quotes or paraphrases another statement, both statements must be analyzed to determine if they constitute hearsay. Fed. R. Evid. 805 addresses this situation:

Rule 805. Hearsay within hearsay.

Hearsay included within hearsay is not excluded under the hearsay rule if each part of the combined statements conforms with an exception to the hearsay rule provided in these rules.

For example, in lawsuit P v. D, where P is suing her employer to recover for a job-related injury, if D calls Z to testify, "Y told me that P said she hurt her back last week cleaning her basement," we have two separate out-of-court statements within Z's testimony:

1. P to Y

2. Y to Z

To overcome a hearsay objection, D must find an exception to the hearsay definition or an exception to the hearsay rule as to each level of potential hearsay.

In this hypothetical, we can easily solve the hearsay issue as to the first statement: P's statement to Y, if offered by D, fits within Rule 801(d)(2)(A). If Y takes the stand and testifies, "P said to me, . . ." then we only have one level of hearsay to deal with (P to Y). Y's credibility can be tested by the oath, by cross-examination, and by the fact-finder observing Y's demeanor. But if the only way to prove that P made the statement is by putting Z on the stand, the second level of hearsay (Y to Z) must be overcome or Z will not be permitted to testify.

D can overcome the hearsay objection as to the second level (Y to Z) in a variety of ways. D might show that the Y-to-Z statement is not hearsay for any of the reasons discussed in Chapter 2, or that the statement falls within one of the exceptions to the hearsay definition (Rule 801(d)(1) or 801(d)(2)), or that it satisfies one of the exceptions to the hearsay rule (Rule 803, 804 or 807). If D cannot do any of these things, however, the hearsay objection must be sustained.

Multiple hearsay issues are discussed from time to time in Chapters 8–10.

§ 7.05 Admissibility Determined by Other Rules

Keep in mind that merely because a statement fits within an exception to the hearsay rule does not automatically mean that it is admissible. The Advisory Committee's Note to Rule 803 reminds us that "[t]he exceptions are phrased in terms of nonapplication of the hearsay rule, rather than in positive terms of admissibility, in order to repel any implication that other possible grounds for exclusion are eliminated from consideration." A statement that fits within a hearsay exception must also be analyzed to determine whether any other provision of the Federal Rules of Evidence requires its exclusion.

CHAPTER

8

RULE 803:
THE "DECLARANT AVAILABILITY IMMATERIAL" EXCEPTIONS

A. "AVAILABILITY OF DECLARANT IMMATERIAL"

§ 8.01 In General

Fed. R. Evid. 803 contains 23 exceptions to the hearsay rule, each of which applies to a more or less precisely defined situation. The rule begins by instructing that a statement fitting into any of the provisions of Fed. R. Evid. 803 "[is] not excluded by the hearsay rule, even though the declarant is available as a witness." This means that in assessing admissibility over a hearsay objection, we don't care whether the declarant could be or has been called as a witness or not; we simply look at the statement and the circumstances in which it was made. If the statement fits within a Fed. R. Evid. 803 exception, the hearsay objection is overruled.

Recall the collision between a bus and an automobile discussed in Chapter 2. A second or two before the collision, a man named Winston Smith heard a woman shout, "Oh, look, the bus is running the red light!" P's lawyer subsequently learns that her name was Julia Albion.

At trial, P wants the jury to hear what Julia Albion shouted just before the crash. To do so, P subpoenas Smith to testify. Ms. Albion's statement is hearsay, but (as you will see in a few more pages) fits within Fed. R. Evid. 803(2), the "excited utterance" exception. D's hearsay objection, therefore, is overruled; Smith can repeat Ms. Albion's hearsay statement while testifying.

As it turns out, Julia Albion lives only three blocks from the courthouse. She is perfectly willing to testify, but for some reason, P would rather have the jury hear about her statement through Smith. P has the right to do so: if a statement fits within a Fed. R. Evid. 803 exception, there is no obligation to call the declarant as a witness, even if the declarant is available.[1]

Suppose instead P does subpoena Ms. Albion. She testifies, "I saw the bus go right through the red light; it never even attempted to stop." This isn't hearsay, because she is relating from the witness stand what she saw. Next, P's attorney asks:

Q. Did you say anything at the time?

A. Yes. Just before the bus collided with the car I shouted out, "Oh, look, the bus is running the red light!"

---

[1] This is always true insofar as the hearsay rule is concerned. Remember, though, that in criminal cases, whenever a prosecutor offers hearsay evidence against a defendant, the state must also satisfy the Sixth Amendment Confrontation Clause. *See* Chapter 6.

D's hearsay objection will still be overruled, because (as you will learn in § 8.02) Ms. Albion's statement fits within the excited utterance provision of Fed. R. Evid. 803(2). She (the declarant) is not only available, she's actually testifying, but that doesn't affect the applicability of a Fed. R. Evid. 803 provision, because as to Fed. R. Evid. 803 exceptions, the availability of the declarant is immaterial.

After Ms. Albion completes her testimony, P calls Winston Smith. Direct examination proceeds:

Q. . . . Where were you at one o'clock in the afternoon on April 4, 1999?

A. I was on the corner of Broadway and 48th Street in Manhattan.

Q. Did anything unusual occur?

A. Yes. I heard a woman shout, "Oh, look, the bus is running the red light!" A second later I heard a crash.

D's hearsay objection is still (or again) overruled: because declarant's statement fits within a Fed. R. Evid. 803 provision, it is immaterial whether declarant was available to testify or has already testified.[2]

B. COMMON ORAL STATEMENTS

1. Spontaneous Declarations: Rules 803(1) and 803(2)

§ 8.02 In General

Fed. R. Evid. 803(1) and 803(2) provide as follows:

> **Rule 803. The following are not excluded by the hearsay rule, even though the declarant is available as a witness:**
>
> **(1) Present sense impression. A statement describing or explaining an event or condition made while the declarant was perceiving the event or condition, or immediately thereafter.**
>
> **(2) Excited utterance. A statement relating to a startling event or condition, made while the declarant was under the stress of excitement caused by the event or condition.**

These provisions are closely related. The common theme is lack of time to forget or fabricate. Fed. R. Evid. 803(1) statements are assumed to be reliable on the theory that if a statement is made during or immediately after the declarant perceives something, there is no appreciable risk of misremembering, and he is unlikely to have time to fabricate a false statement about it. Fed. R. Evid. 803(2) statements are considered reliable because (as the Advisory Committee puts it) "circumstances may produce a condition of excitement that temporarily stills the capacity of reflection and produces utterances free of conscious fabrication." Of course, if the event is exciting enough to "still the capacity of reflection," it also may interfere with declarant's ability to perceive or communicate accurately; nevertheless, the common law recognized an excited utterance exception, and Fed. R. Evid. 803(2) codifies it.

Thus, both provisions rely upon spontaneity to reduce the risk of fabrication and lapses in memory.

Because 803(1) and 803(2) are so closely related, many statements will satisfy both. Still, there are differences, and to overcome a hearsay objection, an attorney must persuade the judge that a statement satisfies *all* of the requirements of at least one of these provisions; it would not suffice to satisfy some of the requirements of 803(1) and some of 803(2).

---

[2] If Ms. Albion has already testified as to what she saw and what she said, D may succeed in excluding Smith's testimony on Fed. R. Evid. 403 grounds (needless presentation of cumulative evidence).

In older cases, statements that fall within these exceptions were sometimes described as coming within the *"res gestae."* That Latin phrase, which means "the thing itself," appears in so many different legal contexts, many totally unrelated to hearsay, that by now it has about as many uses as a switch-hitting utility infielder-outfielder.[1] In other words, it has so many different meanings it has been rendered almost meaningless. For that reason, most courts avoid using it.

The requirements for these two provisions, and the issues likely to arise, are as follows:

Rule 803(1): present sense impression

1. Declarant must have had *first-hand knowledge* of the facts asserted in the statement.
2. *Nature of the event or condition and its effect on declarant.* Any event or condition will suffice; there is no need to show that it had any particular effect on the declarant.
3. *Subject-matter of the statement.* The statement must "describe or explain" the event or condition.
4. *Spontaneity; lapse of time between the event or condition and the statement.* The statement must have been made "while the declarant was perceiving the event, or immediately thereafter."

5. *Sixth Amendment Confrontation Clause. See* § 8.07.

Rule 803(2): excited utterance

1. Declarant must have had *first-hand knowledge* of the facts asserted in the statement.
2. *Nature of the event or condition and its effect on declarant.* The rule requires that the event or condition be "startling" and caused the declarant "stress or excitement."
3. *Subject-matter of the statement.* The statement need only "relate to" the event or condition.
4. *Spontaneity; lapse of time between the event or condition and the statement.* The statement need not have been made during or immediately after the event; it suffices that, at the time declarant made the statement, he or she "was under the stress of excitement caused by the event or condition."
5. *Sixth Amendment Confrontation Clause. See* § 8.07.

The party offering the statement must persuade the judge by a preponderance of the evidence that the exception's requirement has been satisfied.[2]

§ 8.03   First-hand Knowledge Requirement

To satisfy either rule, the offering party must persuade the judge that the declarant perceived the event or condition that is the subject matter of the statement. (There is no requirement that the declarant *participate* in the event; perception is enough.)

Proof that the declarant perceived the event or condition can be made in a variety of ways. Assume, for example, that P needs to establish that X was driving a VW Rabbit on a certain morning. DL, who lived across the street from X at the time, commented to his wife that morning, "X is driving the VW again today; I wonder if something is wrong with the Mercedes." This will qualify under Fed. R. Evid. 803(1) if it is clear that DL in fact saw X driving the VW.

If DL is a witness at trial, he can simply testify, "I saw X pull out of the driveway, and I remember commenting to my wife, 'X is driving the VW today; I wonder if something is wrong with the Mercedes.' " If declarant is not a witness, someone else can testify to facts establishing declarant's perception. DL's wife could testify, for example, "DL was standing at the window and said to me, 'X is driving the VW today; I wonder if something is wrong with the Mercedes.' " Because we know from DL's wife's testimony that DL was looking out of the window at the time he made the statement, we can comfortably conclude that DL in fact saw X in the Volkswagen.

Suppose DL's wife is blind, or had her back turned to DL when he made the statement. In that case, it is less clear that DL actually saw X in the VW. (It is also less clear that the statement was made

---

[1] This is a baseball metaphor. If you do not understand it, worry not. I promise you it will not be on the exam.

[2] In United States v. Bourjaily, 483 U.S. 171, 176 (1987), the Supreme Court, citing Fed. R. Evid. 104(a), held that the offering party must persuade the judge by a preponderance of the evidence that the requirements of any hearsay exception have been satisfied.

"at or near the time" that he saw whatever it is he saw.) Still, it would be well within judicial discretion to conclude that the statement fits within Fed. R. Evid. 803(1). In other words, the statement itself, together with surrounding circumstances, can suffice to establish DL's first-hand knowledge of the event.

When the declarant is an unidentified bystander, on the other hand, the Advisory Committee Note to Fed. R. Evid. 803(1) and 803(2) observes that pre-FRE cases "indicate hesitancy in upholding the statement alone as sufficient" to establish that declarant perceived the event first-hand. Such hesitancy, according to the Advisory Committee, "would under appropriate circumstances be consistent with" these rules. In other words, a judge has discretion to reject a statement attributed to an unidentified bystander even if the statement itself indicates the bystander saw the event. A judge is most likely to do so if she thinks the witness who claims to have heard such a statement is lying. In a traffic accident case, for example, P, a pedestrian, claims D, who was driving a Lincoln Continental, ran the light and knocked him down, causing permanent soft-tissue back injuries; D denies it ever happened. P and D are the only eyewitnesses available at trial, but P wants to testify that, just before being struck, he heard an unidentified man shout out, "O my gosh, the Lincoln is running the light!" The judge may be sorely tempted to exclude this testimony as too pat and too convenient to be believable. Although a judge should not consider witness credibility in determining admissibility, such a result (as the Advisory Committee delicately put it) "would under appropriate circumstances be consistent with the rule."

§ 8.04 Nature of Event or Condition; Effect on Declarant

Any event or condition may suffice to be the subject matter of a statement of present sense impression (Fed. R. Evid. 803(1)): "I see X is driving her VW today." "I smell ammonia." "This feels very smooth." "It tastes salty."

To qualify as an excited utterance, by contrast, Fed. R. Evid. 803(2) requires a showing that the event or condition was "startling" and caused the declarant "stress" or "excitement." A colleague of mine tells his students, "If it begins with 'Oh my gosh' and ends with an exclamation point, it's an excited utterance." That should give you a pretty good idea.

The offering party can prove that a startling event occurred, and that it had the necessary effect on the declarant, in a variety of ways. W1 could testify, for example, "I heard a crash, came running around the corner, and saw DL. He was very upset, actually shaking. He pointed to the intersection and said, 'A bus just ran the red light and broadsided that car!' " The wreckage of the two vehicles proves the event occurred; DL's shaken state is persuasive evidence that he saw it and was upset by it.

§ 8.05 Subject Matter of the Statement

To fit within Fed. R. Evid. 803(1) (present sense impression), the statement must be closely tied to the event or condition that prompted it, i.e. must "describe or explain" the event or condition.

A Fed. R. Evid. 803(2) statement (excited utterance) need not be so narrowly connected to the event or condition; it suffices that the statement "relates to" whatever prompted the statement. *Murphy Auto Parts Co. v. Ball*, 249 F.2d 508, 511 (1957), *cert. denied*, 355 U.S. 932, a pre-Rules case that is still in some evidence casebooks, provides a useful example. Two cars collided. The Balls were injured, and sued James Murphy, the owner-operator of the other vehicle, and his employer, Murphy Auto Parts, which was owned by his stepfather. Murphy Auto Parts carried more insurance than the individual defendant, and therefore, in legal parlance, was the "deep pockets defendant" in the case; but to show that the company was liable, the Balls had to show that James Murphy was on an errand for the company at the time of the collision. To do so, Mrs. Ball testified that, just after the collision, James jumped out of his car and said, "I'm sorry, I hope your son isn't hurt, I had to call on a customer and I was in a bit of a hurry to get home." The D.C. Circuit Court, per Circuit Judge (later Chief Justice) Burger, overruled Murphy Auto Parts' hearsay objection because the statement "related to" the exciting event (the collision), and therefore came within the excited utterance exception.

§ 8.06   Spontaneity; Passage of Time Between the "Event or Condition" and Declarant's Statement

Spontaneity is the underlying justification for both of these provisions. Evidence that suggests the declarant thought about what to say or considered the long-range implications of her statement detracts from its spontaneity and weighs against admissibility. For example, the fact that a statement is in response to a question may, under appropriate circumstances, suggest reflection rather than spontaneity.

The passage of time between the event or condition and the statement is a key factor in each rule, as well as a significant distinguishing feature between them. Fed. R. Evid. 803(1) (present sense impression) requires that the statement be made "while the declarant was perceiving the event or condition, or immediately thereafter." The Advisory Committee Note observes that often "precise contemporaneity is not possible, and hence a slight lapse is allowable." A lapse of a few seconds generally will not prevent a statement from qualifying under Fed. R. Evid. 803(1), but if the span between perception and statement is measured in minutes, courts often (but by no means always) conclude that 803(1) no longer applies.

Fed. R. Evid. 803(2) (excited utterance) requires that the statement be made "while the declarant was under the stress of excitement caused by the event or condition." The Advisory Committee Note comments that "the standard of measurement is the duration of the state of excitement," so long as the "condition of excitement . . . temporarily stills the capacity of reflection and produces utterances free of conscious fabrication." When declarant was unconscious or in shock for much of the period between the event and the statement, courts generally hold that the declarant's "condition of excitement" continues or resumes when declarant regains consciousness. Even when declarant has not suffered any physical injury or loss of consciousness, courts have admitted, as excited utterances, statements made many minutes, and even several hours, after the "startling event or condition," so long as there is sufficient evidence that declarant is still under the influence of the startling event.

Courts are particularly willing to overlook or discount lengthy delays in cases involving young children; delays of several hours and even days are sometimes excused.

§ 8.07   Sixth Amendment Confrontation Clause

In *White v. Illinois*, 502 U.S. 346 (1992), the Supreme Court stated that the "spontaneous declaration" exception is firmly rooted and that such statements have "independent evidentiary significance." "A statement that has been offered in a moment of excitement—without the opportunity to reflect on the consequences of one's exclamation—may justifiably carry more weight with a trier of fact than a similar statement offered in the relative calm of the courtroom."[1]

It is clear, therefore, that Fed. R. Evid. 803(2) is a "FRIES" exception, and that any statement that satisfies Fed. R. Evid. 803(2) automatically satisfies the Confrontation Clause.

The same is probably true of present sense impression statements admitted per Fed. R. Evid. 803(1): although such statements lack the excitement of Fed. R. Evid. 803(2) statements, they retain the key ingredients of spontaneity and lack of opportunity to reflect or fabricate.

§ 8.08   Questions

Q. 1. P brings a wrongful death action against the power company, alleging that its negligence caused the electrocution of X, her husband, a lineman. The Company, by contrast, asserts that X's own negligence caused his death, because X failed to be certain that the power was turned off before he began working on a damaged line.

---

[1] White v. Illinois, 502 U.S. 346, 356 (1992). Similarly, in Idaho v. Wright, 497 U.S. 805, 820 (1990), the court, albeit in dictum, commented, "such statements are given under circumstances that eliminate the possibility of fabrication, coaching, or confabulation, and that therefore the circumstances surrounding the making of the statement provide sufficient assurance that the statement is trustworthy and that cross-examination would be superfluous."

At trial P calls W1, also an employee of the company. W1 testifies that he and X were sent to inspect a section of power line; that X climbed the pole, made a preliminary inspection, then went back to their truck; that on emerging from the truck, X told W1, "I radioed the plant, and they told me the power is shut off"; that X again climbed the pole, began working on the line, and was then electrocuted.

The company interposes a hearsay objection to W1's testimony about what X said regarding his radio conversation with personnel at the power plant. How should P respond? How should the judge rule?

Ans. X's statement to W1 ("I radioed . . . they told me the power is off"), is hearsay, because P is offering it to prove the truth of the matter asserted (i.e. to prove that "they" told X the power was off). But it should be admitted, because X's statement to W1 satisfies all of the requirements of Fed. R. Evid. 803(1):

1) X, the declarant, had first-hand knowledge of the "event" in question (his conversation with power plant personnel).

2) While there is nothing "startling" about X's conversation with power plant personnel, Fed. R. Evid. 803(1) doesn't require that the event be "startling."

3) X's statement to W1 "described" his conversation with power plant personnel.

4) X's statement to W1 was made "immediately after" his conversation with power plant personnel.

5) This is civil litigation, not a criminal case, so the Sixth Amendment Confrontation Clause need not be considered.

Q. 2. Suppose five minutes had elapsed between X's conversation with power plant personnel and his statement to W1, instead of just a few seconds. Would this make his statement to W1 inadmissible hearsay?

Ans. Not necessarily. While a longer time period increases the hearsay risks of impaired memory and opportunity to fabricate, X would have had no conceivable motive to lie to W1 about his conversation with power plant personnel, and it is unlikely that he would misremember such an important piece of information.

Trial judges have substantial discretion in deciding whether the requirements for a hearsay exception have been satisfied, and plaintiff is a widow, perhaps with young children, suing a multimillion dollar utility company. It is not unknown for hearsay exceptions to expand somewhat in such cases.

Q. 3. D is charged with murdering V, his former girlfriend, on June 1.

The prosecutor seeks to elicit testimony from W, a friend of V, who will testify that V approached her about one o'clock in the afternoon, trembling and pale, literally shaking, more upset than W had ever seen her. Asked what was the matter, V replied that D had tried to kill her that morning; that he had picked her up to take her to school, stopped along route, threatened to kill them both if she didn't take him back, and fired a shot in the air as she broke away. (The only corroboration of V's statement is that she had missed an 8 a.m. class that morning, and that she appeared extremely nervous and upset at 1 p.m. that afternoon.) After V calmed down and had a chance to reflect, she insisted that W promise not to tell anyone for fear of getting D in trouble.

Later that day V was shot and killed, and D is charged with the crime. Is W's testimony about V's statement admissible over a hearsay objection?

Ans. The prosecutor should cite Fed. R. Evid. 803(2).

1) Declarant (V) had first-hand knowledge of her encounter with D.

2) Being shot at and threatened certainly qualifies as a startling, stressful event. On the other hand, aside from the statement itself, the only corroboration that the event ever occurred (that V missed a class that morning and was extremely upset at 1 p.m.) is tenuous at best.

3) V's statement to W certainly "relates to" the event; in fact, it describes it.

4) The lapse of time is the main potential barrier here to admissibility. Still, in the trial on which this problem is based, the trial judge admitted W's testimony, and the appellate court affirmed. Even though the event had occurred an indefinite number of hours before declarant made the statement, "[t]he lapse of time between [the] event and the statement relating to it did not significantly erode the stress of excitement resulting to [declarant] from the event. Personal observations by [declarant's] best friend and her choral music teacher vouch for the physical and emotional manifestations . . . of the continued existence of that stress or excitement at the time of the utterance . . ." *State v. Robinson*, 94 N.M. 693, 616 P.2d 406 (1980).

5) Fed. R. Evid. 803(2) is FRIES, so D's Sixth Amendment Confrontation Clause objection should be overruled as well.

2. State of Mind: Rule 803(3)

§ 8.09   In General

Rule 803(3) provides as follows:

Rule 803. The following are not excluded by the hearsay rule, even though the declarant is available as a witness:

(3) Then existing mental, emotional, or physical condition. A statement of the declarant's then existing state of mind, emotion, sensation, or physical condition (such as intent, plan, motive, design, mental feeling, pain, and bodily health), but not including a statement of memory or belief to prove the fact remembered or believed unless it relates to the execution, revocation, identification, or terms of declarant's will.

In § 2.07 we saw that when declarant's state of mind is a fact in issue, a statement about something else, from which we must *infer* declarant's state of mind, is *not* hearsay, but that a direct statement by the declarant as to her state of mind *is* hearsay. Fed. R. Evid. 803(3) provides that many (but not all!) hearsay statements directly stating declarant's state of mind are admissible over a hearsay objection.

Application of Fed. R. Evid. 803(3) raises the following issues:

1. *Declarant's first-hand knowledge.* The rule admits only statements by a declarant concerning his or her *own* state of mind, so first-hand knowledge is not really an issue. Regardless of whatever psychologists may tell us, Fed. R. Evid. 803(3) accepts that, for hearsay purposes at any rate, a person knows what he thinks, feels, wants, intends, fears, etc.

2. *Relevance of declarant's state of mind.* To understand the application of Fed. R. Evid. 803(3), it is important to pinpoint how evidence of the declarant's state of mind can be relevant to a lawsuit. State of mind can be relevant in a wide range of circumstances. The following are among the most common.

   (a)   State of mind is often an element of a crime, cause of action or defense. *See* § 8.10.

   (b)   A statement by the declarant as to pain, mental feeling or bodily health is often relevant in personal injury and similar actions. *See* § 8.11.

(c) A statement by the declarant as to his then-existing *intent* is a basis from which we can infer the declarant's subsequent conduct. This is sometimes referred to as the *"Hillmon* doctrine." *See* § 8.12.

(d) A statement by the declarant as to his then-existing intent to do something with another person is a basis from which we can infer that other person's subsequent conduct. This is sometimes referred to as "second party *Hillmon.*" *See* § 8.13.

3. *"Then-existing" state of mind v. "backward-looking" statements.* The rule covers only statements by the declarant about her state of mind at the time she is speaking, not statements about what she felt, thought, etc. at some time in the past. *See* § 8.14.

4. *Victim's fear of defendant.* In homicide cases, prosecutors often offer, and judges sometimes admit, testimony that a few days before V was killed, V told a friend that he or she was afraid that the defendant was going to kill him or her. Do such statements fall within Fed. R. Evid. 803(3)? *See* § 8.15.

5. *Will cases.* The rule recognizes an important exception to the "then-existing" restriction in litigation concerning declarant's will: in such cases, "backward-looking" statements are admissible. *See* § 8.16.

6. *Sixth Amendment Confrontation Clause. See* § 8.17.

§ 8.10 State of Mind as an Element of a Crime, Cause of Action, or Defense

In many civil lawsuits and in almost all criminal cases, a litigant is required to prove what a person's state of mind was. Failure to offer such proof will result in a directed verdict. To determine the mental element of a given crime, cause of action or defense, we look at the substantive law that defines that crime, cause of action or defense. Examples:

1. In a murder prosecution, the prosecutor must prove that the defendant killed the victim *intentionally* or with *malice aforethought;* while the defense might be that the defendant acted in the *reasonable belief* that he had to use deadly force in self-defense.

2. In an extortion trial, the prosecutor must prove that D placed the victim in *fear of death or bodily harm.*

3. In a libel action brought by a "public figure," P must establish that D's defamatory remarks were uttered *knowingly, or with reckless disregard of whether,* they were false.

4. In a fraud suit, P must prove that D did what she did with the *intent to defraud.* Often this involves showing that D *knew* that certain representations she made were untrue. D, on the other hand, might want to show that these representations were not "material" because P *did not rely* on D's representations.

In each instance, statements that shed light on the key person's state of mind (D in example 1; the extortion victim in example 2; D in example 3; both D and P in example 4) are highly relevant. Fed. R. Evid. 803(3) allows many such statements to be admitted even if they are hearsay.

Questions

Q. 4. An indictment charges D with first degree murder, alleging that, acting intentionally and with premeditation, she shot and killed Dr. T at four o'clock in the afternoon on June 1, 1999. (Dr. T had been D's long-time lover, but had jilted her for another woman a month before he died.) D, however, insists it was all a tragic accident. Her breakup with Dr. T had been quite amicable; she had gone to his home that day to return some items he had loaned her, including a .38 caliber pistol; that as she was handing it to him it slipped from her hand, fell to the ground, and discharged one bullet, which struck him in the chest and killed him.

What is the "mental element" of the crime D is charged with?

Ans. The indictment spells it out: D is accused of killing Dr. T "intentionally and with premeditation." Thus, any evidence that either side can offer concerning how D felt toward Dr. T on or near June 1 is highly relevant in assessing her guilt or innocence.

Q. 5. At trial, the prosecutor calls W1, a friend of D's, who will (reluctantly) testify that when D found out on May 10 that Dr. T was seeing another, younger woman, D exclaimed, "That louse! He's nothing but a two-timing gutter rat! He doesn't deserve to live!" If D objects that this is hearsay, how should the prosecutor respond? How should the judge rule?

Ans. Fed. R. Evid. 801(d)(2)(A). D said it; the prosecutor, her party-opponent in the case, is offering it. Objection overruled. If a statement satisfies Fed. R. Evid. 801(d)(2)(A), there is no reason to cite any other provision of Article VIII.

Q. 6. On cross-examination, D has W1 testify that on May 30, D told W1, "I hope I can persuade Dr. T to come back to me, but if not—well, I'll always be grateful to him anyway, and I wish him every happiness." If the prosecutor interposes a hearsay objection, what is D's best response, and how should the judge rule?

Ans. Fed. R. Evid. 803(3). D's statement was of her "then-existing state of mind" toward Dr. T. This is relevant because (if the jury believes that she said it and that she meant it at the time) it tends to negate the "mental state" element of the indictment (i.e. that she visited Dr. T on June 1 with a premeditated plan to kill him). Objection overruled.

Note that W's testimony may be manufactured—she may be lying to help D beat a murder charge; or D may have already decided to kill T, and may have made the statement to W1 as part of a plan to manufacture a defense. Fed. R. Evid. 803(3) does not, however, authorize the judge to exclude a statement merely because the judge thinks the witness is lying or doubts that the declarant was sincere when she made the statement. If the statement satisfies the rule's requirements, it comes in; it is up to the jury to decide (1) whether she in fact said it, and if so, (2) whether she meant it, and (3) if so, whether that grateful and benevolent attitude toward Dr. T existed at the time he was killed by shots fired from the gun she happened to be holding in her hand.

§ 8.11 Mental Feeling, Pain, Bodily Health

In litigation where someone's mental or physical condition is an issue, statements by that person describing mental feeling, pain, or bodily health may be admissible over a hearsay objection under Fed. R. Evid. 803(3). In a personal injury action, for example, P, and D both may seek to offer out-of-court statements by P, such as "My back hurts"; "Thank you, I'm feeling much better, the pain is almost gone"; "I still can't concentrate; I feel so lethargic all the time." So long as such statements describe declarant's then-existing mental or physical feeling, they fit within the scope of Fed. R. Evid. 803(3).

§ 8.12 Intent as a Basis to Infer Declarant's Subsequent Conduct: *"Hillmon* Doctrine"

If X, on March 4, told Y, "I plan to leave tomorrow for Colorado," or "This time tomorrow I'll be on my way to Colorado," that statement is relevant as tending to prove that X in fact left for Colorado on March 5. In *Mutual Life Ins. Co. v. Hillmon*, 145 U.S. 285, 295–297 (1892), the Supreme Court held that such a statement of intent, if offered as proof that the declarant subsequently did what he'd said he intended to do, is within the "state of mind" exception to the hearsay rule. The Advisory Committee Note to Fed. R. Evid. 803(3) makes it clear that the *Hillmon* rule, "allowing evidence of intention as tending to prove the doing of the act intended, is . . . left undisturbed."

Now suppose that on March 4, X had said to T, "Last week Z offered me a job in Crooked Creek, so tomorrow I'm leaving for Colorado." If this statement is offered to prove that X left for Colorado on March 5, the statement clearly fits within the *Hillmon* doctrine: if offered for that purpose, it is no different, really, than the statement in the first paragraph of this section. On the other hand, if this statement is offered as proof that Z *had offered X a job* in Crooked Creek, it falls outside the scope of 803(3), because X's statement that Z had offered him a job looks backward to something that (according to X) has already happened.

Question

Q. 7. Suppose both facts (whether Z offered X a job, and whether X left for Colorado on March 5) are relevant to the lawsuit. We've just seen that X's statement to T in the previous paragraph is admissible over a hearsay objection if offered to prove that X left for Colorado on March 5, but is inadmissible hearsay if offered to prove that Z had offered him a job there. How can we resolve the conflict?

Ans. There are several potential solutions.

(a) The judge could redact the statement, instructing T to testify only that X said "I'm leaving for Colorado tomorrow."

(b) If T testifies to the entire statement, the judge could issue a limiting instruction, per Fed. R. Evid. 105: the jury should consider the statement only regarding whether X left for Colorado on the 5th, but not as evidence that Z had offered X a job.

(c) If the risk of unfair prejudice on the job offer issue substantially outweighs the statement's legitimate probative value on whether X left for Colorado on the 5th, the judge should exclude the statement per Fed. R. Evid. 403.

§ 8.13 "Second-party *Hillmon*": Declarant's Statement of Intent to Do Something With Z, as Proof of Z's Subsequent Conduct

D is charged with killing X, whose body was found behind a barn. The last person known to have seen X alive is W, who will, if permitted, testify that "X told me, 'D and I are meeting tonight in back of the barn, to settle our dispute once and for all.' " The prosecutor offers this evidence, not (or not just) to prove that X went behind the barn that night, but to prove that *D met* with X behind the barn that night. This differs from straightforward application of the *Hillmon* doctrine because declarant X's statement of intent is being offered to prove not what X subsequently did, but what a second party (D) subsequently did.

For years prior to the enactment of the FRE, "Second-party *Hillmon*" was a matter of considerable debate among judges and scholars. The House Judiciary Committee Report on the Federal Rules rejected second-party *Hillmon*: "the Committee intends that [Fed. R. Evid. 803(3)] be construed to limit the [*Hillmon* doctrine], so as to render statements of intent by a declarant admissible only to prove his future conduct, not the future conduct of another person." Some courts, following the House Judiciary Committee lead, apparently have rejected second-party *Hillmon* outright; others have admitted such statements only when independent evidence strongly corroborates that the second party in fact engaged in the conduct predicted in declarant's statement.

Question

Q. 8. Borachio (D1) and Conrade (D2) are charged with assault and robbery. The indictment alleges that on March 1, 1999, they shot and seriously wounded Leonato and stole $5,000 from him.

As her first witness at trial, the prosecutor calls Don John, who will testify that before his conviction on narcotics charges in the summer of 1999, he was a crack dealer. Don John testifies that in late February of '99 (as best as he can remember, the 25th), Conrade told him, "Me and Borachio will be lookin' to score an eighth of a key soon. We been scopin' out a bad dude, and we're gonna take him off in just a couple of days."

(a) Why is this relevant?

Ans. Conrade's statement, "Me and Borachio . . . we're gonna take [a bad dude] off in just a couple of days," tends to prove that Conrade (the declarant) and Borachio (the "second party") were planning to rob someone soon so they could purchase cocaine. Thus, the statement tends to prove that Conrade and Borachio subsequently did precisely that.

(b) Both defendants object: hearsay. Ruling?

Ans. Conrade's objection is easily overruled, per Fed. R. Evid. 801(d)(2)(A) or 803(3). As to the latter, Conrade's statement of intent is admissible to prove that he later did what he said he intended to do.

The prosecutor cites 803(3) to Borachio's objection as well. But Borachio is not the declarant here. Hence, 803(3) admits Conrade's statement against Borachio only if we accept "second-party *Hillmon.*" At this point in the trial, the prosecutor has offered no corroboration of Borachio's alleged involvement in any robbery; hence, the statement should not be admitted.

Incidentally, if this question sounds familiar, it should: In Chapter 5, I used the same facts to illustrate the requirements of Fed. R. Evid. 801(d)(2)(E). (Question 5–15, § 5.21.) In §§ 5.17–5.19, we saw that 801(d)(2)(E) does not admit a statement against a nondeclarant defendant unless the offering party can satisfy that rule's requirements (which in essence go to the propriety of the statement's use against the nondeclarant defendant) by a preponderance of the evidence. Imposing the same requirement on second-party *Hillmon* is a logical middle ground between automatic exclusion of evidence which may be both needed and reliable, and admission of unreliable evidence.

§ 8.14 Declarant's "Then-existing" State of Mind

Fed. R. Evid. 803(3) admits, over a hearsay objection, statements by the declarant as to his *"then-existing* state of mind." By "then-existing" the rule means, existing at the time the declarant made the statement. "I am happy," "I feel depressed," "I'm hungry," "I don't trust her," "I plan to fly to Cleveland tomorrow" are all statements of the declarant's "then-existing" state of mind, because in each, the declarant is telling the listener what he is thinking or feeling or planning to do as he is speaking. By contrast, statements such as "I didn't like her back then," "Boy, was I hungry," "at the time I intended to take the job," etc. are *not* statements of the declarant's "then-existing" state of mind, because declarant is not telling us what she *is* thinking, feeling, or planning; rather, she's telling us what she thought, planned or felt *at some time in the past.* Similarly, declarant's out-of-court statement, "I remember that X hit Y first" would not be admissible under Fed. R. Evid. 803(3) as proof that X hit Y first. As Fed. R. Evid. 803(3) states, except in will cases, the rule does not "includ[e] a statement of memory or belief to prove the fact remembered or believed . . ."

Questions

Q. 9. P brings a personal injury action, alleging he suffered serious injury and considerable pain when he was run over by D's horse while out jogging. Consider the applicability of Fed. R. Evid. 803(1)–803(3) to each of the following:

(a) W1 will testify that as she passed P lying on the path, P shouted "Oh, my knee, my leg! It feels like it's broken! Oh, I can't stand it!"

Ans. This statement is admissible under any of these provisions.

(b) W2 will testify that as they were standing by the water cooler at work, P said, "I was knocked down by a horse last week, and I've felt dizzy and weak ever since."

Ans. "I feel dizzy" would be admissible Fed. R. Evid. 803(1) or 803(3), but "I was knocked down by a horse last week" probably would not be. It is not spontaneous enough for 803(1) or (2) and is backward-looking, so cannot fit within 803(3). (Nor, probably, will it satisfy Fed. R. Evid. 803(4). *See* §§ 8.19, 8.21.)

Q. 10. D is charged with murdering X. The indictment alleges that she shot and killed him at 4 p.m. on June 1. At trial the government introduces evidence that D and X had been lovers for many years, until X dumped D for a younger woman. D's defense is that she was merely returning several things to X, including a revolver he had loaned her; that it fell and went off accidentally, with tragic results. D wishes to have W2, a homicide detective, testify that when he arrested her at 6 p.m. on June 1, she cried, "I loved X! I could never do anything to hurt him!" The prosecutor objects: hearsay.

(a) D responds: Fed. R. Evid. 803(3). How should the judge rule?

Ans. A judge might understandably be tempted to reject this statement simply because it is so self-serving: D's protestations of a lack of criminal intent are precisely what we'd expect from someone who is facing a murder charge. On the other hand, it is questionable whether a judge may properly exclude a statement that appears to satisfy the Fed. R. Evid. 803(3) requirements, merely because the judge doesn't believe the statement is true.

The better basis to exclude the statement is that it isn't really about her state of mind toward X at 6 p.m., when she made the statement; rather, the statement looks backward in time to 4 p.m., when X was shot.

Under a strict application of Fed. R. Evid. 803(3), the evidence should be excluded, although decisions can be found admitting such statements. (I don't want to shock you, but judges occasionally bend the rules a bit to help a defendant toward whom they feel some sympathy.)

(b) D responds: 803(2), excited utterance. How should the judge rule?

Ans. Sustained. Two hours is a long time, and the statement is so self-serving that it may well be the product of reflection and fabrication. That a statement is self-serving is a valid factor to consider in applying Fed. R. Evid. 803(1) or 803(2), because the self-serving nature of the statement casts doubts on its spontaneity.

§ 8.15 Homicide Cases: Victim's Fear of Defendant

V is found murdered, and D is charged. At trial, the prosecutor wants to call W1 who will, if permitted, testify that a few days before V was killed, V told W1, "I'm afraid D is going to kill me." Similarly, W2 will testify that V told her, "I believe D is planning to kill me." D objects: "Hearsay." The prosecutor responds: "Fed. R. Evid. 803(3): V's state of mind." Ruling?

The prosecutor's response appears to be valid: belief and fear are states of mind, and in each case V was telling a friend what she[1] believed at the time, i.e. her "then-existing state of mind." Ah, but how is V's state of mind relevant? In each case, the statement is one of *belief*: V told W2 that she "*believes*" D is planning to kill her, and told W1 that she is afraid D will kill her; and fear, in this context, is another way of expressing a *belief* that something will happen.

Flip back for a moment to § 8.09, and re-read the text of Fed. R. Evid. 803(3).

V's statements are relevant only if we accept V's "statement of belief . . . to prove the fact . . . believed." Fed. R. Evid. 803(3) explicitly provides that a declarant's "statement of belief [is] not admissible" for that purpose. The judge should sustain the defendant's objection.

Besides, such statements are often simply too speculative to have much legitimate probative value, while the risk of unfair prejudice from such an uncross-examinable accusation "from the grave" is likely to be substantial. The statement should also be excluded on Fed. R. Evid. 403 grounds.

---

[1] This scenario occurs with some frequency where a defendant is accused of killing his wife, ex-wife, girlfriend or ex-girlfriend. It also occurs in cases where one alleged criminal is accused of killing another, for example in a dispute over who will control drug selling on a particular block or when a higher-up in a criminal organization suspects an underling of keeping more than his allotted share of the merchandise or profits.

Do not be surprised, though, to find cases in which courts cite Fed. R. Evid. 803(3) to admit such statements. Sometimes judges rely on labels ("statement of the victim's state of mind") without thinking things through.[2] And sometimes a judge will bend the rules a bit to help a prosecutor convict someone who (in the judge's opinion) deserves to be convicted.

Questions

Q. 11. D is accused of killing V, whose raped and strangled body was found in a motel in the next town. The state presents evidence that D and V had lived together for several months; that V moved out; that D kept trying to get V to "take him back"; that he constantly called her, came to the school where she taught, and followed her frequently. Evidence is introduced that the semen found in and on the victim matches D's DNA; his fingerprints were found in the hotel room.

(a) In addition, W1 will testify that, a few days before V was killed, she told W1, "D is going to kill me soon. I just know it!" Objection, hearsay. Ruling?

Ans. Sustained. V's belief that D would kill her is not admissible under Fed. R. Evid. 803(3) to "prove the fact believed."

(b) After the state rests, the defendant takes the stand and admits that he took V to the motel on the evening in question, but insists that she went willingly, and they made passionate and consensual love. Then they fell asleep. A few hours later, D insists, he woke up, got dressed and drove off, looking for food; when he returned to the hotel, V was dead. Someone must have broken in and done it while he was away.

In rebuttal, the state recalls W1 and proffers her testimony anew. Defendant renews the hearsay objection. Ruling? Is there an argument the state can make now that was not available in question (a)?

Ans. Now the prosecutor has a plausible non-hearsay use for the evidence: V's belief that D would kill her is relevant to rebut the defendant's testimony that V went with him willingly and consented to have sex. The evidence carries an obvious Fed. R. Evid. 403 risk, but a judge could legitimately admit the evidence and give a limiting instruction: "You may consider V's statement, that she believed the defendant would kill her soon, in deciding whether she went with D willingly and consented to have sex with him. You should not consider it, however, as evidence that D killed her." Granted, the likelihood that a jury could, or would, follow that instruction is, shall we say, not too great. But it would still be within a judge's discretion to allow the prosecutor to introduce V's statement.

§ 8.16 Will Cases

The rule admits backward-looking statements if they relate "to the execution, revocation, identification, or terms of declarant's will."[1] Whether such statements are inherently reliable is open to question. On the other hand, because litigation about a declarant's will occurs only after declarant is deceased, the need for such evidence, particularly in cases where the will has been lost or where doubts have been cast upon the document's authenticity, is obvious. This is an exception in which need for the evidence trumps doubts about its reliability.

Questions

Q. 12. X dies; D, the executor of her estate, files a document purporting to be X's will. P, her son, challenges the document (in which P was left only $100 and the rest of X's assets are to go

---

[2] That's why they are only judges, rather than (ahem) law professors.

[1] It would make more sense simply to create, or recognize, a separate exception for statements by a declarant about the existence or contents of his or her will, rather than tacking it onto the end of the "state of mind" exception. The two were linked together at common law, however, and the FRE retained this approach.

to D, a second cousin) as a forgery. After P presents his case, D calls W1, who will testify that on July 1, X told W1: "I'm signing my new will tomorrow. I warned my son that if he didn't stop drinking and gambling I'd disinherit him, and tomorrow I'm going to do just that." P objects: hearsay. Ruling?

Ans. Overruled. This is straightforward *Hillmon* doctrine: X's statement of intent is offered to prove that she subsequently did what she said she intended to do. This, in turn, tends to support the authenticity of the contested document.

Q. 13. D also calls W2, who will testify that on July 9, X told W2: "I feel quite depressed. I signed a new will last week leaving my son only $100." Objection, hearsay. Response, 803(3). Ruling?

Ans. Overruled. This is backward-looking, so normally Fed. R. Evid. 803(3) would be inapplicable; but in a will case, backward-looking statements *are* admissible.

§ 8.17 Sixth Amendment Confrontation Clause

The Supreme Court probably would categorize most Fed. R. Evid. 803(3) statements as having "independent evidentiary significance." If it is important to decide what DL knew, thought, feared, hoped, felt or planned on January 1, 1999, her statements about her state of mind on that date would be significant even if (assuming she was available at trial) she took the stand and testified as to what she remembered knowing, thinking, fearing, etc. back on that date.

Fed. R. Evid. 803(3) is also "firmly rooted": the Court recognized it more than a century ago in *Hillmon*.

Thus, in most respects, of Fed. R. Evid. 803(3) is a "FRIES" exception, and statements that satisfy the exception automatically satisfy the Confrontation Clause.

Two aspects of Fed. R. Evid. 803(3), however, may not be "FRIES."

First, "second-party *Hillmon*" statements. American courts have accepted such statements at least since the 1820's, and the Supreme Court cited one such case approvingly in the *Hillmon* decision itself. On the other hand, many courts have rejected "second-party *Hillmon*" altogether. Some courts might be willing to accept "second-party *Hillmon*" statements in civil cases but not when offered by a prosecutor in a criminal case. The law is unclear.

Second: the "will case" aspect of Fed. R. Evid. 803(3). There is nothing inherently reliable about a declarant's statement concerning the contents of a will she might have executed months, years or even decades before—if she executed a will at all. (This is a subject about which people have been frequently known to lie or misremember.) Thus, although the law has long recognized this exception in litigation about the contents of a declarant-testator's will, should the issue ever arise in a criminal case, a court very likely would conclude that such a statement is not inherently reliable enough to satisfy the "firmly rooted" prong of the Confrontation Clause. Moreover, if the actual contents of a will ever became an issue in a criminal case, a testator's backward looking statement on the subject certainly would not have "evidentiary significance" independent of the document itself. Thus, before a prosecutor could call W to testify as to what DL said about the contents of DL's will, the prosecutor would either have to produce the will, call DL as a witness, or demonstrate that DL was unavailable.

§ 8.18 Questions

Q. 14. In a civil action (P v. D), a relevant fact is whether X made an oral employment contract on December 31 to pay Y $1,000 per week for one year. Consider the admissibility over a hearsay objection of each of the following:

(a) P calls W1, who will testify that on December 29, X told W1, "I'm going to offer Y a job at $1,000 per week for the coming year."

Ans. Admissible, Fed. R. Evid. 803(3), per the *Hillmon* doctrine, to prove that X subsequently made the offer. (The Sixth Amendment Confrontation Clause need not be considered, since this is a civil, not a criminal, case.)

(b) P calls W2, who will testify that on December 28, X said, "Y and I are going to sign a contract on the 31st: he'll work for me for a year at $1,000 a week."

Ans. This is "second-party *Hillmon*": declarant X's statement of intent to do something is offered as proof that someone else (Y) did something. At least absent corroboration, it should be excluded.

(c) P calls W3, who will testify that on January 4, Y said, "Boy, am I glad my money troubles are over! I just started a new job with X on the first of the year—at a thou a week!"

Ans. This might look admissible under Fed. R. Evid. 803(3): it is Y's statement about his then-existing "gladness," which is certainly a state of mind. But this law suit isn't about whether Y was "glad" or not, it is about whether X offered and Y accepted an oral employment contract at $1,000 per week.

Thus, on the issue on which the statement is relevant, the statement looks backward: it is relevant only if we accept Y's assertion that he had started working for X. (If Y had simply said, "I work for X," that statement, if offered to prove that Y worked for X at the time, would fall outside Fed. R. Evid. 803(3); so would a statement such as "I'm glad I work for X.")

Q. 15. D shot and killed X after they argued, and D is accused of murder. D claims she acted in self-defense, which requires a showing that she acted in the reasonable belief that she had to use deadly force to protect herself from death or serious injury. At trial, D calls W1, who will testify that a few days before D and X had the fatal encounter, D said, "I'm afraid X is out to get me, because she thinks I've been messing around with her husband." Admissible, over a hearsay objection?

Ans. It depends on why D is offering it. If D is trying to prove that X really *was* "out to get" her, it is not admissible. But if it is offered to support D's defense that she had a *reasonable belief* that she would have to defend herself against possible violence from X, it is admissible evidence of D's then-existing state of mind per Fed. R. Evid. 803(3). (That D was afraid of violence from X a few days before the fatal encounter supports the inference that D was still afraid of X on the day X was killed.)

The Sixth Amendment Confrontation Clause need not be considered, because here it is the defendant, not the prosecutor, who is offering the hearsay.

Q. 16. In a different homicide trial, L is accused of killing M; L's defense is a straightforward denial of all involvement. At trial the prosecutor calls W1, who will, if permitted, testify that a few days before M was shot, M told W1, "I'm afraid L is out to get me, because he thinks I've been messing around with his wife." Admissible, over a hearsay objection? If so, should the evidence be excluded on any other ground?

Ans. The prosecutor may argue that Fed. R. Evid. 803(3) overcomes the hearsay objection, at least as to the first portion of M's statement ("I'm afraid L is out to get me").

But the evidence should be excluded. Fed. R. Evid. 803(3) does not admit a declarant's "statement of belief [i.e. M's fear that L was 'out to get' him] . . . to prove the fact . . . believed [i.e. that L was in fact 'out to get' M]." *See* § 8.15.

Superficially, this question looks a lot like the previous one, in which we admitted D's pre-homicide statement that she was afraid of V. But there is a fundamental difference between the two questions. In *this* question, evidence relates, not to the *defendant's fear of the victim*, but the *victim's fear of the defendant.* Unlike the previous question, where the defendant's state of mind (fear of the victim) *was* an element of the crime or defense, here, the *victim's* fear is not an element of the crime or defense. M's statement is relevant, therefore, only if we assume he could accurately gauge the state of *someone else's* mind ("L thinks . . .") and could accurately predict what L would do ("L's out to get me").

Q. 17. Assuming D in problem 15 and L in problem 16 are married to each other, can this marriage be saved? If so, is it worth it?

3. Statements for Purposes of
Medical Diagnosis or Treatment: Rule 803(4)

§ 8.19 In General

Fed. R. Evid. 803(4) provides as follows:

> **Rule 803. The following are not excluded by the hearsay rule, even though the declarant is available as a witness:**
>
> **(4) Statements for purposes of medical diagnosis or treatment. Statements made for purposes of medical diagnosis or treatment and describing medical history, or past or present symptoms, pain, or sensations, or the inception or general character of the cause or external source thereof insofar as reasonably pertinent to diagnosis or treatment.**

Statements that fall within this provision are considered trustworthy because the declarant has a strong motive to be truthful and accurate when providing information on which health care providers will be diagnosing a condition or devising a treatment scheme. Moreover, because the declarant is (usually) describing her own symptoms, the risk of misperception or misremembering are also thought to be comparatively minor.

Application of Fed. R. Evid. 803(4) involves the following issues:

1. *First-hand knowledge and second-party statements.* Under appropriate circumstances, statements are admissible even if the declarant is speaking about a second party, not herself. *See* § 8.20.

2. *Purpose.* A statement falls within Fed. R. Evid. 803(4) only if it was made "for purposes of medical diagnosis or treatment." *See* § 8.21.

3. *Person to whom the statement was made.* The Advisory Committee Note points out that "the statement need not have been made to a physician. Statements to hospital attendants, ambulance drivers, or even members of the family might be included" so long as they were made for purposes of diagnosis or treatment.

4. *"Pertinent"; cause; fault.* Statements are admissible only to the extent that they are "pertinent" to diagnosis or treatment. While this often incudes information concerning the cause of the patient's condition, statements attributing fault or blame are not included within the rule. *See* § 8.22.

5. *Interplay with other rules. See* § 8.23.

6. *Sixth Amendment Confrontation Clause. See* § 8.24.

§ 8.20 First-hand Knowledge; Second-party Statements

When a patient describes her own condition and symptoms ("Doctor, my back has been hurting ever since I —"), she is relating facts of which she has first-hand knowledge; such statements pose no particular difficulties.

Suppose, though, the patient is an infant, or an adult who is unable to communicate with health care personnel. For example, at four in the afternoon a baby's mother tells a doctor, "He started acting cranky and fussy this morning, right after he had a jar of Beechbaby's strained applesauce. He wouldn't eat his lunch, didn't even want to nurse. At around one-thirty I noticed he was feeling feverish, and even after I gave him baby aspirin, he felt warm." In subsequent litigation (against, perhaps, the Beechbaby Food Company), the doctor should be permitted to testify as to the mother's statements, because her statements fit within 803(4): she made those statements for purposes of medical diagnosis and treatment and she has first-hand knowledge of what happened, even though she is describing someone else's condition, not her own.

Suppose instead the statement is: "Doctor, my husband came home this evening complaining of heartburn. He said he had some very spicy pastrami for lunch and it's been bothering him all afternoon. He took a bicarb and lay down and now he's hot all over and he's drooling and I can't wake him up!" (Let us assume she and her husband are suing the restaurant at which he purchased the sandwich.) This situation differs a bit from the two previous ones, because here the declarant lacks first-hand knowledge of some important information (the nature of the ailment at its onset, when the symptoms started, and their probable cause). But should it be excluded as unreliable for this reason? She obtained the information from her husband. *He* had first-hand knowledge of these facts; it's unlikely he misperceived or misremembered them. Unless specific reasons exist to doubt the trustworthiness of what the husband told his wife, there is no logical reason to exclude those aspects of what she said to the doctor.

On the other hand, in this situation we are dealing with multiple hearsay: (1) husband to wife; (2) wife to doctor. The second level clearly comes within Fed. R. Evid. 804(4): she said what she said to the doctor to help the doctor diagnose and treat her husband. Level one, husband to wife poses the difficulties.

a. That the husband complained of heartburn that night comes within Fed. R. Evid. 803(3), but the part of the statement that is most important for litigation purposes, that his trouble started with the pastrami sandwich, does not, because that part of the statement is backward looking.

b. Husband to wife might come within Fed. R. Evid. 803(4), but only if the judge concludes that he told her about the sandwich and the heartburn for purposes of seeking diagnosis or treatment. A sympathetic judge might agree. A skeptical judge might reason that a passably intelligent adult male would not need his wife's advice before taking a bicarb or antacid for heartburn.

c. If the judge concludes that the husband's statement to the wife does not come within Fed. R. Evid. 803(4), plaintiffs might argue that Fed. R. Evid. 807, the "residual" exception, applies. Fed. R. Evid. 807 is covered in Chapter 10.

§ 8.21 "For Purposes of Medical Diagnosis or Treatment"

Fed. R. Evid. 803(4) is used most often in physical injury or similar suits. P is injured; he tells Dr. PW1 what hurts, how long it has hurt, and why. Dr. PW1 forms an opinion of the nature and extent of the injury or ailment and decides on a regime of treatment. Months or years later, P files suit against D, alleging D's negligence caused his injury.

Prior to trial, P's attorney arranges for him to be examined by Dr. PW2. Dr. PW2 will not participate in any way in the treatment of P's condition; he is being consulted solely so he can give expert testimony about the nature, severity and duration of P's ailment. As part of his examination of P, PW2 asks P a detailed series of questions about P's condition and medical history.

At trial, P calls Dr. PW1, to have her testify as to her diagnosis and the treatment she prescribed. In explaining her conclusions, prognosis, and treatment, Dr. PW1 will naturally want to include what P told her during that first visit and during subsequent examinations and treatment.

Similarly, P calls Dr. PW2, to have him testify as to his diagnosis of P's condition. In explaining his conclusions, Dr. PW2 will naturally want to include what P told him during his examination of P.

Prior to the enactment of the Federal Rules, the law recognized a hearsay exception only for statements made with the ultimate goal of seeking *medical treatment*. P's statements to PW1 were admissible as proof of the truth of the matter asserted, because P made those statements so PW1 could diagnose, and thus prescribe a treatment for, P's condition. P's statements to Dr. PW2, by contrast, fell outside the pre-Federal Rules hearsay exception, because P's appointment with Dr. PW2 wasn't for purposes of treatment, but only to help PW2 form a *diagnosis* so he could give expert testimony at trial.

This may seem like a logical enough distinction, but there is a complicating factor. Rules governing expert testimony permit an expert to spell out to the jury the information on which the expert based his opinion: information which would include statements P had made to PW2. When this occurred, the judge would have to instruct the jury that P's statements to PW2 were not admissible to prove the truth of the matter asserted, but only to inform the jury of the basis upon which PW2 formed his opinion. If this arcane distinction doesn't make much sense to you, you can imagine how much it made to the typical jury.

Fed. R. Evid. 803(4) solves this dilemma by providing that statements made for purposes of diagnosis *or* treatment fall within the scope of the hearsay exception. Thus, PW2, like PW1, can repeat statements made to him by P without the need of a limiting instruction.

§ 8.22 "Pertinent"; Cause; Fault

The rule includes only statements that are reasonably "pertinent" to treatment or diagnosis. This often includes an explanation of the cause of the injury or ailment, but not an allocation of fault. If the patient tells the doctor, "As I was crossing the street I was struck by a car *that ran a red light,*" the first part of the statement would be admissible but the italicized portion would not be.

Courts sometimes encounter difficulties applying this requirement with statements made to a psychiatrist or psychologist, because arguably almost anything could be "pertinent" in that setting, including attributions of fault.

§ 8.23 Interplay with Other Rules

If a statement about a physical sensation doesn't satisfy Fed. R. Evid. 803(4) because it was not made for purposes of diagnosis or treatment, it still may be admissible under Fed. R. Evid. 803(1)-(3).

Fed. R. Evid. 803(4) is often used together with Fed. R. Evid. 803(6) or 803(8), the business and public record exceptions. *See* § 8.49. Fed. R. Evid. 803(4) is often used together with rules regulating expert testimony. This is discussed briefly in § 8.21.

The law recognizes a privilege for statements made by a patient to a doctor. (*See* Article V of the Federal Rules of Evidence.) The privilege entitles the patient to prevent a litigant from forcing the doctor to repeat such statements. Fed. R. Evid. 803(4) in no way defeats this privilege. On the other hand, if P is suing for personal injuries, P has every right to waive the privilege and elicit such testimony from doctors P calls as witnesses. Once P does so, D can also elicit such testimony from doctors who examined P. As a practical matter, therefore, the privilege does not very often interfere with the admissibility of such statements.

§ 8.24 Sixth Amendment Confrontation Clause

In *White v. Illinois*, 502 U.S. 346, 356 (1992), the Supreme Court held that "a statement made in the course of procuring medical services, where the declarant knows that a false statement may cause misdiagnosis or mistreatment, carries special guarantees of credibility that a trier of fact may not think replicated by courtroom testimony." Thus, such statements have "independent evidentiary significance" and sufficient indicia of reliability to survive a Confrontation Clause challenge. In other words, Fed. R. Evid. 803(3) is a "FRIES" exception.

Statements made to expert witnesses purely for the purposes of diagnosis for expert testimony, on the other hand, have less inherent reliability, because the declarant makes such statements to obtain expert testimony, not treatment. My best guess is that such statements would not be considered "firmly rooted," would not have "independent evidentiary significance," and would not survive a Confrontation Clause objection.

§ 8.25 Questions

Q. 18. P sues for compensation for on-the-job injuries she claims she suffered on June 1, 1998. During a pretrial deposition, W1, P's husband, testified that when P came home from work that evening, she said, "My back is killing me! My supervisor ordered me to lift some heavy boxes and now I can hardly stand up!" P's attorney intends to elicit the same testimony from WI at trial. If D makes a hearsay objection, what are P's best arguments for admission? How should the judge rule?

Ans. (a) Fed. R. Evid. 803(4)

Because the statement was not made to a health care professional, the first question is whether it falls within Fed. R. Evid. 803(4) at all. The Advisory Committee Note observed that statements to non-doctors, including family members, can come within the rule. To satisfy 803(4), though, P must persuade the judge that what she said was pertinent to and "for purposes of diagnosis and treatment." The facts don't give much indication of this, and unless P can make that showing, 803(4) is not likely to apply.

If P made the statement to her husband purposes of "diagnosis or treatment"—because, even though he is not a health care professional, she respects her husband's judgement about how to treat aches and pains—then most of it should be admitted under Fed. R. Evid. 803(4), but not all. W1 should be permitted to testify that his wife said "I hurt my back lifting heavy boxes and now it's so bad I can hardly stand up," but not that the injury occurred at work or that her supervisor ordered her to lift them.

(b) We would arrive at the same result under Fed. R. Evid. 803(3). P's husband can repeat the portions of the statement in which she told him about her then-existing sensations: "My back is killing me! . . . I can hardly stand up!" The middle portion of her statement ("supervisor . . . boxes") looks backward in time, though, and for that reason is not admissible under 803(3).

(c) P can also argue that a sharp jab of pain was a "startling event"; that her statement therefore was an excited utterance, Fed. R. Evid. 803(2); and that her explanation ("supervisor . . . boxes") "related to" the event and is therefore admissible. A sympathetic judge might accept this argument and admit, but to do so would probably be stretching the rule a bit.

Keep in mind that even if the judge excludes the middle portion of the statement, *P* can still testify about how she hurt her back; P's *testimony* doesn't involve hearsay. All that would be excluded is W1's testimony about part of what P said when she arrived home that night.

Q. 19. Later in the trial, P calls W2, a chiropractor who treated P's back injury. W2 will, if permitted, testify that on June 7, when she first visited his office, P told him, "I hurt my back on June 1 at work when my supervisor told me to move some heavy boxes." Admissible, over D's hearsay objection?

Ans. P's best argument is Fed. R. Evid. 803(4). A strict application of the rule, however, would admit only "I hurt my back on June 1 moving some heavy boxes," and the judge would likely tell the jury to consider only that much of the statement. Reason: while the doctor needs to know how P injured herself ("lifting some heavy boxes"), it is not pertinent to treatment for him to know that P did so on orders of her supervisor.

Q. 20. D is accused of sexually assaulting V, a nine-year-old boy. V's mother learned of the assault when V came crying to her and said, "D made me do bad things and it hurts!" When his mother asked "What bad things?" V described them. Can the mother testify as to what V said, if D interposes hearsay and Confrontation Clause objections?

Ans. The prosecutor will cite two rules: excited utterance, Fed. R. Evid. 803(2); statement for purposes of medical treatment, Fed. R. Evid. 803(4). A judge could legitimately admit the statement under either. For example, that the child came crying to his mother strongly suggests he was still "under the stress" of the startling event. But some courts are very skeptical about admitting the portion of the statement in which the child names the alleged perpetrator.

As to the Confrontation Clause, the Supreme Court, in *White v. Illinois*, 502 U.S. 346, 356–357 (1992), held that both of these exceptions satisfy the Confrontation Clause in a child molestation case whose facts resemble this problem.

Q. 21. The next day, the mother took the child to a doctor. The child told the doctor, "D made me [etc.]." Is the doctor's testimony about the child's statements admissible, over hearsay and Confrontation Clause objections?

Ans.

(a) Fed. R. Evid. 803(2) probably will not apply here, because many hours, perhaps a full day, has elapsed between the event and these statements.

(b) Fed. R. Evid. 803(4) overcomes the hearsay objection so far as *what* was done to the child, because the doctor will need this information to diagnose and treat the child's physical injuries. Whether it overcomes the objection as to the identity of the perpetrator is a closer question. D should argue that 803(4) does not admit statements relating to fault or blame. Unless the prosecutor can come up with a counterargument that brings the identity of the perpetrator within the scope of information pertinent for diagnosis and treatment, D should succeed in excluding the fact that the child identified him to the doctor as the perpetrator.

The prosecutor can argue that the identity of the perpetrator is important in helping diagnose and treat the child for at least two reasons. (1) The information could be vital in assessing the risk that the child may have contracted a sexually transmitted disease. (2) A doctor would need to know the perpetrator's identity in diagnosing and treating the emotional impact of the assault. Courts are sharply divided about the admissibility of the part of a child's statement identifying the perpetrator.

(c) *Confrontation clause. See* § 8.24. If the part of the statement identifying the perpetrator survives a hearsay objection, it will also survive a Confrontation Clause challenge.

C. COMMON WRITTEN STATEMENTS

1. "Refreshing Recollection," Rule 612; "Recorded Recollection" Rule 803(5)

§ 8.26 Rule 612: "Refreshing Recollection"

When a witness takes the stand at trial, the preferred form of testimony comes from the witness' unaided memory. As every trial lawyer quickly learns, however, a witness' unaided memory can be remarkably unreliable, particularly under the pressure and tension of direct and cross-examination. Whenever possible, therefore, an attorney should employ a variety of techniques to enhance a witness's recollection. The most frequently used methods are preparation and repetition. Prior to trial, a lawyer should rehearse the direct and probable cross-examination with a willing witness as often as time permits. When documents or written memoranda exist concerning the subject matter of the witness' testimony, the lawyer should urge the witness to study them prior to trial to further enhance his memory.

Nevertheless, a cooperative witness may suffer a lapse of memory on the witness stand. When this occurs, the attorney need not forgo eliciting the information; instead, the law provides a variety of options. The first step is attempting to refresh the witness' recollection. The most direct is simply to supply the missing information to the witness in the guise of a question:

Q. Ms. White, tell us, please, who attended the meeting.

A. Let's see, quite a few people were there—um, there was Bashful, and Dopey, and Grumpy, and Happy, and Sleepy, and Sneezy.

Q. Anyone else?

A. Not that I recall.

Q. What about Doc. Was he there?

A. Oh, yes, that's right, he was there, too.

This may not be quite as impressive to the jury as if Ms. White could rattle off all seven names without prompting, but it gets the information out, and that's the important thing.

Suppose, though, that the important details are too complex to be put into a simple question; or suppose the witness gets very confused and flustered. When this happens, the attorney can attempt to refresh the witness' recollection by showing her a document or memorandum (or anything else, for that matter).

Q. Ms. White, tell us who was there.

A. Um, let me see. There was Greasey and Weepy and Sleazy and—no, wait, that's not right—

Q. Your Honor, may I show the witness a document to refresh her recollection?

(Judge): Yes. Have it marked first as an exhibit for identification.

(The clerk marks the document.)

Q. Ms. White, examine Defense exhibit 12 for identification. Does that refresh your recollection?

A. Yes. Thank you.

Once Ms. White has refreshed her recollection, the attorney can resume direct examination.

This technique of using a writing to refresh a witness' recollection during testimony can also be used on an uncooperative witness who professes to a lack of memory to avoid testifying to certain facts. The attorney may confront the witness with a writing under the guise of refreshing his recollection in an effort to browbeat the witness into saying what the witness would prefer to keep unsaid.

The use of a document to refresh memory is governed by Fed. R. Evid. 612,[1] which provides, in pertinent part:

Rule 612. Writing Used to Refresh Memory

[I]f a witness uses a writing to refresh memory for the purposes of testifying, either—

(1) while testifying, or

(2) before testifying, if the court in its discretion determines it is necessary in the interests of justice,

an adverse party is entitled to have the writing produced at the hearing, to inspect it, to cross-examine the witness thereon, and to introduce in evidence those portions which relate to the testimony of the witness. . . .

---

[1] Procedural aspects of Fed. R. Evid. 612 are not covered here.

(Matthew Bender & Co., Inc.)

Note that Fed. R. Evid. 612 is *not* a hearsay exception, and does not permit the party using a writing to refresh a witness' memory to introduce it, or ask the witness to read it aloud, or in any other way get its contents directly before the jury. In fact, Fed. R. Evid. 612 is included within the Federal Rules, first, to make clear that the party using 612 can*not* offer the document in evidence, and second, to ensure that the *other* party in the suit has the right to examine, use, and offer the document in evidence if it chooses to do so.

Thus, if, while W1 is testifying, D's attorney shows W1 a document to refresh W1's memory, D's attorney must then also show the document to P's attorney. P's attorney can cross-examine W1 about the document and, if she thinks it will help her case, can introduce the relevant portions of the document into evidence.

What happens, though, when a witness—cooperative, neutral, or hostile—asserts, sincerely or not, that she cannot remember the event (or the important details) in question, even after the attorney has attempted to use a writing to refresh her memory? Depending upon circumstances, an attorney may have a number of alternatives (or none at all). One such alternative is Fed. R. Evid. 803(5).

§ 8.27 Rule 803(5): "Recorded Recollection"

Fed. R. Evid. 803(5) provides as follows:

> **Rule 803. The following are not excluded by the hearsay rule, even though the declarant is available as a witness:**
>
> **(5) Recorded recollection. A memorandum or record concerning a matter about which a witness once had knowledge but now has insufficient recollection to enable the witness to testify fully and accurately, shown to have been made or adopted by the witness when the matter was fresh in the witness' memory and to reflect that knowledge correctly. If admitted, the memorandum or record may be read into evidence but may not itself be received as an exhibit unless offered by an adverse party.**

In essence, the law establishes a sequence of preferences. The first preference is testimony by unaided memory; next comes testimony by refreshed memory (the Fed. R. Evid. 612 procedure). If the witness simply cannot recall the important details, even after attempting to refresh his memory by looking at a Fed. R. Evid. 612 writing, a memorandum that satisfies Fed. R. Evid. 803(5) is an accepted substitute: instead of testifying from memory, the witness reads the document aloud to the jury.

§ 8.28 Read, But Not Received

Because a memorandum or record admitted under Fed. R. Evid. 803(5) is considered a substitute for testimony (albeit less preferred), it is treated the same way testimony would be: the witness reads it aloud to the jury, just as if the witness would speak aloud to the jury if testifying from memory. The party using Fed. R. Evid. 803(5) cannot offer the document as an exhibit for the jury to examine in the courtroom or (once jury deliberations begin) in the jury room; if this were allowed, the jury might give the memorandum greater emphasis than it gives to "live" testimony, the preferred form of evidence.

The other party in the suit may, however, offer the document into evidence, if, for example, she thinks it may help her impeach the witness.

§ 8.29 Rule 803(5): Requirements and Issues

Application of Fed. R. Evid. 803(5) imposes the following requirements and raises the following issues:

1. *Declarant must testify*: The person whose memorandum is to be offered under Fed. R. Evid. 803(5) must be on the witness stand when it is offered. *See* § 8.30. (To emphasize this point, a Fed. R. Evid. 803(5) declarant is hereinafter referred to as "DL/W"—i.e., declarant-witness.) DL/W's testimony must suffice to establish the remaining requirements listed below.

2. *First-hand knowledge.* The declarant/witness must testify that at one time he had first-hand knowledge of the facts at issue.

3. *Lacks sufficient recollection.* DL/W must testify that he now "has insufficient recollection . . . to testify fully and accurately." To satisfy this requirement, the party who will offer evidence via Fed. R. Evid. 803(5) should first attempt to refresh the witness's recollection (Fed. R. Evid. 612). *See* § 8.34.

4. *Memorandum or record.* DL/W must identify (authenticate) the document, tape recording, or whatever that is being offered as a substitute for his "live" testimony. *See* § 8.31.

5. *"Made or adopted."* DL/W must testify that he "made or adopted" the memorandum or record "at or near the time of the condition or event, while the event was still fresh in DL/W's memory." *See* § 8.35.

6. *Accuracy.* DL/W must testify that the memorandum or record correctly recorded the facts that he once knew. *See* § 8.36.

7. *Read but not received.* When Fed. R. Evid. 803(5) has been satisfied, the memorandum or record is read aloud to the judge and jury, but cannot be physically moved into evidence by the offering party. *See* § 8.28.

8. *Sixth Amendment Confrontation Clause. See* § 8.36.

§ 8.30 Declarant/Witness

A memorandum or record can be offered in evidence under Fed. R. Evid. 803(5) only if, and while, a person who (a) had first-hand knowledge of the facts in question, and who (b) made or adopted the memorandum or record, is testifying on the witness stand. This is so because only the declarant can give the testimony necessary to demonstrate that the memorandum satisfies the rule's requirements. Moreover, this assures that the party against whom the 803(5) statements are offered has an opportunity to cross-examine the person who supplied the information contained in the memorandum or record. Even if the declarant/witness doesn't remember very much about the facts in question, cross-examination can help the jury assess his credibility as a person and the reliability of the memorandum.

To require the declarant to be a witness, as Fed. R. Evid. 803(5) does, may seem inconsistent with Fed. R. Evid. 803 generally, which is, after all, entitled, "Availability of declarant immaterial." The Advisory Committee conceded that, conceptually, this rule does not fit very comfortably into Fed. R. Evid. 803, but decided to put it there anyway.

§ 8.31 "Record or Memorandum"

The rule does not require that the "record or memorandum" take any particular form, so long as the information is recorded in some way; on paper (handwritten or typed), on floppy or hard disk, dictated onto a cassette tape, etc.

§ 8.32 A Straightforward Example

W1 was the manager of the XYZ store. On September 10, 1998, she conducted an inventory of its merchandise. That night a fire broke out and everything in the store was destroyed. (Fortuitously, W1 brought the inventory form with her when she left the store.) Subsequently, XYZ sues its insurance company to collect on the policy. The case goes to trial in June, 2003.

To prove how much merchandise was on hand, XYZ calls W1 to the stand. Direct examination proceeds as follows.

Q. 1. Describe how you conducted the inventory.

Ans. After the store closed for the night, I counted how many pieces we had of each item of merchandise, and wrote the number down on our monthly inventory sheet.

Q. 2. You personally counted each item before recording it on the list?

Ans. That's right.

Q. 3. Do you recall, today, how many pieces of each item of merchandise you had in stock that night?

Ans. Oh, no. The store carried hundreds of items; I couldn't even remember that then, let alone three years later!

Q. 4. Your Honor, may I have this document marked as Plaintiff's exhibit 17? [It is so marked.] Ms. W1, please examine Plaintiff's 17. Do you recognize it?

Ans. Yes, that's the inventory I filled out on September 10, 1998.

Q. 5. How do you know?

Ans. I recognize the form as the kind we used; I see where I wrote the date down on it; and its got my signature on the bottom.

Q. 6. Read it over, please. [W1 does so.] Could you now testify from memory as to how many of each item were on stock on September 10?

Ans. Sorry, no, I can't.

Q. 7. Are you satisfied now that this inventory correctly recorded the merchandise on hand on September 10, 1998?

Ans. Oh, yes. I was always very careful when I took inventory.

XYZ: Your Honor, I now offer Plaintiff's 17 in evidence.

[Judge]: Without objection, it is so received.

[Whereupon, it is read into the record.]

This sequence of questions methodically takes W1 through each of the requirements of Fed. R. Evid. 803(5). Q1 and Q2, and W1's answers, establish that W1, the declarant/witness, once had first-hand knowledge of the information on the form: she personally counted each piece of merchandise. Q3 establishes that W1 cannot testify fully and accurately without refreshing her recollection; Q6 establishes that she cannot do so even after examining the form. Q4 and Q5 identify and authenticate the document as the document in question. Q7 establishes that the inventory list accurately reflects the information of which W1 had first-hand knowledge at the time she was counting each item of merchandise.

§ 8.33 Multiple-person Documents

Often a record or memorandum is a collaborative effort; more than one person participates in its creation. This is no automatic bar to using the document under Fed. R. Evid. 803(5); the Advisory Committee Note states that "[m]ultiple person involvement in the process of observing and recording is entirely consistent with the exception." The Senate Judiciary Committee gives, as examples, "employer dictating to secretary, secretary making memorandum at direction of employer, or information being passed along a chain of persons. . ." Again, the key requirement is that someone who had first-hand knowledge of the facts in question testifies to the accuracy of the memorandum.

Questions

Q. 22. In the inventory discussed in § 8.32, suppose two employees worked together to take inventory. W1 testifies that she and W2 spent several hours doing the inventory; that W2 examined each shelf or storage bin and told W1 what it contained, and W1 kept a tally on a company form. W1 testifies that she recalls what kinds of merchandise were in the warehouse, but cannot remember how many of each had been there at the time. She is shown a document (which P's attorney first had marked as Plaintiff's exh. 1 for identification) and is asked, "do you recognize it?"

"Yes, that's the form I wrote the inventory down on, based on what W2 told me. It's in my handwriting and I put the date on it, here."

Plaintiff's counsel seeks to have the contents of exhibit one read into evidence. D objects: hearsay. In response, P cites Fed. R. Evid. 803(5). Ruling?

Ans. Objection sustained. Fed. R. Evid. 803(5) requires that a showing that, at one time, the witness/declarant (W1) had first-hand knowledge of the information recorded in the document. W1 did not have such knowledge, because he didn't do the actual counting; W2 did.

Q. 23. Is the inventory admissible if W1 further testifies that after all of the merchandise was inventoried in this fashion, W2 read W1's list over, said "Yup, that's right," and signed it?

Ans. No. Fed. R. Evid. 803(5) requires that the person who had first-hand knowledge (in this case, W2) testify, to authenticate and vouch for the accuracy of the list. It is not enough that W1 assert that W2 vouched for it.

Q. 24. W2 now takes the stand and testifies that he is sure that he counted accurately the number of each items and reported accurately to W1. Does W1's list now qualify under Fed. R. Evid. 803(5)?

Ans. Yes. The Advisory Committee and Senate Judiciary Committee cite approvingly to cases upholding admissibility in this kind of situation. The key, again, is that W2, the person who once had first-hand knowledge, testifies that he in fact perceived the facts in question and communicated them accurately to W1.

Q. 25. If W2 is unavailable, how can P get the list into evidence, using only rules we have covered thus far?

Ans. The difficulty is that the information on W1's list represents two statements, not one:

(1) W2's verbal statement to W1 ("There are 27 midget widgets"); and

(2) W1's written statement (putting the number "27" on the inventory form next to the listing, "midget widgets").

Fed. R. Evid. 803(5) is not by itself enough to overcome D's hearsay objection, because (in the absence of W2's testimony) 803(5) only provides a hearsay exception for the second statement; it doesn't cover the first. But, as Fed. R. Evid. 805 provides (*see* § 7.04), "Hearsay included within hearsay is not excluded under the hearsay rule if each part of the combined statements conforms with an exception to the hearsay rule provided in these rules." Applied to this case, because we have already found a hearsay provision to cover the second statement, we can overcome the hearsay objection if we can find a provision to cover the first statement (W2's verbal report to W1).

(1) Suppose at trial W1 could testify, "I clearly recall W2 calling out, 'There are 27 midget widgets.' " If D objected that this is hearsay, how should P respond?

W2's statement to W1 is hearsay, but it should nonetheless be admissible, because it satisfies Fed. R. Evid. 803(1). It is W2's "statement describing a . . . condition [the number of midget widgets], made while [W2] was perceiving the [number of widgets], or immediately thereafter."

(2) W1 cannot now recall how many midget widgets W2 told him there were on the shelves that day. But that is no barrier to admissibility, because instead of his memory, W1 can rely on his list.

(Matthew Bender & Co., Inc.)

In other words, each listing on the inventory is W1's 803(5) of W2's 803(1). That's how multiple hearsay works: no matter how many different levels of hearsay are included within an item of evidence, the hearsay objection is overcome if an Article VIII provision can be found for each level of hearsay.

§ 8.34 "Lacks Sufficient Recollection"

The party seeking to use Fed. R. Evid. 803(5) need not show that the witness lacks all recollection of the event or condition described in the memorandum (which some courts, prior to the Federal Rules, foolishly insisted upon). It is enough that the witness "lacks sufficient recollection to testify fully and completely."

Occasionally a witness will feign insufficient memory, in the hopes that he can evade the scrutiny of cross-examination (by answering "I'm sorry, I can't remember" to all questions) while getting his story across to the jury through a memorandum that qualifies under Fed. R. Evid. 803(5). The judge has at least some discretion in deciding whether a witness' protestations of lack of memory are true.

The reverse situation also sometimes arises, particularly in criminal trials: a witness will claim lack of memory because she doesn't want to testify at all. Assume, for example, that D and W1 were charged with a burglary. Prior to trial, the prosecutor agreed to allow W1 to plead guilty to a lesser charge in exchange for her testimony against D. W1 took the plea, but when D goes to trial, W1 is suddenly "unable to remember" anything whatsoever about the burglary she pleaded guilty to only a few weeks before. In such a case, the prosecutor may attempt to qualify a document (such as a signed confession) as W1's "recorded recollection" under Fed. R. Evid. 803(5). If it appears that W1 is deliberately trying to avoid testifying, many judges will give the prosecutor the benefit of the doubt in deciding whether the 803(5) requirements have been satisfied.

§ 8.35 "Made or Adopted"

It is not necessary to show that the witness himself wrote the memorandum or record; it suffices if the witness "adopted" someone else's memorandum while the events in question were still fresh in the witness' memory.

Questions

Q. 26. At a board meeting of ABC Corporation, DL, an ABC officer, boasted that he had used a variety of tactics to avoid hiring women for managerial positions. W1 and X attended that meeting. Incensed at what DL said, X that night wrote a memo detailing DL's remarks. The next day X showed his memo to W1, who agreed that X had accurately related what DL had said.

P, a woman who had been turned down for a managerial position, subsequently filed a Title VII sex discrimination suit against ABC. The corporation defends by asserting that P was denied the job solely because the man it hired instead of P was better qualified.

Learning of P's suit, X sends P a copy of his memo; it is so detailed that if P can get it into evidence she will have an airtight case. Unfortunately, X is not available to testify at trial, and W1 can no longer remember precisely what it was that DL said.

If P attempts to use X's memo to prove what DL said at the meeting, how many different levels of hearsay are involved?

Ans. Two. First, there is DL's verbal statement ("DL to the board"). Second, there is X's written memorandum ("X to paper"). Thus, we have another "multiple hearsay" issue.

Q. 27. Is X's memo admissible, over a hearsay objection?

Ans. Yes.

(1) If W1 could remember DL's statements, he could repeat them, over a hearsay objection, per Fed. R. Evid. 801(d)(2)(D). DL, an officer of ABC Corp., is its agent; his statements, on matters within the scope of his authority, are attributable to ABC.

(2) W1 cannot testify fully and accurately about what DL said; but if X's memorandum can qualify as W1's "recorded recollection," this is an acceptable substitute for W1's testimony from memory. X's memo would thus be W1's Fed. R. Evid. 803(5) of DL's Fed. R. Evid. 801(d)(2)(D).

(3) To qualify X's memo as W1's Fed. R. Evid. 803(5), P must show that W1 "adopted" X's memo in accordance with the rule.

To do so, P calls W1 as a witness. W1 testifies that he and X attended the meeting and heard what DL said; that it was about gender discrimination; but that he can no longer recall the important details.

While W1 is still on the stand, P has X's memorandum marked as an exhibit for identification.

Q. Do you recognize this document?

A. Yes. This is a memo X showed me the day after the board meeting, detailing what DL said.

Q. Did you read it when he showed it to you?

A. Yes.

Q. When you read it, were you satisfied that it was accurate?

A. Yes. I remember commenting to X that he wrote it exactly as I remembered it.

Q. Read it to yourself, please. [W1 does so.]

Having read it, do you now recall what it was that DL said?

A. The general thrust, but not precisely, no.

Q. But are you satisfied now that this memorandum accurately reflected what DL said?

A. Yes.

The document is now admissible as a memorandum of W1's recorded recollection. Even though W1 did not write it, he "adopted" it (satisfied himself that it was accurate) while the events in question were still fresh in his memory.

Q. 28. If the trial judge permits P to employ this procedure, may she now offer the memo into evidence as an exhibit?

Ans. No. The last sentence of Fed. R. Evid. 803(5) states, in pertinent part, "If admitted, the memorandum or record may be read into evidence but may not itself received as an exhibit . . ." *See* § 8.28.

Q. 29. Can ABC offer the exhibit into evidence? Why might ABC want to do so?

Ans. ABC may do so. The final clause of the last sentence of Fed. R. Evid. 803(5) specifically permits it. ABC might want to offer it as an exhibit if its lawyer thinks that to do so will help impeach W1's testimony. Perhaps, for example, the memo "sounds" more impressive than it looks— perhaps it is written on the back of a third grade homework assignment, in a semilegible scrawl with crossouts and circles and arrows, adorned with coffee stains and doodles in the margins. Whether to offer it in evidence is a tactical decision for ABC's attorney.

§ 8.36 Accuracy

To qualify a writing under Fed. R. Evid. 803(5), the declarant/witness must testify that she made or adopted it "when the matter was fresh in [her] memory" and that it accurately reflected the first-hand knowledge she had at the time she made or adopted it. This poses two questions: (1) how much time may elapse between the event and writing the memorandum; and (2) what kind of testimony will satisfy the "accuracy" requirement.

Time. There is no rigid cut-off; minutes, days, weeks and perhaps even longer periods should in appropriate cases create no insurmountable barriers. Once the witness testifies that she made or adopted the memorandum while the events were fresh in her mind, the judge has discretion whether to accept this testimony. Relevant factors include amount of time passed, the nature of the event or fact in question, its importance to the witness/declarant when it occurred, and the degree of detail in the writing.

Foundation testimony. Testimony such as "I remember being very careful to get it down on paper correctly" or "I remember thinking, when I read X's memorandum, that X described it accurately" suffices. So would "I'm sure I wouldn't have filed it until I was satisfied it was accurate," or "I always check reports like these for accuracy before I file them." A bit weaker, but still probably sufficient, would be testimony such as "I really don't remember anything about the incident, but I'm sure I wouldn't have signed if I had any doubts about its accuracy."

Keep in mind that foundational testimony of some kind is a *prerequisite* to using Fed. R. Evid. 803(5). A stubborn witness probably can frustrate an attorney, simply by refusing to acknowledge that he considered the memorandum accurate at the time he wrote, signed or verbally adopted it.

§ 8.37 Sixth Amendment Confrontation Clause

Fed. R. Evid. 803(5) requires the declarant to testify as a witness. This assures a defendant the opportunity to cross-examine him; hence, to satisfy the requirements for 803(5) automatically satisfies the Confrontation Clause, as well.

Some scholars argue that if the witness professes complete lack of memory on the subject, the Confrontation Clause is left unsatisfied because the defendant is denied an opportunity to conduct "meaningful" cross-examination. The Supreme Court rejected this argument with regard to Fed. R. Evid. 801(d)(1)(C) (*see* §§ 4.02, 4.05), and courts generally reject this argument with regard to Fed. R. Evid. 803(5), as well. It is up to the defense attorney to make the witness look foolish and perhaps untruthful by asking the witness a series of questions which the witness answers with "I don't remember."

§ 8.38 Questions

Q. 30. D, an investment advisor, is indicted for mail fraud. The indictment alleges that on February 1, 1999, as part of a scheme to defraud, she mailed investment advice concerning the DEF Company to X, a client, containing factual assertions that she knew were not true.

During the preindictment investigation, in November of 1999, FBI Agent W1 interviewed W2, D's research director. W2 told W1:

D showed me the letter she was planning to send to X. I told her, "Am I missing something? You know that DEF hasn't shown a profit in the last three years!"

D just smiled and said, "You know it and I know it, but X doesn't know it." Then she put the letter in the envelope and licked it shut.

A few days later Agent W1 showed W2 her typed notes of their discussion. W2 signed the bottom of the form, just below the words, "I affirm under penalty of perjury that the statements contained in this memorandum are accurate to the best of my knowledge."

At trial, in April of 2002, the prosecutor calls W2 as a witness, expecting him to testify to the same facts as he had told Agent W1. Instead, W2 says he can no longer remember anything relating to X, although he acknowledges that he probably knew a good deal about the X account at the time. The prosecutor has Agent W1's form marked as Government exhibit 6 for identification, shows it to W2, asks him to read it silently to himself, and then asks,

Q. Does this refresh your memory?

A. Sorry, it doesn't.

Q. Well, do you recognize this piece of paper?

A. 'Fraid not.

Q. Is that your signature at the bottom of the page?

A. Yes.

Q. To the best of your knowledge, today, are the statements in that memorandum accurate?

A. I told you, I don't remember anything about the X account, I don't remember meeting with D about it, and I don't remember this piece of paper!

Q. Do you see where it says, just above where you signed, "I affirm under penalty of perjury that the statements contained in this memorandum are accurate to the best of my knowledge"?

A. Yes.

Q. I ask you again: To the best of your knowledge, today, are the statements in that memorandum accurate?

A. I guess they are, yes, or I wouldn't have signed them.

The prosecutor asks W2 to read the memorandum aloud. D's attorney objects: hearsay; Sixth Amendment Confrontation Clause. How should the judge rule?

Ans. Once again, we have a multiple hearsay issue to deal with: D's statement to W2, and W2's adoption of Agent W1's memorandum.

The first level, D's statement to W2, poses no problem. D, the declarant, is a party; it is offered in evidence by the Government, D's party-opponent. Fed. R. Evid. 801(d)(2)(A). If W2 could (or would) remember what D said, the hearsay objection could be overruled without a second thought.

But because W2 can't (or won't) remember what D said, the prosecutor has to use Agent W1's memorandum, as a substitute for W2's testimony, to prove that D made the crucial statement to W2. It's close, but the judge could properly overrule the objection, because W2's direct examination satisfies all of the Fed. R. Evid. 803(5) requirements.

D's best arguments against admissibility relate to the "fresh in memory" and accuracy requirements.

"Fresh in memory." W2 didn't adopt Agent W1's memorandum until nine months after the event in question occurred. That's a rather long time. Still, is nine months an excessive period, under the circumstances? If your boss (in essence) told you, "I am about to knowingly defraud a client," do you think you would have trouble remembering it nine months later?

Vouching for accuracy. W2's endorsement of the memorandum was reluctant and lukewarm at best; but (particularly if the judge concludes that W2 is simply trying to avoid testifying against D), the judge can legitimately rule that the "vouching" requirement has been satisfied.

Regarding the Confrontation Clause, *see* § 8.37.

Q. 31. Suppose instead that when the prosecutor asked, "To the best of your knowledge, today, are the statements in that memorandum accurate?" W2 had answered:

No, I don't see how they can be. I'm sure that D never said those things to me. She's not that kind of person. And besides, if she said anything like that, I'm sure I'd remember it! I guess I must have signed this form without reading it.

Can the prosecutor use Fed. R. Evid. 803(5) to get the facts in the memorandum before the jury?

Ans. I don't think so. If W2 stonewalls and insists that the memorandum is not accurate, the prosecutor is probably stymied.

(Matthew Bender & Co., Inc.)

Q. 32. Suppose, in the previous problem, the prosecutor calls Agent W1, who testifies, "When I showed my memorandum to W2, I asked him to read it out loud to me. He did so. I asked him, 'Is that accurate?' He said it was, and I asked him to sign it and he did." Would this suffice to qualify the memorandum under Fed. R. Evid. 803(5)?

Ans. Probably not. The traditional view is that the witness who had first-hand knowledge (W2) of the key events (D's conversation with W2) is the one who must endorse the accuracy of the memo; here, instead, the prosecutor is trying to use W1 to prove that W2 endorsed its accuracy.

2. Records of Regularly Conducted Activity (the "Business Record" Exception): Rule 803(6)

§ 8.39 In General

Fed. R. Evid. 803(6) provides as follows:

> **Rule 803. The following are not excluded by the hearsay rule, even though the declarant is available as a witness:**
>
> **(6) Records of regularly conducted activity. A memorandum, report, record, or data compilation, in any form, of acts, events, conditions, opinions, or diagnoses, made at or near the time by, or from information transmitted by, a person with knowledge, if kept in the course of a regularly conducted business activity, and if it was the regular practice of that business activity to make the memorandum, report, record, or data compilation, all as shown by the testimony of the custodian or other qualified witness, unless the source of information or the method or circumstances of preparation indicate a lack of trustworthiness. The term "business" as used in this paragraph includes business, institution, association, profession, occupation, and calling of every kind, whether or not conducted for profit.**

This provision, like so many others in Article VIII, is based on the twin considerations of reliability and necessity.

The necessity for such a rule is obvious. It is often impractical and inconvenient, and sometimes impossible, to identify, let alone call as a witness, every person who participated in making a typical business record. Picture, for example, a salesman who jots down on a company form the particular items he sold to each customer on whom he called during a business trip. At the end of each day, he calls the home office and tells someone in the sales department how much of which items he sold to each customer. That employee in turn writes down each item on another company form. The next day, someone else types information from that form into the company computer. Once in the computer, the information is automatically available to the shipping, accounting and salesman compensation departments.

To identify, let alone call as a witness, everyone who participated in the creation of the record would pose absurd difficulties. Under Fed. R. Evid. 803(6), a party need only call one witness, "the custodian or other qualified witness," who need not have participated in any way in the creation of the record, to secure its admissibility over a hearsay objection.

The reliability of business records is based on three considerations: reliance, routine practice, and duty. The typical business enterprise relies upon the accuracy of its records in deciding what to ship, whom to bill, what bills to pay, how to plan for the future, and so on. Thus, the enterprise has a very powerful motive to assure that its records are accurately made and kept. To qualify, moreover, the rule requires that each participant in creating and keeping the record must act in accord with established business procedures, and must have a business duty to perceive, transmit or record the information.

There is a bit of schizophrenia lurking in Fed. R. Evid. 803(6). The common law antecedent of Fed. R. Evid. 803(6) covered only "business records," and generally adhered to a fairly narrow, traditional, commercial definition of "business." The Advisory Committee sought to broaden its scope, and therefore chose not to use the word "business"; instead, its title and its language referred only to "regularly conducted activity" The House Judiciary Committee thought this was too broad; it amended the text of the rule (but not its title!) to restrict it to records of "regularly conducted *business* activity," and provided a fairly traditional definition of "business." The Senate Judiciary Committee preferred the broader, Advisory Committee approach, and deleted the references to "business" from the Senate version of the bill. The Conference Committee restored the narrower House version, but broadened the definition of "business" somewhat.

Fed. R. Evid. 803(6) imposes the following requirements and raises the following issues:

1. *Original source of information.* The person who provides the information that is recorded in the "business record" must

    (a)　have first-hand knowledge of the information, and

    (b)　must have a regular "business duty" to acquire and report the information. *See* § 8.40.

2. *"Record."* The evidence must be in some physical (or physically reproducible) form: on paper, on tape, on computer disk, etc. "Mental business records" don't qualify.

3. *"Business/regularly conducted activity."* To qualify, the record must relate to an activity that fits within the rule's definition of "business." *See* § 8.41.

4. *Making the record: time, duty, "regularity."* The record must be made "at or near the time" the events recorded in the record occurred; it must be made by someone who had a "business duty" to make the record; and it must be part of the "regular course of business" to make the record. *See* § 8.42.

5. *Keeping the record.* It must also be part of the "regular course of business" to keep the record. *See* § 8.43.

6. *Subject matter.* A record that qualifies as a Fed. R. Evid. 803(6) record can be used to prove "acts, events, conditions, opinions, or diagnoses." *See* § 8.44.

7. *Multiple hearsay.* One particularly noteworthy feature of this exception is that it *sometimes* (not always!) "compresses" what might otherwise be several levels of hearsay into one; this simplifies securing admissibility, but adds confusion in assessing whether a record consists of multiple hearsay. *See* § 8.45.

8. *Procedure for admission.* The rule establishes a streamlined procedure for admitting such records: generally it suffices to call the record custodian to identify the record and give pro forma foundation testimony. *See* § 8.46.

9. *Trustworthiness clause.* A record that appears to qualify for admission may be excluded if "the source of information or the method or circumstances of preparation indicate lack of trustworthiness." This clause requires the judge to assess declarant credibility to a greater extent than normal. *See* § 8.47.

10. *Sixth Amendment Confrontation Clause. See* § 8.48.

11. *Interplay with other rules. See* § 8.49.

§ 8.40　Original Source of Information

Although the rule is not exactly a model of clarity, its language and legislative history, taken together, require that a person who provides the information that is recorded in the "business record" must:

    (a)　have first-hand knowledge of the information, and

(b)   must have a regular "business duty" to acquire and report the information.

In the typical business record situation, this causes no difficulties. A salesman who sells merchandise to a customer, for example, has first-hand knowledge of what he sold, thereby satisfying subparagraph (a). He also has a regular, routine business duty to report this back to the home office, thereby satisfying subparagraph (b). (The company, after all, needs the information so it knows whom to bill and for how much, how much commission to pay the salesman, etc.) Similarly, a research chemist in a corporation's research and development department has first-hand knowledge of the experiments she conducts, and, like any good scientist, it is part of the regular conduct of her "business" as a research scientist to record each step in the experiment and the information she acquires as a result.

Problems sometimes arise, however, with regard to each subpart of Fed. R. Evid. 803(6)'s "original source of information" requirement.

Johnson v. Lutz, 253 N.Y. 124, 170 N.E. 517, 518 (1930) is the classic example of information that fails to satisfy subparagraph (a), the first element of the "original source of information" requirement. A police officer, investigating a traffic accident, included in his report information given to him by civilian bystanders who were at the scene when the officer arrived.[1] The officer (and his report) satisfied subparagraph *(b)*: it was part of his regular duties to acquire and report the information that the bystanders told him. But while this satisfies subparagraph (b), it does not satisfy subparagraph *(a)*, because the officer was not the original source of the information about how the collision occurred. (The bystanders, assuming they saw the accident, had first-hand knowledge; but because *they* had no "business duty" to provide the information,[2] they cannot satisfy paragraph *(b)*.)

Another way of looking at *Johnson v. Lutz* is to analyze it in terms of multiple hearsay. It involved two different levels of hearsay. First, the bystanders made statements to the officer ("bystanders to officer"). Second, the officer included what they said in his report ("officer to paper"). Fed. R. Evid. 803(6) covers the second level of hearsay, but because the bystanders had no business duty to provide the officers with information, Fed. R. Evid. 803(6) cannot cover the first level.

The fact that the bystanders' statements do not come within Fed. R. Evid. 803(6) does not necessarily mean they are inadmissible. Consider the following:

Questions

Q. 33. Suppose P calls the officer as a witness at trial. Direct examination proceeds:

Q. Officer, what happened that day?

A. I heard a squeal of brakes, the sound of an impact, and several people screaming; it came from the next block. I went to where the sound came from, and saw a motorcycle crushed under the wheels of a truck. As I got there, several bystanders called to me, —

(By D's attorney): Objection, your honor! Hearsay!

(Judge): Sustained.

Q. Officer, how much time elapsed from when you heard the squeal of brakes and so on, to when you arrived at the accident and the bystanders started telling you something?

A. It could not have been more than 30 seconds.

Q. These bystanders you mentioned: describe their demeanor.

A. They were pretty upset. One man was crying, and I remember a woman's hand was shaking while she pointed toward the intersection.

---

[1] If the same situation arose today, we would probably look to Fed. R. Evid. 803(8), the official records exception, rather than Fed. R. Evid. 803(6), the business record exception; but the analysis would be precisely the same under either rule.

[2] A citizen has a moral duty to cooperate with law enforcement officials, but there is no *legal* duty to do so (unless he or she is served with a subpoena).

Q. How many bystanders gave you statements?

A. Several. Two gave me their names and addresses.

Q. Tell us, officer, what the bystanders said to you?

(By D's attorney): Objection, your honor! Hearsay!

How should the judge rule?

Ans. First of all, if your answer even mentions Fed. R. Evid. 803(6), you weren't paying attention to the question. In this question, the officer is on the witness stand, testifying from memory. Therefore 803(6) has no role in the problem at all.

The judge should overrule the objection. Following D's initial objection, P's attorney elicited testimony from the officer that clearly qualifies the bystanders' statements to him as excited utterances. (If you don't see why, review Fed. R. Evid. 803(2), §§ 8.02–8.06.)

Q. 34. The officer's report contains the following:

I heard a squeal of brakes, the sound of an impact, and several people screaming; it came from the next block. I went to where the sound came from, and saw a motorcycle crushed under the wheels of a truck. I arrived at the scene no more than 30 seconds after hearing the crash. As I got there, several bystanders called to me that the truck ran the stop sign at the intersection and knocked down and ran over the motorcycle. They were terribly upset, shaken, pale. When I looked, I could see why. The cyclist was obviously dead [etc.]

P's attorney calls the officer as a witness.

Q. Officer, did you investigate this accident?

A. Yes, I did.

Q. Tell us, please, what you saw, what you heard, and what you did after you arrived there.

A. I'm sorry, counselor. This accident was more than five years ago and I've investigated hundreds of traffic accidents since then. I'm afraid the details tend to run together in my memory.

What options are available to P's attorney?

Ans. First, he should have the officer's report marked as an exhibit for identification; then he should ask the officer to read the report to himself, to see if it refreshes his recollection (Fed. R. Evid. 612).

If that doesn't work, P's attorney has a two-level hearsay problem: "bystanders to officer" and "officer to paper." But it is clear from the report itself that the bystanders' statements qualify as excited utterances (just as in the previous problem). Therefore, P's only remaining problem is how to prove that the bystanders made their statements. In the previous problem, P accomplished this through the officer's testimony. Since in this problem the officer does not remember the events well enough to testify, P must use the report to prove what the bystanders said and under what circumstances. To do so, P must find an Article VIII provision to overcome the objection that the report is hearsay.

P has two options: (1) ask the officer the questions necessary to qualify his report under Fed. R. Evid. 803(5); or (2) ask the officer the questions necessary to qualify his report under Fed. R. Evid. 803(6).

Because we can find a hearsay provision to overcome each level of hearsay, the objection should be overruled, and the entire report, including the bystanders' statements, should be admissible, either under Fed. R. Evid. 803(2) and 803(5) or Fed. R. Evid. 803(2) and 803(6).

Q. 35. Suppose the officer is not available as a witness. What are P's options?

Ans. P can, of course, try to locate the bystanders and subpoena them. But if that doesn't work (or even if it does), P will want to get the officer's report into evidence.

The officer's report still involves two levels of hearsay: "bystanders to officer" and "officer to paper." The bystanders' statements to the officer will still come within Fed. R. Evid. 803(2), but Fed. R. Evid. 803(5) is no longer available as a means of proving that they made the statements contained within the report, because 803(5) requires putting the person who made or adopted the report (the officer) on the stand.

As you will see more fully in § 8.46, however, under Fed. R. Evid. 803(6), the report *is* admissible—even if the officer is unavailable.

Note that in the last two problems, we had to resort to multiple hearsay analysis to attempt to overcome a hearsay objection, because the key statements in the report did not satisfy the Fed. R. Evid. 803(6) "original source of information" requirement. That requirement is satisfied only if the person who provided the information contained in the report had *both* first-hand knowledge of the information *and* a regular business duty to acquire and report the information.

Problems also sometimes arise with regard to the second subpart of the Fed. R. Evid. 803(6) original source of knowledge requirement, if the person who acquires the knowledge has no business duty to report it.

Questions

Q. 36. X supervises several employees in a company's warehouse. Her duties include submitting weekly reports on how well each worker does his or her job, how well each gets along with others, etc.

X happens to be something of a nutrition faddist. She makes a point of noticing what each worker brings for lunch from home, and includes this information in her weekly reports. X's superiors don't complain about these unorthodox additions to her reports (she may be a bit nutty, but she's a good supervisor), which provide them with a bit of comic relief as they lunch on yogurt or sun-dried tomato bagels and veggie-spread lite cream cheese.

One evening after returning home from work, Z, a warehouse employee, falls sick. Eventually doctors diagnose the ailment: food poisoning. Z sues a neighborhood supermarket, alleging that it sold him spoiled lunchmeat.

(a) To corroborate his own testimony that he ate the supermarket's lunch meat earlier on the day he took ill, Z wants to introduce the weekly employee evaluation form that X filled out for the week in question. D (the food store) objects: hearsay. Does Fed. R. Evid. 803(6) overcome the objection?

Ans. No. X's report of what Z had to eat that day satisfies the first element of the "original source of information"—she saw what Z ate, so she had first-hand knowledge; but it fails to satisfy the second element, since she had no business duty to acquire or report the information.

(b) How else might Z attempt to offer the same evidence?

Ans. Z can call X as a witness. If X remembers that Z ate lunchmeat that day, X can testify from memory. If not, Z can use X's report for the week to refresh X's memory (Fed. R. Evid. 612). If that doesn't work, Z can attempt to qualify the relevant portion of X's report as X's "recorded recollection" under Fed. R. Evid. 803(5).

§ 8.41 "Business"

Fed. R. Evid. 803(6) provides that to fit within the exception, the record must have been made and kept "in the course of a regularly conducted business activity." The rule defines "business" as including "business, institution, association, profession, occupation, and calling of every kind, whether or not conducted for profit." This language was included "in order to make it clear that the records of institutions and associations like schools, churches and hospitals are admissible under this provision."[1] So are records

---

[1] Conference Committee Report.

of illegal activities (e.g. a diary of bribes paid to public building inspectors) and illicit organizations (e.g. a narcotics network's records of drugs bought and sold), if the records meet the other requirements of the rule.

An individual's business records are likewise admissible. Thus, for example, a lawyer's appointment book comes within Fed. R. Evid. 803(6); so do a doctor's medical records of his patients. But purely private records (e.g. an individual's personal check book or diary) probably do not, no matter how meticulously and regularly kept.

§ 8.42 Making the Record: Time, Duty, "Regularity"

The record must be made "at or near the time" the events recorded in the record occurred, close enough in time to minimize the risk that the person providing the information might misremember. It must be made by someone who had a "business duty" to make the record. This can be the same person who acquired the information in the first place, or it can be another employee or participant in the business, so long as both are acting in accordance with a business duty. Finally, it must be a *regular* part of the business to make the record. A special record of an extraordinary event, for example, would not qualify as a Fed. R. Evid. 803(6) record.

§ 8.43 Keeping the Record

The party offering the document must also show that it was a regular practice of the business to keep the kind of record that is being offered in evidence. It would not suffice, for example, if a witness testified, "We generally don't hang on to this kind of record, but I happened to find these in a shoe box in the back of the closet."

§ 8.44 Subject Matter of the Record

A record that qualifies as a Fed. R. Evid. 803(6) record can be used to prove "acts, events, conditions, opinions, or diagnoses." Courts applying Fed. R. Evid. 803(6) have admitted records of: hotel telephone logs; written prescriptions issued by a clinic and filled by a pharmacy; an elevator maintenance logbook; an office lease (to prove who the lessee was); a charitable organization's checking account records; a company's employee evaluation forms; computerized benefit and payroll records; corporate officials' diaries describing business meetings; appraisals of the value of a major league baseball team; hospital emergency room records of symptoms, diagnosis and treatment; and on, and on. Note that this list of examples include objectively verifiable data (hotel logs, payroll forms, checks paid, elevator maintenance) and matters of judgment open to disagreement and dispute (employee evaluations, financial appraisals, medical diagnoses).

As to the latter category ("diagnoses and opinions"), the only significant restriction as to subject matter is the "trustworthiness" clause. An opinion recorded in a business record should be admitted only to the extent that the opinion would be admissible if offered by a witness while testifying. If the topic is one that only an expert witness could testify about (medical diagnoses, financial appraisals, and so on), then an opinion recorded in a business record will be admitted only if the person expressing the opinion is qualified as an expert on that subject. A doctor's diagnosis or opinion as to the cause, extent and duration of someone's injury, included in a hospital record, would be admissible as proof of the cause, extent or duration of the injury; a janitor's opinion on the same subject, even if "regularly" recorded in the hospital record (!), would not be admissible.

§ 8.45 Multiple Hearsay; "Compression"

Business records can quite often pose multiple hearsay problems. *See*, for example, questions 33–35. Consider also the following.

Questions

Q. 37. P was injured on June 1 when a shelf fell on him, and he is suing his former employer, claiming permanent disability. (At issue: the extent and permanency of injuries, and P's claim for punitive damages because D allegedly knowingly maintained an unsafe workplace.) Immediately after the mishap P was rushed to the hospital. The hospital emergency room's admitting form contains the following.

> Patient suffered back injury when poorly-built temporary shelving fell on him. He complains of intense pain and lack of sensation in lower body. Legs show a lack of reflexive response. He has a large bruise in his mid-to-lower back, with a deep laceration just above the waist.

P offers this record into evidence. Assuming he satisfies the procedural requirements (*see* § 8.46), is it admissible, over a hearsay objection?

Ans. Most of it is; some of it is not.

The entire record is, of course, a business record of the hospital. It was made by a hospital employee who is a health care professional, who had a business duty to acquire the information (by asking questions and by conducting a physical examination). The record was (let us assume) made and kept in accord with the rule. Still, it is incorrect to treat the record as if it was one statement; it consists, really, of four separate statements (one in each sentence). Each has to be analyzed separately.

(1) "Patient suffered back injury when poorly-built temporary shelving fell on him."

This statement cannot be admitted pursuant to Fed. R. Evid. 803(6) alone, because the person who wrote the report, the admitting nurse, did not have first-hand knowledge of how the injury occurred. (She, after all, was not with P when the shelf fell.) Thus, this part of the report is multiple hearsay: someone (presumably P) told the nurse how P was injured ("P to nurse"); the nurse entered the information into the hospital admitting record ("nurse to paper"). This statement is admissible over a hearsay objection, therefore, only if some other Article VIII provision can be found for the first level of hearsay.

The provision that comes most readily to mind is Fed. R. Evid. 803(4). The declarant (presumably P) made this statement to the nurse "for purposes of diagnosis." But 803(4) covers only part of the statement: "Patient suffered back injury when . . . shelving fell on him." It does not cover aspects of the statement that attribute fault ("poorly built").

Thus, Fed. R. Evid. 803(4) and 803(6), taken together, overcome the hearsay objection as to most of the first sentence in the report; but the trial judge would have to redact the inadmissible words before allowing the report to be circulated to the jury.

(2) "He complains of intense pain and lack of sensation in lower body."

The analysis is basically the same. This is double hearsay, but it is admissible: P to nurse, Fed. R. Evid. 803(3) or 803(4); nurse to paper, Fed. R. Evid. 803(6).

(3) "Legs show a lack of reflexive response."

This is only one level of hearsay: the nurse examined P, and wrote what she observed into the admitting record. Objection overruled, Fed. R. Evid. 803(6).

(4) "He has a large bruise in his mid-to-lower back, with a deep laceration just above the waist."

This, similarly, is only one level of hearsay: the nurse examined P, and wrote what she observed into the admitting record. Objection overruled, Fed. R. Evid. 803(6).

Sometimes, however, what looks like multiple hearsay isn't.

Q. 38. ABC Realty maintains a large apartment complex. As part of its regular maintenance, public areas (walkways, stairways, etc.) in each building are inspected every three months by employees, who submit regular reports of the results of their inspections.

In litigation (P v. D), a fact at issue is the condition of the north and south staircases of building 1224 Tara Drive on September 14, 1999. ABC's maintenance records for September–December, 1999 are subpoenaed. They contain the following notation:

On Thurs. aft. 9/4/99, the undersigned and R. Butler conducted an inspection of 1224 Tara. Most of building is in good repair. The undersigned noticed [etc. Several paragraphs later:]

On Mon. 9/8 R. Butler reported that the staircase on the north side of the building is in good repair but that the tread on the south side staircase is becoming worn on several steps between the 2nd and 3rd floor & again between 4 and 5.

The report is dated September 10, 1999, and is signed, "S. O'Hara."

P establishes the required foundation (*see* § 8.46) and offers the report; D objects: hearsay.

How many levels of hearsay are there in O'Hara's report?

Ans. Even though there are *two* statements involved in this record ("Butler to O'Hara"; "O'Hara to paper"), *they are treated for Fed. R. Evid. 803(6) purposes as if they were only one statement.* Why? Because both declarants, Butler and O'Hara, had a business duty to ABC Realty to acquire and report the information. When one employee, acting pursuant to a business duty, reports first-hand information to another, who then, acting pursuant to a business duty, records what the first has said into a business record, multiple statements are "compressed" into one if the record itself qualifies under Fed. R. Evid. 803(6).

Q. 39. Is the report admissible over a hearsay objection?

Ans. Yes, assuming the proper foundation for admissibility is established (*see* § 8.46). The only real issue is whether the record was made "at or near the time" the conditions described in the report were perceived. Butler inspected the staircases on September 4; he reported to O'Hara what he saw on September 8. We don't know whether Butler's report to O'Hara was a formal typed memo, a handwritten note or a casual comment in the elevator. O'Hara completed her report on the 10th; again, we don't know what kind of notes she took to assure she would not forget important details between the 4th and the 10th. But assuming the proper foundation was established, we do know that O'Hara's report was prepared in accordance with an established procedure and that such reports were relied upon by ABC Realty for business purposes. Delays of four to six days between observation and the final report should not cast sufficient doubts on trustworthiness to raise a serious question.

§ 8.46 Procedures for Admission

Fed. R. Evid. 803(6) provides a party can establish that a record qualifies as a Fed. R. Evid. 803(6) business record "by the testimony of the custodian or other qualified witness. . . ." "Qualified witness" means someone (such as the company's "record custodian," such as someone who works in a company's file room) who can (a) identify and authenticate the record in a way that satisfies Article IX of the Federal Rules, and (b) testify about the company's record-making and record-keeping process. The witness need not have any first-hand knowledge whatsoever about the particular document in question; he need not have participated in its creation; he need not even have been an employee when that record was created. He should, however, be able to testify in general terms about the following:

- how the kind of record about to be offered into evidence is made;

- that it is (or was) part of the company's regular practice to make such records;

- that the original source of the information in this type of record has first-hand knowledge of and a business duty to report that information;

- that this type of record is made from information that is reported and recorded at or near the time of the event, condition, opinion or diagnosis recorded in the record;

- how the company uses that kind of record;

- that it is part of the regular practice of the company to keep such records, and how it does so; and

- how the witness retrieved this particular record from the company's files.

Such testimony establishes that the document in question satisfies the Fed. R. Evid. 803(6) requirements.

Computerized records differ from paper records in that the computer can reorganize, sort and categorize data if directed to do so by specific commands or by special programs. This presents no barriers to admissibility so long as a qualifying witness can explain in general terms that such reorganization of the data is done in the routine course of business.

Sometimes a record made by one company is incorporated into the records of a second company. Assume, for example, that when the regional office of Greaseburger Fast Food, Inc. ships its all grease-patties (specially coarse), fetid cheese, etc., it prepares a shipping slip detailing the quantity of each item that is to be delivered to each individual franchise. There is no reason why a local franchise could not routinely adapt its copy of the regional office's shipping slip as its own business record of what it received. That document would be admissible as a business record of the local franchise—but only if, as part of the routine, an employee of the local franchise checked to make sure that the regional office's shipping slip was accurate.

§ 8.47 The "Trustworthiness" Clause

Even after a "qualified witness" gives the necessary foundation testimony described in the previous section, Fed. R. Evid. 803(6) provides that the record may be excluded if "the source of information or the method or circumstances of preparation indicate lack of trustworthiness."

The trustworthiness clause provides a good illustration of shifting burdens of proof. To secure admission of a document under Fed. R. Evid. 803(6), the party offering the document must call a "qualified witness" and elicit the foundational testimony outlined in § 8.46. Once the offering party has produced the required testimony, the burdens of production and persuasion shift: the document is admissible over a hearsay objection unless the other party can persuade the judge that the document is insufficiently trustworthy.

The leading case on trustworthiness, cited in the Rule's legislative history, is *Palmer v. Hoffman*, 318 U.S. 109 (1943), which is unfortunate, because it is a badly written opinion. Following a railroad grade crossing accident in which someone was killed, the engineer gave a lengthy, extremely self-serving statement to company and state investigators, denying that he or the company had done anything wrong. Thereafter the engineer became unavailable. In a subsequent wrongful death action brought by decedent's plaintiff against the railroad, the company sought to offer the engineer's statement into evidence. The Supreme Court quite reasonably concluded that the lower courts were correct in excluding the statement, but did a poor job explaining its reasons.

First, the Court said, the engineer's statement was not a record made in the "regular course" of the railroad's business, because the business of the railroad is running a railroad, not investigating accidents. This rationale ignored the fact that it was a regular part of the railroad's operating procedures to investigate all accidents and take statements from all employees who had knowledge of what had happened. (To do so was certainly "good business" on the railroad's part. Very few of us would willingly ride a railroad that did not bother to investigate all accidents.) Despite the flawed reasoning, some courts, citing *Palmer*, for many years held that accident reports can never be accepted as business records.

Second, the Court rejected the engineer's statement as untrustworthy because it had been prepared in anticipation of potential litigation. This may seem a more appropriate basis for the holding, until you consider that an experienced attorney does *everything*, e.g. negotiates a contract, drafts a will or separation agreement, etc., in anticipation of potential litigation. (Your clients will want you to help them arrange their affairs to avoid litigation if possible, while increasing the chances of winning if a matter does go to litigation. Thus, you must "anticipate potential litigation" in order to avoid it.)

Thus, neither of the articulated bases for *Palmer* is now considered good law. Accident reports can be business records; so can documents, of whatever nature, that were prepared in anticipation of possible litigation. The trustworthiness issue focuses instead on the specific facts surrounding the document that is being offered in evidence. Are there specific circumstances surrounding this particular document, or the procedure by which it was produced, or the quality of the foundational testimony, that create serious and unanswered questions about the document's trustworthiness? If so, it should be excluded; if not, Fed. R. Evid. 803(6) overcomes the hearsay objection.

It is not possible to compile an exhaustive list of circumstances that might cast doubt on the trustworthiness of business records. The fact that a document is prepared solely for use in pending litigation may be a significant factor. If a record includes opinion on a subject requiring expertise, it would be untrustworthy if those whose opinions are reported are not qualified to give expert opinions. The same result should be reached if the report purports to have been prepared by X, but X denies having done so. And so on.

§ 8.48   Sixth Amendment Confrontation Clause

In *Ohio v. Roberts,* 448 U.S. 56, 66 (1980), the Supreme Court classified the business record exception as firmly rooted; indeed, the historical roots of the exception go back more than two centuries. And there is little reason to question that such records have independent evidentiary significance. It seems clear, therefore, that Fed. R. Evid. 803(6) is a "FRIES" exception: a record that qualifies under the rule will also overcome a Confrontation Clause objection.

§ 8.49   Interplay with Other Rules

As discussed in previous sections, Fed. R. Evid. 803(6) often involves multiple hearsay. Hospital records, for example, frequently include statements that may fall within Fed. R. Evid. 803(1)–803(4). Accident reports may require application of Fed. R. Evid. 801(d)(2)(A), 801(d)(2)(D) or 803(2).

Keep in mind that other rules may also be used to secure admission of a document over a hearsay objection. If the person who wrote the record testifies at the trial, it may be admissible under Fed. R. Evid. 801(d)(1)(A)–(C) or 803(5). If the person who wrote the record is unavailable as a witness, provisions of Fed. R. Evid. 804(b) may apply (*see* Chapter 9).

If a party in a lawsuit is offering a document that was written by the opposing party, Fed. R. Evid. 801(d)(2)(A) answers the hearsay objection; there is no need to satisfy the more demanding requirements of 803(6). Similarly, if the document was written by the agent of the opposing party, the offering party can overcome the objection by satisfying either Fed. R. Evid. 801(d)(2)(C), 801(d)(2)(D), or 801(d)(2)(E) instead of 803(6).

The two preceding paragraphs simply belabor the basic point that when a party offers an out-of-court statement in evidence, she can overcome a hearsay objection by satisfying the requirements of *any* Article VIII provision. The fact that a document was prepared as part of a "business" does not restrict the offering party to using only Fed. R. Evid. 803(6).

3.   Rule 803(7): Absence of Entry in Business Record

§ 8.50   In General

Fed. R. Evid. 803(7) provides as follows:

Rule 803. The following are not excluded by the hearsay rule, even though the declarant is available as a witness:

(7) Absence of entry in records kept in accordance with the provisions of paragraph 6. Evidence that a matter is not included in the memoranda, reports, records, or data compilations, in any form, kept in accordance with the provisions of paragraph (6), to prove the nonoccurrence or nonexistence of the matter, if the matter was of a kind of which a memorandum, report, record, or data compilation was regularly made and preserved, unless the sources of information or other circumstances indicate lack of trustworthiness.

The Advisory Committee Note to this provision says pretty much all there is to say about it:

Failure of a record to mention a matter which would ordinarily be mentioned is satisfactory evidence of its nonexistence. . . . While probably not hearsay as defined in Fed. R. Evid. 801, [pre-Federal Rules of Evidence] decisions may be found which class the evidence not only as hearsay but also as not within any exception. [Fed. R. Evid. 803(7) has been drafted] in order to set the question at rest in favor of admissibility. . . .

In other words, such evidence is not hearsay, but in case some judge doesn't get the message and insists that it *is* hearsay, it is admissible over a hearsay objection.

To satisfy the rule, a party must call a "qualified witness" who can testify that the company has a regular procedure for making records of the kind of event or condition in question; that such records are made and kept in the regular course of business, and so on; that he or she conducted a diligent search of the relevant records; and that this search produced no evidence of the event or condition in question. The testimony should proceed much along the same lines as the foundation testimony outlined in § 8.46.

It would not suffice, however, for a witness to testify that he was told by other employees that they searched the records and found nothing. You would have to call the witness who actually searched the records.

4. Public Records and Reports: Rule 803(8)

§ 8.51 In General

Fed. R. Evid. 803(8) provides as follows:

Rule 803. The following are not excluded by the hearsay rule, even though the declarant is available as a witness:

(8) Public records and reports. Records, reports, or data compilations, in any form, of public offices or agencies, setting forth (A) the activities of the office or agency, or (B) matters observed pursuant to duty imposed by law as to which matters there was a duty to report, excluding, however, in criminal cases matters observed by police officers and other law enforcement personnel, or (C) in civil actions and proceedings and against the Government in criminal cases, factual findings resulting from an investigation made pursuant to authority granted by law, unless the sources of information or other circumstances indicate lack of trustworthiness.

This rather unwieldy provision closely parallels Fed. R. Evid. 803(6): what the latter does for the records of "civilian" businesses, Fed. R. Evid. 803(8) does for government offices and agencies. Like Fed. R.

Evid. 803(6), it is based on the twin considerations of reliability and necessity; the comments made in § 8.39 relating to necessity and reliability with regard to 803(6) apply equally to Fed. R. Evid. 803(8). Moreover, the law recognizes a presumption that public servants are honest and impartial and carry out their official duties carefully and efficiently. Additionally, just as Fed. R. Evid. 803(6) covers the records of a wide range of businesses, from the multinational corporation to the individual potter or seamstress, Fed. R. Evid. 803(8) applies to the records of any government agency, from the United States Department of Defense or the British Foreign Ministry to a village Board of Selectmen or a local school board.

Nevertheless, while the parallels between Fed. R. Evid. 803(6) and 803(8) are many and obvious, there are significant differences, too. These are discussed in the succeeding sections.

§ 8.52   The Three Subsections

Fed. R. Evid. 803(8) divides public records into three categories, and promulgates a somewhat different rule for each. Thus, the first step in applying Fed. R. Evid. 803(8) is to determine within which of its subsections the record most logically falls. Although this not always a simple matter (some records can fall within more than one of the categories, for example), the basic distinctions are fairly clear.

Fed. R. Evid. 803(8)(A): activities of the office or agency.

This provision includes records that reflect what the agency and its agents did, but not what the agency or its agents saw or heard or concluded. It covers records of the internal functioning the agency (e.g. individual employee pay and time records; inventories of equipment on hand; etc.) and the routine, non-judgmental actions of the agency or its agents. Thus, for example, Fed. R. Evid. 803(8)(A) permits a litigant to use a record from the Department of the Treasury to prove that a particular social security check was issued and mailed to a specified individual. Likewise, records of the Federal Deposit and Insurance Corporation are admissible to prove that a particular bank was federally insured. Similarly, Fed. R. Evid. 803(8)(A) would permit records from the Occupational Safety and Health Administration to be used to prove that an OSHA inspector visited a particular job site. (Fed. R. Evid. 803(8)(A) would not, however, suffice to secure admission of records of what the OSHA inspector saw when she visited the workplace, or the conclusions she arrived at after her inspection; to admit those records would involve Fed. R. Evid. 803(8)(B) and 803(8)(C), respectively.)

So long as the record is properly authenticated (*see* § 8.53) and no serious question exists as to trustworthiness (*see* § 8.54), few significant restrictions apply to the use of Fed. R. Evid. 803(8)(A).

Fed. R. Evid. 803(8)(B): matters observed and reported pursuant to duty.

To qualify under this provision, (a) the report must be based upon information obtained first-hand by a government agent or employee; (b) the agent must have an official duty to observe and report on the event or condition in question; and (c) the agency must have an official duty or purpose to observe and report on such matters. The "matters observed" are generally restricted to objectively verifiable facts. Examples include an OSHA inspector's description of conditions she observed at a workplace; a U.S. Customs Service record that a particular car (make, model, year, license number) crossed the border from Mexico to the United States on a particular date; weather bureau records of the weather conditions in a particular location; and an accident investigation report, filed by a police officer, describing the collision scene and extent of damages (but a statement of the officer's conclusions as to what caused the collision or who was at fault would not be within the scope of Fed. R. Evid. 803(8)(B)).

Fed. R. Evid. 803(8)(B) is subject to a significant restriction that 803(8)(A) is not: a prosecutor cannot use Fed. R. Evid. 803(8)(B) to offer records of "matters observed" by "law enforcement officers." *See* § 8.57.

Rule 803(8)(C): factual findings.

If a government expert or agency has investigated a matter, this provision directs that a report setting out his, her or its conclusions is admissible over a hearsay objection. The provision includes diagnoses and opinions, and reports that state conclusions as to cause, fault and blame. In essence, this means that instead of (or in addition to) calling expert witnesses to give their opinions about certain events, a litigant can introduce into evidence a report that satisfies Fed. R. Evid. 803(8)(C).

Fed. R. Evid. 803(8)(C) has a major restriction: a government prosecutor may not use the rule. *See* § 8.58.

§ 8.53 Procedure for Admission

Before a public record may be introduced into evidence, it must be authenticated. This can be done through the same procedure set out for business records, by calling a record "custodian or other qualified witness" (*see* § 8.46). Alternatively, a public record can be authenticated pursuant to Fed. R. Evid. 902. The document might be self-authenticating (Fed. R. Evid. 902(1), or it can be accompanied by an affidavit of authenticity by an official who is authorized to certify to the authenticity of such documents (Fed. R. Evid. 902(2), 902(4)).

§ 8.54 Trustworthiness

It is not completely clear from the language or legislative history of Fed. R. Evid. 803(8) whether the rule's trustworthiness clause qualifies each subdivision, or only 803(8)(C). Logically, it should apply to all three subdivisions. If a record can be shown to be untrustworthy, it simply should not be allowed as proof of the matter asserted within it.

As with Fed. R. Evid. 803(6), if the offering party shows that a document satisfies any subsection of Fed. R. Evid. 803(8), it should be admitted unless the opposing party persuades the judge that the record is untrustworthy.

§ 8.55 Rule 803(8)(A): Activities of the Office or Agency

Fed. R. Evid. 803(8)(A) provides as follows:

> **Rule 803. The following are not excluded by the hearsay rule, even though the declarant is available as a witness:**
>
> **(8) Public records and reports. Records, reports, or data compilations, in any form, of public offices or agencies, setting forth (A) the activities of the office or agency, . . . unless the sources of information or other circumstances indicate lack of trustworthiness.**

To demonstrate the similarities and differences between Fed. R. Evid. 803(8)(A) and Fed. R. Evid. 803(6), the Fed. R. Evid. 803(6) outline is reproduced here, with appropriate changes. Fed. R. Evid. 803(8)(A) imposes the following requirements and raises the following issues:

1. *Original source of information.* Implicit within the rule is the requirement that the record is based upon information provided by an agency employee with first-hand knowledge. This need not be proven, however; if the document is properly authenticated, it is presumed to satisfy this requirement unless the opposing party can show otherwise.

2. *"Record."* The evidence must be in some physical (or physically reproducible) form: on paper, on tape, on computer disk, etc. "Mental public records" don't qualify.

3. *"Public office or agency."* This requirement is basically self-explanatory. It presumably would not include an audit of a government agency commissioned by the agency but conducted by a private firm.

4. *Making the record: time, duty, "regularity."* Unlike Fed. R. Evid. 803(6), Fed. R. Evid. 803(8)(A) does *not* require that the agency made the record as part of the "regular course of business".

An extraordinary record of an extraordinary event therefore might well satisfy Fed. R. Evid. 803(8)(A), assuming the opposing party was unable to raise a successful trustworthiness challenge.

Moreover, Fed. R. Evid. 803(8)(A) does not explicitly require that the record be made "at or near the time" the events recorded in the record occurred; nor does it require that the record be made by someone who had an "official duty" to make it. On the other hand, if the opposing party could show that a long delay occurred between the event and the recording of it, or that the person who made it was without a duty to do so, this might cast strong doubts on the report's trustworthiness.

5. *Keeping the record.* Similarly, Fed. R. Evid. 803(8)(A) does not explicitly require that it be part of the "regular course of business" to keep the record.

6. *Permissible contents: activities of the office or agency.* This provision includes records that reflect what the agency and its agents did, but not what the agency or its agents saw or heard or concluded. It covers records of the internal functioning of the agency (e.g. individual employee pay and time records, inventories of equipment on hand, etc.) and the routine, non-judgmental actions of the agency or its agents. *See* § 8.52.

7. *Multiple hearsay.* Fed. R. Evid. 803(8)(A) often "compresses" what might otherwise be several levels of hearsay into one. *See* § 8.45.

8. *Procedure for admission. See* § 8.53.

9. *Trustworthiness clause. See* § 8.54.

10. *Sixth Amendment Confrontation Clause.* Fed. R. Evid. 803(8)(A) clearly is firmly rooted and as such as independent evidentiary significance; hence it is a "FRIES" exception. Thus, if the record satisfies Fed. R. Evid. 803(8)(A), it also satisfies the Confrontation Clause.

§ 8.56   Rule 803(8)(B): Matters Observed and Reported Pursuant to Duty

Fed. R. Evid. 803(8)(B) provides as follows:

> **Rule 803. The following are not excluded by the hearsay rule, even though the declarant is available as a witness:**
>
> **(8) Public records and reports. Records, reports, or data compilations, in any form, of public offices or agencies, setting forth . . . (B) matters observed pursuant to duty imposed by law as to which matters there was a duty to report, excluding, however, in criminal cases matters observed by police officers and other law enforcement personnel, . . . unless the sources of information or other circumstances indicate lack of trustworthiness.**

Again, the same basic outline is used to set out the requirements and issues.

1. *Original source of information.* For a report to qualify under Fed. R. Evid. 803(8)(B), an agent of the public office, must have observed first-hand the condition or event described in the report.

2. *"Record."* The evidence must be in some physical (or physically reproducible) form: on paper, on tape, on computer disk, etc. "Mental public records" don't qualify.

3. *"Public office or agency."* This requirement is basically self-explanatory. It presumably would not include matters observed by a private investigator commissioned by a public agency to conduct an investigation. On the other hand, it may include at least some kinds of reports from private individuals or companies who are under a legal duty to report such matters to a public agency.

(Matthew Bender & Co., Inc.)

4. *Making the record: time, duty, "regularity."* Unlike Fed. R. Evid. 803(8)(A), for a report to qualify under Fed. R. Evid. 803(8)(B), it must be shown that the office or agent *did* have an official duty to observe and to report the event or condition in question.

The "duty" requirement should not be read too literally. The offering party need not show that the agency is explicitly required by statute to observe and report on the kind of events or conditions in question; it is enough that the subject matter of the report is reasonably within the subject-matter jurisdiction of the agency.

Fed. R. Evid. 803(8)(B) does not explicitly require that the record be made "at or near the time" the events recorded in the record occurred. On the other hand, if the opposing party could show that a long delay occurred between the event and the recording of it, this might cast strong doubts on the report's trustworthiness.

5. *Keeping the record.* Fed. R. Evid. 803(8)(B) requires that the record be *made* pursuant to a legal duty (*see* points 4, above, and 6, below), but does not explicitly require that it be *kept* pursuant to duty.

6. *Permissible contents: "matters observed pursuant to duty imposed by law as to which matters there was a duty to report."* To qualify,

   a. the report must be based upon information obtained first-hand by a government agent or employee;

   b. the agent must have an official duty to observe and report on the event or condition in question; and

   c. the agency must have an official duty or purpose to observe and report on such matters.

The "matters observed" are generally restricted to objectively verifiable facts, not value judgments and opinions, and generally cannot include statements made or information provided by private citizens (unless those statements also come within some provision of Article VIII). For examples of reports that satisfy Fed. R. Evid. 803(8)(B), see § 8.52.

7. *Multiple hearsay.* Fed. R. Evid. 803(8)(B) often "compresses" what might otherwise be several levels of hearsay into one. *See* § 8.45.

8. *Procedure for admission. See* § 8.53.

9. *Trustworthiness clause. See* § 8.54.

10. *Sixth Amendment Confrontation Clause.* Fed. R. Evid. 803(8)(B) reports may or may not be found to have "independent evidentiary significance." With the exception of law enforcement reports (see below), they probably are firmly rooted.

11. *Law enforcement exclusionary clause. See* § 8.57.

§ 8.57 Rule 803(8)(B): Law Enforcement Exclusionary Clause

Fed. R. Evid. 803(8)(B) excludes from its scope "in criminal cases matters observed by police officers and other law enforcement personnel." This language was added on the floor of the House of Representatives. Like many floor amendments to pending legislation, this one is well-intended but sloppily worded.

The discussion on the floor of the House when the clause was added reveals that its purpose is to avoid "trial by memo book," i.e. to prevent a prosecutor from offering a police officer's investigative report in evidence, without calling the officer to the witness stand. Without a law enforcement exclusionary clause, its sponsors feared, a defendant might be denied the opportunity, guaranteed in the Sixth Amendment Confrontation Clause, to confront and cross-examine his accusers.

All well and good: a prosecutor should not be permitted to offer an investigator's surveillance report in lieu of the investigator's testimony. But the law enforcement exclusionary clause, as written, prohibits a good deal more. For one thing, it denies the prosecutor the right to offer such reports even if the investigator *does* testify. Second, it appears to exclude *all* law enforcement reports of "matters observed," even simple, objectively verifiable, ministerial matters. Third, as written the clause prohibits the defendant, as well as the prosecutor, from offering a surveillance report prepared by a "police officer or other law enforcement personnel."

Application of the law enforcement exclusionary clause raises the following issues.

1. *Defining "other law enforcement personnel."* Courts, logically, have concluded that the phrase includes any public official, whether or not he or she has the power to make an arrest, whose job involves active participation in or involvement with law enforcement. Thus, for example, a Drug Enforcement Administration crime lab chemist is a "law enforcement personnel"; a lab report is not admissible if the chemist doesn't testify. Similarly, Internal Revenue Service personnel, in a tax evasion case, are considered "law enforcement personnel."

2. *Routine law enforcement reports of a non-adversarial nature.* Several courts have carved an exception to the exclusionary clause to allow a prosecutor to use such reports. Examples: a report by a customs inspector that a car with a particular license plate crossed the Mexican-American border on a particular night (all such numbers are routinely recorded); a report by a Marshall that he served a court injunction on a union leader; a report by members of the Royal Ulster Constabulary that rifles of specified make, model and serial numbers were found in Northern Ireland on a particular date.

3. *Admissibility of report if witness testifies.* Granted that a police chemist or crime lab technician is a "law enforcement personnel"; even so, if she testifies at trial, there is no logical reason to exclude her lab report: her presence at trial gives the defendant the right to confront and cross-examine her.

4. *Use of "law enforcement reports" by the defense.* Several courts, adhering to what Congress meant rather than what it said, have admitted such reports when offered by the defense.

5. *Use of Fed. R. Evid. 803(6) in lieu of Fed. R. Evid. 803(8)(B). See § 8.60.*

§ 8.58   Rule 803(8)(C): "Factual Findings"

Fed. R. Evid. 803(8) provides as follows:

> **Rule 803. The following are not excluded by the hearsay rule, even though the declarant is available as a witness:**
>
> **(8) Public records and reports. Records, reports, or data compilations, in any form, of public offices or agencies, setting forth . . . (C) in civil actions and proceedings and against the Government in criminal cases, factual findings resulting from an investigation made pursuant to authority granted by law, unless the sources of information or other circumstances indicate lack of trustworthiness.**

Fed. R. Evid. 803(8)(C) provides that if a government expert or agency has investigated a matter, a report setting out his, her or its conclusions is admissible over a hearsay objection. In *Beech Aircraft v. Rainey*, 488 U.S. 153, 170 (1988), the Supreme Court unanimously held that the provision includes not only objectively verifiable factual conclusions, but also diagnoses, opinions, and reports that state conclusions as to cause, fault and blame. Thus, the Court held, a report including a Navy lieutenant commander's conclusions, after a thorough investigation, as to what probably caused a Navy training flight to crash was admissible in a wrongful death action brought by the husband of the flight instructor and by the wife of the pilot trainee who died in the crash.

In essence, this means that instead of (or in addition to) calling expert witnesses to give their opinions about certain events, a litigant can introduce a government agency's report into evidence as proof of what happened or why.

Federal courts have upheld admissibility of government agents' or agencies' factual findings in a variety of settings. Examples:

- In a personal injury suit arising out of a collision between a truck and an auto, an accident report prepared by a police officer, concluding that the auto had probably run the red light.

- In a wrongful death action brought after a military training flight resulted in the death of the instructor and trainee, a report prepared by a military investigator, concluding that the most probable cause of the crash was pilot error, rather than a malfunction of the plane.

- In suits alleging discrimination in housing, employment or education, investigative field reports and factual findings made by hearing examiners.

- In a products liability action against a tampon manufacturer, epidemiological studies prepared by the Center for Disease Control analyzing the statistical relationship between tampon use and incidence of toxic shock syndrome (even though the raw data was based upon interviews, questionnaires, and reports submitted to CDC by individual patients, doctors, and state health officials).

Note, too, that the factual findings of government offices and agencies are admissible in civil litigation regardless of whether that agency (or any agency) is a party.

For the sake of consistency, the basic Fed. R. Evid. 803(6)–803(8) outline is used to set out the requirements and issues.

1. *Original source of information.* Fed. R. Evid. 803(8)(C) does *not* require that a public agency or officer have first-hand knowledge of the events or conditions in question. (See, for example, the toxic shock syndrome litigation example outlined above.)

2. *"Record."* The evidence must be in some physical (or physically reproducible) form: on paper, on tape, on computer disk, etc.

3. *"Public office or agency."* The "factual finding" must be one made by a governmental body, not a private company or individual. If a public agency accepts a "private" factual finding after a careful evaluation of it, on the other hand, it logically should fit within Fed. R. Evid. 803(8)(C).

4. *Making the record: time, duty, "regularity."* The factual finding must be one that "result[s] from an investigation made pursuant to authority granted by law." There is no "regularity" requirement; Fed. R. Evid. 803(8)(C) covers reports of temporary investigative agencies created for the sole purpose of investigating a particular matter, as well as reports of established agencies acting in accord with routine practice. Timeliness is relevant only to the extent that it effects trustworthiness.

5. *Keeping the record.* Fed. R. Evid. 803(8)(C) imposes no explicit requirements in this regard.

6. *Permissible contents: "factual findings resulting from an investigation made pursuant to authority granted by law."* See examples listed above.

7. *Multiple hearsay.* An agency's "factual finding" may properly be based heavily on hearsay, so long as the investigation was sufficiently trustworthy.

8. *Procedure for admission. See* § 8.53.

9. *Trustworthiness clause. See* § 8.59.

10.   *Sixth Amendment Confrontation Clause.* Fed. R. Evid. 803(8)(C) may only be used "in civil actions and proceedings and against the government in criminal cases"; the prosecutor in a criminal case cannot use the rule. Thus, for example, a prosecutor cannot offer a government chemist's lab report in evidence, at least without calling the chemist. Hence, Confrontation Clause issues simply do not arise with regard to Fed. R. Evid. 803(8)(C).

§ 8.59   Rule 803(8)(C): Trustworthiness Clause

The Advisory Committee Note on Fed. R. Evid. 803(8) discussed at some length the application of the trustworthiness clause to Fed. R. Evid. 803(8)(C):

Factors which may be of assistance in passing upon the admissibility of evaluative reports include:

(1) the timeliness of the investigation;

(2) the special skill or experience of the official [conducting the investigation];

(3) whether a hearing was held and the level at which conducted;

(4) possible motivational problems suggested by *Palmer v. Hoffman.* [For a discussion of *Palmer,* see § 8.47.]

Others no doubt could be added.

The formulation of an approach which would give appropriate weight to all possible factors in every situation is an obvious impossibility. Hence the rule, as in [Fed. R. Evid. 803(6)], assumes admissibility in the first instance but with ample provision for escape if sufficient negative factors are present.[1]

The final point made in the Advisory Committee Note bears repeating. Once the party offering the evidence establishes that the report was prepared by a government office, agency, officer or agent (federal, state, local or foreign) pursuant to authority granted by law, it should be admitted unless the adverse party can point to or prove "sufficient negative factors" to overcome the presumption of trustworthiness.

§ 8.60   Prosecutorial Use of Rule 803(6) in Lieu of Rule 803(8)(B) or 803(8)(C)

As a general rule, a party can overcome a hearsay objection by satisfying any provision of Fed. R. Evid. 803 or 804 she chooses; as long as the evidence meets the requirements of any one provision, it is irrelevant that the evidence fails to meet the requirements of other provisions. For example, if a statement satisfies Fed. R. Evid. 803(3) (state of mind), it is admissible over a hearsay objection even if it does not also satisfy Fed. R. Evid. 803(1), 803(2), 803(4), 804(b)(1), etc. Several federal courts have correctly concluded, however, that this normal approach should *not* apply if a prosecutor tries to make an end run around the law enforcement exclusionary clauses of Fed. R. Evid. 803(8)(B) and 803(8)(C) by offering a document under Fed. R. Evid. 803(6). In the leading case,[1] the government, rather than calling the Drug Enforcement Administration chemist in a narcotics case, was permitted to offer the chemist's lab report under Fed. R. Evid. 803(6) to prove that the drugs in question were contraband. The Second Circuit reversed the conviction. The law enforcement exclusionary clauses were included in Fed. R. Evid. 803(8)(B) and 803(8)(C), the court stressed, to protect a defendant's constitutionally guaranteed right to confront and cross-examine his accusers. Allowing a prosecutor to resort to Fed. R. Evid. 803(6) in lieu of Fed. R. Evid. 803(8)(B) and 803(8)(C) would frustrate Congressional intent and perhaps violate the Sixth Amendment.

---

[1] Advisory Committee Note to Fed. R. Evid. 803(8)(C).

[1] United States v. Oates, 560 F.2d 45, 65–67 (2d Cir. 1977).

§ 8.61 Questions

Q. 40. P brings a personal injury action against D Manufacturing Company, alleging that he suffered injuries when he slipped and fell on an oil slick as he and his wife were walking along the sidewalk in front of D's factory. D denies liability and also contests P's claim of serious injury.

At trial, P offers in evidence a report filed by DL, an attendant in the ambulance that responded to P's wife's call for help. The report contains the following statements.

(1) Metropolitan Hospital Ambulance # 14 was dispatched at 9:21 a.m. on 7/7/99 in response to a report of an injury in front of 1509 Westminster Lane. Arrived at 9:40.

(2) Injured person (IP) was lying on the sidewalk near a large oil spot.

(3) IP complained of intense back and leg pain.

(4) IP states he slipped and fell on the oil.

D objects that the report is hearsay. P cites Fed. R. Evid. 803(8). Ruling?

Ans. First, we need to know whether "Metropolitan Hospital" is a public or private hospital. If it is a private hospital, admissibility should be analyzed under Fed. R. Evid. 803(6). If it is a public hospital, the judge should rule as follows:

1. Paragraph 1 is admissible under Fed. R. Evid. 803(8)(A). The fact that the ambulance was dispatched to, and arrived at, 1509 Westminster is a record of the "activities of the agency."

2. Paragraph 2 is admissible under Fed. R. Evid. 803(8)(B), assuming the ambulance attendant is required by hospital regulations to describe (i.e to observe and record) the existing circumstances when he arrived at the scene of an injury.

3. Paragraph 3 is admissible under Fed. R. Evid. 803(8)(B), assuming the attendant is required to learn what he can about the nature and extent of the injured person's injury.

Note, by the way, that Paragraph 3 involves multiple statements: P's statement to the attendant, and the attendant's act of recording P's statement on the form. P's statement is covered by Fed. R. Evid. 803(3) and 803(4); Fed. R. Evid. 803(8)(B) covers the attendant's recording of P's statement.

4. Paragraph 4 is more problematic. Like paragraph 3, it involves double hearsay. The attendant very likely is expected to take a statement, if possible, as to how the injury occurred; thus, his act of recording P's statement is covered by Fed. R. Evid. 803(8)(B). P's statement may or may not be admissible under Fed. R. Evid. 803(1) or 803(4).

(Paragraph 4 is not the attendant's "factual finding" as to what happened; it is simply a record of what P claimed.)

Q. 41. P alleges that D Corporation, her former employer, denied her a promotion, and fired her, because she spurned the sexual advances of X, her immediate supervisor. In compliance with Title VII of the Civil Rights Act of 1984, P's attorney filed a complaint with the Equal Employment Opportunity Commission (EEOC), which referred it to the appropriate State Civil Rights Commission (SCRC), which in turn assigned the matter to Y, an SCRC caseworker. Y, a recent college graduate who had majored in psychology, separately interviewed P and X, and submitted a report in which he concluded:

"Without question, there had been a personality clash between P and X. After reviewing all the facts, however, it is clear to me that X did not made unreasonable sexual advances to P and that D Corporation did not violate state law in failing to promote, and in firing, P."

Not satisfied with this result, P's attorney files a Title VII suit in Federal District Court. After P presents her evidence and rests, D Corporation seeks to introduce Y's report to the SCRC to prove that P had not been unfairly discriminated against on the basis of sex.

Is Y's report admissible, over a hearsay objection, under Fed. R. Evid. 803(8)(C)?

Ans. At first glance, the answer appears to be yes: Y's conclusion is (in the language of Fed. R. Evid. 803(8)(C)) a "factual finding resulting from an investigation made pursuant to authority granted by law." It is therefore admissible, "unless the sources of information or other circumstances indicate lack of trustworthiness." Thus, to keep it out, P will have to attack the report's trustworthiness.

An attack on trustworthiness should include consideration of the factors discussed in the Advisory Committee Note and the Senate Judiciary Committee Report:

(1) The timeliness of the investigation. Timeliness does not seem to be much of a factor for or against trustworthiness in this case.

(2) The special skill or experience of the official [conducting the investigation]. Since Y just recently graduated from college, he cannot be particularly experienced. Chalk up a factor for P. The fact that he was a psychology major is perhaps a plus for D, but not necessarily a big one.

(3) Whether a hearing was held and the level at which conducted. This factor looks at the investigation itself. How thorough was it? Did it utilize procedures that seem fair and thorough? Y's "investigation" does not seem too impressive: all he did was interview the two principals in the case, P and X. It's hard to see why this "procedure" entitles his conclusion to any particular credence.

(4) Possible motivational problems [of the investigating officer or agency]. Examine Y's conclusion again: "X did not make unreasonable sexual advances to P." His choice of words implies that Y considers it acceptable for a male supervisor to make sexual advances to a female subordinate, so long as those advances don't become "unreasonable." This suggests, at the very least, a subconscious bias against P's claim, which undermines the presumption of an impartial investigation.

If I were the judge, I would exclude the report.

D. MISCELLANEOUS EXCEPTIONS

§ 8.62   In General

This subchapter discusses several rarely-used exceptions contained within Fed. R. Evid. 803. Discussion of most of these exceptions is quite brief because they are rarely used, rarely cited and, frankly, there is very little to say about most of them. (If your professor is writing her "tenure piece" on the exception for inscriptions on family tombs and crypts, and asks a 42-point question about it on the final exam, blame her, not me.) Fed. R. Evid. 803(17), 803(18) and 803(22) however, are used with some frequency, and merit more than cursory attention.

§ 8.63   Rule 803(9): Records of Vital Statistics

Fed. R. Evid. 803(9) provides as follows:

Rule 803. The following are not excluded by the hearsay rule, even though the declarant is available as a witness:

(9) Records of vital statistics. Records or data compilations, in any form, of births, fetal deaths, deaths, or marriages, if the report thereof was made to a public office pursuant to requirements of law.

The familiar twin considerations of necessity and reliability justify this provision. It is often difficult to find a witness who was present and recalls a birth, death or marriage that took place many years earlier; and, at the same time, it is unlikely that someone would deliberately falsely report such information.

To secure admissibility of a properly authenticated record (*see* Article IX of the Federal Rules), the offering party need only show that a state or local law required someone to report the birth, death or marriage to a public office, and that the report was made in a way that complied with that law.

Issues sometimes arise as to whether Fed. R. Evid. 803(9) covers only the basic details of the event itself (e.g. date and place of a person's birth; date and place that two people were married; date and place of a person's death), or also includes statements in the document as to the underlying circumstances. If the document is being offered in evidence at a trial in which an underlying circumstance is in dispute (e.g. the identity of the newborn's father, or the cause of deceased's death), most scholars argue that statements in the document about such matters should be admissible only if it is clear that the person who provided the information had a reliable basis for it (e.g. the doctor who attended the deceased as he was dying, or who performed the autopsy, would have a reliable basis for a statement as to cause of death).

§ 8.64 Rule 803(10): Absence of Public Record or Entry

Fed. R. Evid. 803(10) provides as follows:

> **Rule 803. The following are not excluded by the hearsay rule, even though the declarant is available as a witness:**
>
> **(10) Absence of public record or entry. To prove the absence of a record, report, statement, or data compilation, in any form, or the nonoccurrence or nonexistence of a matter of which a record, report, statement, or data compilation, in any form, was regularly made and preserved by a public office or agency, evidence in the form of a certification in accordance with rule 902, or testimony, that diligent search failed to disclose the record, report, statement, or data compilation, or entry.**

Fed. R. Evid. 803(10) can be used to prove two related facts: that a record does not exist, or that an event did not occur. Fed. R. Evid. 803(10) is to public records what Fed. R. Evid. 803(7) is to business records. The necessity for such a rule is clear. Without such a rule it would be difficult for the government to prove, for example, that a defendant failed to comply with laws requiring submission of certain documents (e.g. an income tax return) or information (e.g. draft registration). Similarly, suppose, in 1999, it is important to determine whether a child was born in a public hospital in 1990. The only practical way to try to prove that no such birth occurred would be to show that there is no indication of such a birth in the hospital's records.

To use Fed. R. Evid. 803(10), a party must:

1. establish that a particular public agency regularly made and preserved records of the kind of fact or event in question; and

2. prove that the records of the public agency in question contain no mention or reference to the occurrence of the event or existence of the fact in question.

The nonexistence of a record can be proved in either of two ways:

1. An official in the agency can testify that a diligent search failed to locate such a record or entry.

2. An official in that office can submit a written certification in accordance with Fed. R. Evid. 902 that a diligent search of the office's files failed to locate such a record.

The other party can then exclude the testimony or certificate only by persuading the judge that the office in question did not regularly make and keep such records, or that the search for the record in question was not diligent.

§ 8.65 Rule 803(11): Records of Religious Organizations

Fed. R. Evid. 803(11) provides as follows:

Rule 803. The following are not excluded by the hearsay rule, even though the declarant is available as a witness:

(11) Records of religious organizations. Statements of births, marriages, divorces, deaths, legitimacy, ancestry, relationship by blood or marriage, or other similar facts of personal or family history, contained in a regularly kept record of a religious organization.

This exception simply restates an exception long recognized by the common law. Statements contained in such records are considered trustworthy because generally there is little motivation to fabricate such records.

Much of the information covered by Fed. R. Evid. 803(11) is also covered by Fed. R. Evid. 803(6). Either rule, for example, could be used to introduce the regularly made and kept records of a church, synagogue, or mosque as evidence that M and F were married there on a particular date. In one respect, though, Fed. R. Evid. 803(11) is somewhat broader. It also covers "statements of . . . legitimacy, ancestry, relationship by blood or marriage, or other similar facts of personal or family history" recorded in the record, even though no one who participated in making the record had first-hand knowledge of that information. For example, the religious organization's record of the wedding likely will include information as to when M and F were born, and their parents' names. In subsequent litigation, this record is admissible, not only to prove that the wedding took place (if that should be an issue), but also, for example, as proof of M's birth date or of F's mother's maiden name (assuming this information is recorded in the record). Presumably, M and F supplied this information, even though neither had first-hand knowledge of it. (You don't have first-hand knowledge of your birth date, for example; you were there, of course, but the odds are that you don't remember being born, and even less likely that you remember checking the calendar as someone was cutting your umbilical cord. You know your birthday only because your parents told you.)

§ 8.66 Rule 803(12). Marriage, Baptismal, and Similar Certificates

Fed. R. Evid. 803(12) provides as follows:

Rule 803. The following are not excluded by the hearsay rule, even though the declarant is available as a witness:

(12) Marriage, baptismal, and similar certificates. Statements of fact contained in a certificate that the maker performed a marriage or other ceremony or administered a sacrament, made by a clergyman, public official, or other person authorized by the rules or practices of a religious organization or by law to perform the act certified, and purporting to have been issued at the time of the act or within a reasonable time thereafter.

To survive a hearsay objection, the party offering the document must show:

1. That the person who performed or conducted the ceremony also filled out the certificate (which satisfies the requirement that declarant had first-hand knowledge of the information contained in the certificate).

2. That that person was authorized by law or by the rules of a religious organization to perform the act in question.

3. That the certificate was apparently filled out "at the time of the act or within a reasonable time thereafter."

If the ceremony was performed and the certificate was prepared by a public official (e.g. a judge), an official seal will suffice to make the certificate self-authenticating; otherwise, the party offering the document must authenticate it through witnesses or circumstantial evidence.

§ 8.67 Rule 803(13): Family Records

Fed. R. Evid. 803(13) provides as follows:

> **Rule 803. The following are not excluded by the hearsay rule, even though the declarant is available as a witness:**
>
> **(13) Family records. Statements of fact concerning personal or family history contained in family Bibles, genealogies, charts, engravings on rings, inscriptions on family portraits, engravings on urns, crypts or tombstones, or the like.**

An attorney could have a long and happy career as a litigator without ever having to use this provision. Still, who knows? If, some day, an inscription on the container holding someone's cremated remains is your only proof that your client is the testator's son, and is therefore entitled to a share of the estate (that your client is, in other words, owed on a Grecian urn), it is nice to know you can overcome your opponent's hearsay objection. In a situation involving controversy over a marriage, birth, or death, this provision accords entries in a family Bible or genealogy or the like the same status as the official records of a public agency or religious organization.

§ 8.68 Rule 803(14): Records of Documents Affecting an Interest in Property

Fed. R. Evid. 803(14) provides as follows:

> **Rule 803. The following are not excluded by the hearsay rule, even though the declarant is available as a witness:**
>
> **(14) Records of documents affecting an interest in property. The record of a document purporting to establish or affect an interest in property, as proof of the content of the original recorded document and its execution and delivery by each person by whom it purports to have been executed, if the record is a record of a public office and an applicable statute authorizes the recording of documents of that kind in that office.**

This provision assures that records relating to property will be admissible over a hearsay objection if those records are maintained according to state law.

§ 8.69 Rule 803(15): Statements in Documents Affecting an Interest in Property

Fed. R. Evid. 803(15) provides as follows:

> **Rule 803. The following are not excluded by the hearsay rule, even though the declarant is available as a witness:**
>
> **(15) Statements in documents affecting an interest in property. A statement contained in a document purporting to establish or affect an interest in property if the matter stated**

was relevant to the purpose of the document, unless dealings with the property since the document was made have been inconsistent with the truth of the statement or the purport of the document.

This provision covers documents relating to personal property (bills of sale, receipts, and the like) as well as real property.

The rule imposes three requirements:

1. The statement must "purport[] to establish an interest in property."

2. The statement must be "relevant to the purpose of the document," i.e. the document was drawn for the purpose of defining or changing someone's interest in the property.

3. Subsequent dealings with the property in question must not have been "inconsistent with the truth of the statement or the purport of the document."

The underlying theory of this provision is that statements in "dispositive documents," i.e. documents that apparently define who owns or controls an interest in property, are not made (or signed) until all those with an interest in the property are satisfied that the document is accurate.

Fed. R. Evid. 803(15) includes not only statements directly relating to the property ("X hereby sells Blackacre to Y for the following consideration"), but related statements of fact as well (". . . executed on X's behalf by Z, attorney at law, pursuant to power of attorney granted by X to Z on . . ."). Unlike Fed. R. Evid. 803(16) (*see* § 8.70) there is no requirement that the document be of any particular age.

§ 8.70 Rule 803(16): Statements in Ancient Documents

Fed. R. Evid. 803(16) provides as follows:

Rule 803. The following are not excluded by the hearsay rule, even though the declarant is available as a witness:

> **(16) Statements in ancient documents. Statements in a document in existence twenty years or more the authenticity of which is established.**

The rationale for this rule is simple: necessity. Such documents are often the only way to offer proof of facts from a period sufficiently long ago that there may no longer be witnesses available who have first-hand knowledge and present memory to testify. The likelihood of trustworthiness derives from two sources: the first-hand-knowledge requirement, and the probability that the documents and statements involved were made before the current controversy arose.

The provision changes the common law "ancient document rule" in two ways. First, the common law rule only overcame authentication objections (*see* Fed. R. Evid. 901(b)(8)), not hearsay objections. Second, it required that the document in question be at least 30 years old, not 20.

Any kind of document can qualify (a diary, newspaper article, minutes from a corporate board meeting, private correspondence, etc.) as long as it otherwise satisfies the rule.

§ 8.71 Rule 803(17): Market Reports, Commercial Publications

Fed. R. Evid. 803(17) provides as follows:

Rule 803. The following are not excluded by the hearsay rule, even though the declarant is available as a witness:

(17) Market reports, commercial publications. Market quotations, tabulations, lists, directories, or other published compilations, generally used and relied upon by the public or by persons in particular occupations.

If someone wants to know the price at which XYZ Corp. stock closed at the end of trading, she would probably turn to the stock exchange listings in her daily newspaper. If you need someone's address and phone number, you would look it up in the phone book. A stamp collector or trader interested in ascertaining the value of a rare postage stamp would look in a catalogue published by a well-respected philately company. Because people have enough confidence in such reports and publications to rely upon them in their personal and professional lives, they should be considered reliable enough for use as evidence in court. Fed. R. Evid. 803(17) so provides.

§ 8.72 Rule 803(18): Learned Treatises

Fed. R. Evid. 803(18) provides as follows:

> **Rule 803. The following are not excluded by the hearsay rule, even though the declarant is available as a witness:**
>
> **(18) Learned treatises. To the extent called to the attention of an expert witness upon cross-examination or relied upon by the expert witness in direct examination, statements contained in published treatises, periodicals, or pamphlets on a subject of history, medicine, or other science or art, established as a reliable authority by the testimony or admission of the witness or by other expert testimony or by judicial notice. If admitted, the statements may be read into evidence but may not be received as exhibits.**

As a rule, evidence relating to specialized fields of knowledge must be offered through expert testimony; a party is not permitted to use a treatise or scholarly article to prove facts. In a medical malpractice suit, for example, if plaintiff wants to offer proof of the symptoms of and recommended treatment for a particular disease, he cannot simply read an excerpt from a medical treatise; there is too great a risk that the jury, comprised of lay people who are not knowledgeable about the disease, may not fully understand the discussion of it in the treatise and may be unable to accurately apply that discussion to the facts in the case.

Thus, to offer specialized knowledge in evidence, a party must call an expert witness, who can explain the information to the jury, can relate it to the facts of the case, and thereafter can be cross-examined by the other party. Fed. R. Evid. 803(18) provides that once an expert testifies, either side may, subject to several requirements, introduce relevant statements from treatises, scholarly articles, and the like, to explain or impeach the expert's testimony.

The rule imposes the following requirements and restrictions.

1.   An *expert* witness must testify.

2.   The treatise, article, etc. must be "established as a reliable authority" in the area of knowledge in question. Showing that the treatise, article, etc. is a "reliable authority" can be done in several ways, discussed below.

3.   The witness must cite the treatise on direct examination or be questioned about statements contained in the treatise while being cross-examined.

4.   The statements from the treatise can be read into the record, but the book, article, pamphlet (or whatever) cannot be received as an exhibit.

The operation of the rule can be divided into two scenarios: use by the expert on direct examination, and use by the opposing party on cross.

1. Use by the expert witness during direct examination.

In a medical malpractice suit, X v. Y, X calls Dr. W as an expert. The rules governing expert testimony are spelled out in Article VII of the Federal Rules; suffice it here to say that, in explaining his testimony, Dr. W can testify that he relied on a treatise by ABC, which, he testifies, is recognized as an established authority in the medical field. Where appropriate, Dr. W can read relevant passages of the treatise as part of his testimony.

2. Use to cross-examine the expert.

Suppose the ABC treatise contains statements that contradict Dr. W's testimony. Y's attorney wants to ask Dr. W: "Isn't it a fact that the ABC treatise says, and I quote: . . . [reads quoted passage] . . . Doesn't that contradict what you testified to on direct?" She may do so, without first having to lay a foundation that the ABC treatise is "recognized as an authority in the field," because Dr. W, in his direct examination, already did so.

Suppose further that a different treatise, the DEF treatise, also contains statements that disagree with Dr. W's testimony. Y's attorney may use these statements, too, to cross-examine Dr. W, but first she must establish that the DEF treatise is "recognized as an authority in the field." This can be done in any of several ways.

1. *Ask Dr. W.* "Doctor, are you familiar with the DEF treatise? . . . Is it recognized as an authority in the field?" If Dr. W says "Yes," the requirement is satisfied.

2. *Previous testimony of another expert.* If another expert has already testified at this trial that the DEF treatise is recognized as an authority in the field, that witness (Dr. Z) has already satisfied the requirement, and Y's attorney can use DEF to cross-examine Dr. W. (Dr. W can, of course, answer that *he* doesn't recognize DEF as an authority in the field.)

3. *Judicial notice.* Y's attorney can ask the judge to take judicial notice that the DEF treatise is a recognized authority. (Judicial notice is covered in Article II of the Federal Rules; suffice it here to say Y's attorney shouldn't make such a request unless she has first studied Article II and has the necessary evidence to support her request.) If the judge takes judicial notice that the DEF treatise is recognized as an authority in the field, Y's attorney can use the DEF treatise to cross-examine Dr. W.

4. *Subsequent testimony of another expert.* Alternately, Y can later call another expert witness, who testifies that the DEF treatise is treatise recognized as an authority in the field. Thereafter, Y can recall Dr. W for cross-examination using the DEF treatise.

§ 8.73 Rule 803(19): Reputation Concerning Personal or Family History

Fed. R. Evid. 803(19) provides as follows:

> **Rule 803. The following are not excluded by the hearsay rule, even though the declarant is available as a witness:**
>
> **(19) Reputation concerning personal or family history. Reputation among members of a person's family by blood, adoption or marriage, or among a person's associates, or in the community, concerning a person's birth, adoption, marriage, divorce, death, legitimacy, relationship by blood, adoption, or marriage, ancestry, or other similar fact of his personal or family history.**

The theory underlying this provision is that information about a person's family status that is widely enough known to be "common knowledge" is reliable enough to overcome a hearsay objection, even if no one can be identified who has first-hand knowledge of it.

To qualify as valid "reputation" testimony under Fed. R. Evid. 803(19), the party offering the testimony must lay the same foundation as would be required to admit reputation testimony under Fed. R. Evid. 404(a)–405(a) or 608(a).

See also Fed. R. Evid. 804(b)(4), § 9.15 ("Statement of personal or family history").

§ 8.74   Rule 803(20): Reputation Concerning Boundaries or General History

Fed. R. Evid. 803(20) provides as follows:

> **Rule 803. The following are not excluded by the hearsay rule, even though the declarant is available as a witness:**
>
> **(20) Reputation concerning boundaries or general history. Reputation in a community, arising before the controversy, as to boundaries of or customs affecting lands in the community, and reputation as to events of general history important to the community or State or nation in which located.**

This is another "common knowledge" exception to the hearsay rule. Reliability is assumed because in order to qualify, the party offering the evidence must establish, first, that the belief in question is sufficiently widespread to constitute "reputation," and second, that the belief was firmly established before the controversy that is the subject matter of the present lawsuit arose.

§ 8.75   Rule 803(21): Reputation as to Character

Fed. R. Evid. 803(21) provides as follows:

> **Rule 803. The following are not excluded by the hearsay rule, even though the declarant is available as a witness:**
>
> **(21) Reputation as to character. Reputation of a person's character among associates or in the community.**

This provision assures that if reputation testimony is admissible under Fed. R. Evid. 404, 405 and 608(a), its hearsay character will not require its exclusion.

At common law, only evidence of a person's reputation in his or her residential community was admissible. Fed. R. Evid. 803(21) recognizes that in contemporary society many individuals reside, work, recreate, worship, etc. among different "communities" or groups of associates, and hence eliminates reliance on only the person's geographic residential community for reputation evidence.

§ 8.76   Rule 803(22): Judgment of Previous Conviction

Fed. R. Evid. 803(22) provides as follows:

> **Rule 803. The following are not excluded by the hearsay rule, even though the declarant is available as a witness:**
>
> **(22) Judgment of previous conviction. Evidence of a final judgment, entered after a trial or upon a plea of guilty (but not upon a plea of nolo contendere), adjudging a person**

guilty of a crime punishable by death or imprisonment in excess of one year, to prove any fact essential to sustain the judgment, but not including, when offered by the Government in a criminal prosecution for purposes other than impeachment, judgments against persons other than the accused. The pendency of an appeal may be shown but does not affect admissibility.

In litigation that occurs subsequent to a person's conviction for a crime, the law can treat the conviction in any of several ways.

1. In some circumstances, the prior conviction is treated as conclusive under the doctrine of res judicata, either as a bar or as collateral estoppel. This use of prior convictions is not covered in the Federal Rules of Evidence; it is governed by constitutional principles that have nothing to do with hearsay.

2. The prior conviction may be treated as substantive evidence, i.e. as proof (which the fact-finder in the subsequent trial may accept or reject) that the convicted person in fact did what she was convicted of doing, i.e. that she engaged in certain conduct with a certain mental state. Assume, for example, that F was convicted in 1998 of forging Y's name to a check. Several years later, in a trial totally unrelated to the 1998 forgery, a litigant might offer the fact of F's conviction to prove that in 1998 F signed another person's name to a check with the intent to defraud.

   If offered for this purpose, F's prior conviction constitutes a "statement" (see below) that F forged the check in 1998 with the intent to defraud. If the conviction satisfies the requirements of Fed. R. Evid. 803(22) (not all convictions do), the fact that the prior conviction is hearsay does not require exclusion of the conviction.

   The adverse party can still object that the evidence is irrelevant, or is inadmissible character evidence, or violates Fed. R. Evid. 403. Fed. R. Evid. 803(22) covers only the hearsay objection.

3. The prior conviction may be used for the limited purpose of impeaching a witness's (or a hearsay declarant's) character for truthfulness. This use of a prior conviction is regulated by Fed. R. Evid. 609.

4. Some prior convictions are not admissible or usable for any of these purposes.

The use of a prior conviction as substantive evidence in subsequent litigation (the second category mentioned above) involves hearsay, because when a judge or jury in a criminal trial convicts the accused of a crime, it is making a *statement*: "I, the judge (or, we, the jury) find the defendant guilty of the crime of —." In fact, in finding a defendant guilty, the judge or jury is really making several statements. For example, suppose F is indicted for robbing a liquor store at gunpoint at 12th and Elm at 11 p.m. on June 1. To find F guilty, the jury must conclude that F was in the liquor store at 12th and Elm at 11 p.m. on June 1, that she had a gun, and that she used the gun to force W1, the store clerk, to empty the register and give her the money.

If, in another lawsuit, someone wants to offer the fact of F's conviction as substantive evidence, that conviction is hearsay: it is a statement, made elsewhere than at the trial of the new case currently being litigated, offered to prove the truth of the matter asserted. (*See* Fed. R. Evid. 801(c); *see* § 2.03.) Because we normally expect someone to fight criminal charges that are untrue, and because the prosecutor's burden of proof in a criminal case is so heavy (guilt must be established beyond a reasonable doubt), most convictions are considered highly trustworthy. Convictions that satisfy Fed. R. Evid. 803(22) are therefore admissible over a hearsay objection to prove "any fact essential to sustain the judgment."

Note that only *convictions* are admissible to prove "any fact essential to sustain the judgment." *Acquittals*, by contrast, are *not* admissible in subsequent litigation as proof that the criminal defendant did *not* do what he was charged with. This is because an acquittal is not a finding that the defendant is innocent of the charge; it is only a finding that a reasonable doubt exists as to the defendant's guilt.

Application of Fed. R. Evid. 803(22) imposes the following requirements and raises the following issues:

1. *The nature of the crime.* Only convictions for felonies (i.e. crimes punishable by death or imprisonment in excess of one year) fit within the provision. Misdemeanors (crimes punishable by less than one year imprisonment) do not.

   Note that the rule does not require that the convicted person *actually receive* a sentence of death or imprisonment in excess of one year; it suffices that he or she *could have* received such a sentence.

2. *Manner of conviction.* The conviction comes within the rule only if it came after trial, or as the result of a guilty plea. Convictions by pleas of nolo contendere do not fit within Fed. R. Evid. 803(22).

3. *Use of conviction in subsequent litigation.* Fed. R. Evid. 803(22) overcomes a hearsay objection only if the prior conviction is being offered in evidence "to prove any fact essential to sustain the judgment."

4. *Use in civil litigation and by the defense in criminal trials.* Civil litigants and criminal defendants may use a conviction under Fed. R. Evid. 803(22) "to prove any fact essential to sustain the judgment" regardless of who the convicted person was. The convicted person could be one of the litigants, or a witness, or anyone else.

5. *Use by the prosecutor in a criminal trial.* A prosecutor may use a conviction under Fed. R. Evid. 803(22) "to prove any fact essential to sustain the judgment" only if the person who was convicted in the prior case is also the defendant in the current case.

6. *Pendency of an appeal.* If an appeal of the conviction is pending, the party adversely affected by the evidence may inform the jury of that fact, but the fact that a case is on appeal does not affect admissibility of the conviction.

Operation of the rule is illustrated by the following questions.

Questions

Q. 42. A man and a woman entered a liquor store at 12th and Elm at 11 p.m. on June 1. The man pulled a gun and ordered W1, the liquor store clerk, to empty the cash register into a sack that the woman was holding.

A minute or two after the robbers left the store, W2, who lives nearby, saw a dark-colored Taurus, speeding up Elm Street, sideswipe a Plymouth Voyager parked on Elm between 14th and 15th Streets, doing substantial damage. W2 can testify that the first three letters of the Taurus's license plate are "VCF."

M and F are subsequently charged with the robbery. According to Department of Motor Vehicle records, F at the time owned a Taurus, with license number VCF-123. W3, a neighbor of F, will testify that F's car was dark brown.

F is arrested; M is a fugitive. F goes to trial for the robbery and is convicted. Although robbery carries a maximum possible sentence of fifteen years, because this is her first offense, she has made considerable progress toward kicking her crack cocaine habit, and the judge is a bit of a softy anyway, she is sentenced to five years, all but the first six months of which is suspended, followed by five years probation.

Thereafter, P, the owner of the Plymouth Voyager, sues F for the damage to his vehicle. In P's civil trial, P seeks to prove that F was convicted of the liquor store robbery.

a. How is this relevant?

Ans. It is relevant because it establishes that F was in the vicinity of P's vehicle at the date and time that P's vehicle was damaged, and was in rather a hurry to get away from that vicinity as quickly as she could; this, in turn, makes it more probable than it would be without that evidence that it was F (and F's Taurus), and not anyone else, who sideswiped P's vehicle.

b. Procedurally, how should P seek to offer proof of F's conviction?

Ans. F's conviction is recorded in an official court record. P can therefore subpoena a copy of that record, which can be authenticated under one of the provisions of Fed. R. Evid. 902. P should also subpoena a copy of the indictment and the pleadings, which will contain the details (day, time, place, and manner in which the crime was committed) involved.

c. If F interposes a hearsay objection in the civil suit, is her conviction admissible under Fed. R. Evid. 803(22)?

Ans. Apply the Fed. R. Evid. 803(22) issue-requirement checklist.

1. *The nature of the crime.* Robbery is punishable by up to fifteen years, so F's conviction qualifies, even though F was only sentenced to six months' actual imprisonment.

2. *Manner of conviction.* F was convicted after trial, which satisfies Fed. R. Evid. 803(22).

3. *Use of F's conviction in current litigation.* To convict F of the robbery, it was "essential to sustain the judgment" finding her guilty that the jury concluded, beyond a reasonable doubt, that she was in the liquor store at Elm and 12th at 11 p.m. on June 1. Therefore, her conviction may be offered as a basis from which the jury in the civil case can infer that she was in the vicinity of Elm and 14th–15th shortly after 11 p.m., when time P's Voyager was sideswiped.

4. *Use in civil litigation. . .* P may offer F's conviction against F.

5. *Use by prosecutor. . .* not applicable.

6. *Pendency of appeal.* F can offer evidence that she is appealing her conviction, in the hopes that the jury will disregard the implications of her conviction.

Q. 43. Change the facts slightly. Assume that the brown Taurus, license number VCF 123, was owned, not by F, but by G, a friend and neighbor of F's. Witnesses at F's criminal trial testified that G had loaned F her car for Memorial Day weekend (May 30–June 2).

After F is convicted of robbery, P sues, not F, but G. (State law provides that the owner of a vehicle is responsible for any damage or injury caused by someone driving the car with the owner's consent. Fortunately for all concerned, G's auto insurance insures her against liability for damages caused by anyone to whom G lends her car.) At the trial of the civil case, P offers in evidence the fact of F's conviction for robbery. Admissible, over G's hearsay objection?

Ans. Yes. The analysis of issues 1–3, and 5–6 from the checklist is identical to that in question 42 c. The only difference is that here, P is using F's conviction as evidence against *G*. In civil litigation, this is explicitly permitted by the rule.

Q. 44. Sometime after F is convicted, police apprehend M, and his case goes to trial.

At M's trial, W1 testifies that M "looks like" the man with the gun, but admits that it's been so long he can't be sure. He easily identifies F as the woman participant. Next, the prosecutor calls witnesses who testify that M and F were living together at the time of the robbery.

a. Now the prosecutor wants to prove that F was convicted of being the woman participant in the robbery. How is this relevant?

Ans. It is logical to assume, if F was the female participant, that M, with whom she was living at the time, was the male participant.

b. Is F's conviction admissible against M, if M interposes a hearsay objection?

Ans. No. This question illustrates issue 5 on the list of issues and requirements. Unlike a civil litigant (see question 43), a prosecutor cannot make evidentiary use of F's conviction against anyone but F.

§ 8.77 Rule 803(23): Judgment as to Personal, Family or General History, or Boundaries

Fed. R. Evid. 803(23) provides as follows:

> **Rule 803. The following are not excluded by the hearsay rule, even though the declarant is available as a witness:**
>
> **(23) Judgment as to personal, family or general history, or boundaries. Judgments as proof of matters of personal family or general history, or boundaries, essential to the judgment, if the same would be provable by evidence of reputation.**

Under this provision, if litigation in the past (whether civil or criminal) resulted in a judgment relating to any of the subjects discussed in Fed. R. Evid. 803(19) or 803(20), that judgment is admissible as proof of any fact "essential to the judgment." For a discussion of the phrase "essential to the judgment," see § 8.76.

§ 8.78 Rule 803(24)

This rule has been transferred to Fed. R. Evid. 807. Case law interpreting Fed. R. Evid. 803(24) is now applicable to Fed. R. Evid. 807.

CHAPTER

9

RULE 804:
THE "DECLARANT UNAVAILABLE" EXCEPTIONS

§ 9.01 Introduction

A major difference distinguishes Fed. R. Evid. 804 from Fed. R. Evid. 803. As we have seen, in Rule 803, the declarant's availability or unavailability has no effect on the statement's admissibility (*see* § 8.02). The exceptions to the hearsay rule set out in Rule 804(b), by contrast, may be used *only* if the offering party can first show that the declarant is unavailable, as that term is defined in Rule 804(a).

Thus, to use a Rule 804 exception, the party offering the statement in evidence must:

  (a) Show that the declarant is unavailable, by satisfying the judge that the *declarant* fits within one of the provisions of Rule *804(a)*; and

  (b) Satisfy the judge that the *statement* fits within one of the provisions of Rule *804(b)*.

The traditional rationale for imposing the "declarant unavailable" requirement is that, unlike statements fitting within the Rule 803 exceptions which are (theoretically, at least) considered "just as good" as live, sworn testimony, statements fitting within the Rule 804(b) exceptions are considered less desirable than live, sworn testimony. Such statements are therefore admitted over a hearsay objection only if the declarant is unavailable to testify at trial.

Rule 804(b) contains five exceptions to the hearsay rule which apply in more-or-less precisely defined situations.

§ 9.02 Rule 804(a): "Declarant Unavailable"

[1] In General

Rule 804(a) provides as follows:

> **Rule 804. Hearsay Exceptions; Declarant Unavailable**
>
> **(a) Definition of unavailability. "Unavailability as a witness" includes situations in which the declarant—**
>
>   **(1) is exempted by ruling of the court on the ground of privilege from testifying concerning the subject matter of the declarant's statement; or**
>
>   **(2) persists in refusing to testify concerning the subject matter of the declarant's statement despite an order of the court to do so; or**

(3) testifies to a lack of memory of the subject matter of the declarant's statement; or

(4) is unable to be present or to testify at the hearing because of death or then existing physical or mental illness or infirmity; or

(5) is absent from the hearing and the proponent of statement has been unable to procure the declarant's attendance (or in the case of a hearsay exception under subdivision (b)(2), (3), or (4), the declarant's attendance or testimony) by process or other reasonable means.

A declarant is not unavailable as a witness if exemption, refusal, claim of lack of memory, inability, or absence is due to the procurement or wrongdoing of the proponent of a statement for the purpose of preventing the witness from attending or testifying.

Note that the rule is concerned with the declarant's unavailability *as a witness*. Someone who is present in the courtroom and on the witness stand is still "unavailable" as a witness if he or she comes within 804(a)(1), (2) or (3).

In accordance with Fed. R. Evid. 104(a), the judge, not the jury, decides whether the witness is "unavailable." Also pursuant to Rule 104(a), the judge may consider inadmissible evidence (out of the jury's hearing) in deciding the unavailability issue.

[2] Rule 804(a)(1): Privilege

Rule 804(a)(1) provides:

Rule 804(a) Definition of unavailability. "Unavailability as a witness" includes situations in which the declarant—

(1) is exempted by ruling of the court on the ground of privilege from testifying concerning the subject matter of the declarant's statement; . . .

A detailed discussion of testimonial privileges is far beyond the scope of this book. Suffice it here to highlight a few of the issues that may arise.

As a rule, a party can establish a declarant's unavailability as a witness on grounds of privilege only if the party calls the declarant as a witness and attempts to question her under oath, and the witness properly asserts either one of the common law evidentiary privileges, a privilege recognized under Fed. R. Evid. 501, or her Fifth Amendment privilege against self-incrimination. Under some circumstances, however, a judge could properly accept a lesser showing of unavailability (for example, an affidavit signed by DL attesting that, if called, she will assert her Fifth Amendment privilege).

The judge need not automatically accept the declarant's claim that she is legally privileged not to testify. For example, someone who was convicted of a crime and never appealed the conviction (or whose appeal was denied) can no longer plead the Fifth if asked about the circumstances surrounding the crime. Thus, the judge should deny the claim of privilege and order the witness to testify in such a case. If the witness disobeys the order, she may be held in contempt of court, and incarcerated without a trial until she agrees to testify or the trial ends, whichever comes first. (Such refusal would render the witness unavailable under Rule 804(a)(2).)

A judge may not be able to make an intelligent decision as to whether information is privileged unless she knows what the information is. In *United States v. Zolin*, 491 U.S. 554, 565–566 (1989), the Supreme Court held that in some circumstances, the judge may require the witness to disclose the allegedly privileged information *in camera* before deciding whether the privilege (in that case, the attorney-client privilege) applies.

Remember, too, that a witness' claim of privilege may be valid as to some questions or some subjects but not as to others. The attorney-client privilege only precludes an attorney from revealing confidential conversations she had with her client in the context of the attorney-client relationship; the privilege does not extend to conversations or conduct that occurred outside the attorney-client relationship.

For example, the attorney could not be compelled to testify about her client's participation in a crime which she learned of during a confidential communication. In contrast, she could be compelled to testify about something her client said about a man the client was dating, because that knowledge did not come to her *within* the attorney-client relationship.

[3] Rule 804(a)(2): Refusal to Testify

Fed. R. Evid. 804(a)(2) classifies a declarant "unavailable" if he or she "persists in refusing to testify concerning the subject matter of the declarant's statement despite an order of the court to do so." The situation sometimes arises when a witness has asserted a privilege under Rule 804(a)(1), the judge concludes that the privilege does not apply, and the witness persists in refusing to answer questions. Another common scenario is the refusal of a reluctant state or government witness to testify against a partner (or superior) in crime. If the witness refuses to answer, the judge should order the witness to do so, and warn the witness that continued refusal will result in being held in contempt.

[4] Rule 804(a)(3): Lack of Memory

Fed. R. Evid. 804(a) classifies a declarant as unavailable who "testifies to a lack of memory on the subject matter of the declarant's statement." If the declarant claims not to be able to remember, the attorney seeking to elicit his testimony or introduce the out-of-court statement may employ any Article VIII provision she can satisfy. If the prior statement was given under oath at a proceeding, for example, the attorney may be able to admit it pursuant to Fed. R. Evid. 801(d)(1)(A), if the court agrees that the witness/declarant's current protestation of lack of memory is "inconsistent" with the former statement. This creates an ironic situation in which a judge concludes that a witness is "unavailable" to testify about a matter per Rule 804(a)(2), yet is "available" to be cross-examined about the prior statement per Rule 801(d)(1).

Before seeking a ruling that the witness/declarant is unavailable for lack of memory, the attorney seeking to elicit the information from the witness/declarant should seek to refresh the witness/declarant's recollection, for example by showing the witness a writing or other object (*see* Fed. R. Evid. 612; § 8.26) and, if that doesn't work, should utilize Rule 803(5) if material exists that satisfies that Rule.

If the judge is convinced that the witness-declarant is lying when he claims lack of memory, the judge can order the witness to testify or hold him in contempt, as outlined in the previous section. If the witness continues to refuse, he is either unavailable per 804(a)(2) or 804(a)(3).

[5] Rule 804(a)(4): Death, Illness, Infirmity

This provision is basically self-explanatory. The burden is on the party seeking to introduce the prior statement to establish the declarant's death, illness or infirmity.

[6] Rule 804(a)(5): Absent From the Hearing

Rule 804(a)(5) provides:

Rule 804(a) Definition of unavailability. "Unavailability as a witness" includes situations in which the declarant—

(5) is absent from the hearing and the proponent of statement has been unable to procure the declarant's attendance (or in the case of a hearsay exception under subdivision (b)(2), (3), or (4), the declarant's attendance or testimony) by process or other reasonable means.

It is simple common sense that someone is "unavailable" to testify if his whereabouts are unknown. The same is true if the declarant is outside the jurisdiction of the court (i.e. cannot be subpoenaed) and is unwilling to appear voluntarily.

Even so, civil procedure rules allow litigants to depose an out-of-jurisdiction declarant. Lawyers cannot compel W to travel from Texas to testify at a trial in California; but the attorneys can obtain a court order in Texas requiring W to submit to a deposition in Texas. The deposition would then be admissible under Fed. R. Evid. 804(b)(1), assuming it satisfied that Rule's requirements.

The parenthetical clause in Rule 804(a)(5) provides that, if a party offers a hearsay statement under Rules 804(b)(2), 804(b)(3), or 804(b)(4) and relies on declarant's absence from the hearing under Rule 804(a)(5) to establish his unavailability, to satisfy Rule 804(a)(5) the party must show, not only that she was unable to "procure the declarant's attendance," but also that she was unable to depose him to "procure the declarant's testimony."

§ 9.03 Rule 804(b): The Exceptions

[1] Introduction

The five hearsay exceptions found in Fed. R. Evid. 804(b) have two requirements in common: each requires that the declarant had first-hand knowledge of the facts asserted in the statement, and each requires that the declarant is unavailable to testify pursuant to Rule 804(a).

[2] Rule 804(b)(1): Former Testimony

[a] In General

A witness (W) testifies at a proceeding of some kind (a trial, deposition, preliminary hearing, grand jury proceeding, congressional hearing, coroner's inquest, police departmental disciplinary hearing, etc.). Later, the testimony that W gave at that prior proceeding is relevant at a different proceeding, but W is no longer available to testify. Therefore, one of the parties in the new proceeding offers the transcript of W's former testimony in evidence. Should W's former testimony be admissible, even though, when offered at a new proceeding, it is hearsay? Or would admitting the testimony give one party an unfair advantage over his adversary?

The answer depends upon whether the examination of W at the former proceeding was substantially similar to what would occur if W were available to testify at the current proceeding. If so, then the rights of all of the parties to the current litigation should be adequately protected, and W's former testimony should be admissible. The question is, how much similarity should be required?

At common law, former testimony was admissible only if: (1) all parties at the former proceeding were identical with all parties at the current proceeding; and (2) the issues at the former and the current proceeding also were identical. Only then, the reasoning went, could we be sure that the examination of W at the prior proceeding adequately mirrors what would have happened if W had been available at the current proceeding.

Many judges and scholars, though, protested that this required more similarity than was necessary to assure fairness, and often resulted in the exclusion of evidence that was quite trustworthy. In enacting Fed. R. Evid. 804(b)(1), Congress sought to accommodate these views. The Rule directs that sufficient similarity (and therefore fairness) exists so long as: (1) the issues relating to W's testimony at the current proceeding are the same as they were at the prior proceeding; (2) *the party against whom the former testimony is now offered* (or in civil cases, that party's predecessor in interest) was a party to the former proceeding; and (3) at the prior proceeding, that party had an *opportunity and similar motive* to examine W the way it would examine W now if W were available.

Fed. R. Evid. 804(b)(1) provides:

Rule 804. Hearsay Exceptions; Declarant Unavailable

(b) Hearsay exceptions. The following are not excluded by the hearsay rule if the declarant is unavailable as a witness:

(1) Former testimony. Testimony given as a witness at another hearing of the same or a different proceeding, or in a deposition taken in compliance with law in the course of the same or another proceeding, if the party against whom the testimony is now offered, or, in a civil action or proceeding, a predecessor in interest, had an opportunity and similar motive to develop the testimony by direct, cross, or redirect examination.

Testimony that satisfies Rule 804(b)(1) is considered an acceptable substitute for "live" testimony because it has most of the attributes of "live" testimony. W's testimony at the prior proceeding, of course, must have been under oath. A party at the prior proceeding must have had an opportunity to test W's testimony on direct, cross or redirect examination along the same lines that the party against whom the testimony is currently being offered would do, if W were now available as a witness. The missing factor, of course, is the opportunity of the fact-finder to observe declarant's demeanor while testifying.

Rule 804(b)(1) imposes the following requirements and raises the following issues.

1. *First-hand knowledge.* It must be apparent that W, the witness whose former testimony is now being offered, had first-hand knowledge of what he testified about.

2. *Unavailable.* The offering party must show that W is currently unavailable, per Rule 804(a).

3. *Nature of prior proceeding.* It does not matter whether the prior proceeding was "another hearing of the same or a different proceeding, or . . . a deposition taken in compliance with law in the course of the same or another proceeding," so long as the other requirements of 804(b)(1) are satisfied.

4. *Identity of adverse party.* Former testimony is admissible against a party only "if the party against whom the testimony is now offered, or, in a civil action or proceeding, a predecessor in interest," was a party at the prior proceeding at which the testimony was given.

a. *Criminal trials.* A prosecutor can offer former testimony against a defendant pursuant to 804(b)(1) only if the defendant was a party in the prior proceeding. Similarly, a defendant can offer former testimony against the government only if the government was a party in the former proceeding.

b. *Civil litigation.* The party against whom the former testimony is being offered must have been a party to the prior proceeding, or his "predecessor in interest" must have been a party. How "predecessor in interest" should be defined is a question of some controversy (*see* § 9.05).

5. *Motive to examine.* The issues at the prior proceeding must have been similar enough to those in the current proceeding to assure that the adversely affected party's treatment of W at that proceeding is an adequate substitute for how that party would treat W now, if W were available (*see* § 9.03[2][b]).

6. *Opportunity to examine.* The procedures and other circumstances at the prior proceeding must have been such to give the adverse party an adequate opportunity to examine W on direct, cross or redirect examination (*see* § 9.03[2][b]).

7. *Offering the testimony.* Almost always, former testimony is offered in the form of a transcript, which must be authenticated in accordance with Fed. R. Evid., Art. IX. If no transcript is available, W's former testimony may be proved by someone who was present and recalled what W said.

8. *Objections.* Suppose objections should have been made at the prior proceeding, but weren't? Suppose a proper objection was made, but W's testimony was nonetheless allowed to stay in the record? (*See* § 9.04.)

9. *Other rules.* Keep in mind that prior testimony may be offered under Article VIII provisions other than 804(b)(1), including, in appropriate circumstances, Rules 801(d)(1)(A), 801(d)(1)(B), 801(d)(2)(A), 803(5), and 807, and may be used to refresh a witness' memory under Rule 612.

10. *Sixth Amendment Confrontation Clause.* Prior testimony is a "weaker substitute" for live testimony, and lacks independent evidentiary significance. Thus, a prosecutor could not rely on the prior testimony exception unless the declarant is unavailable. But this poses no particular difficulties, because Rule 804 so provides.

In *Ohio v. Roberts*, 448 U.S. 56, 73–77 (1980), the Court held that former testimony (in that case, at a preliminary hearing) that meets certain guarantees of trustworthiness is firmly rooted and thus satisfies the Confrontation Clause. Testimony that meets Rule 804(b)(1)'s requirements appears to satisfy the *Roberts* test.

Questions

Q. 1. Cars driven by P and D collide in an intersection, and P sues. At trial, P calls W1, who testifies that he saw D run a red light and crash into P's car. The jury finds for P, but an appellate court remands for a new trial. At the second trial, P offers a transcript of W1's testimony; D makes a hearsay objection. Ruling?

Ans. Objection sustained. P has made no showing that W1 is unavailable to testify at the second trial.

Q. 2. P offers an affidavit from his investigator, attesting that W1 has sold his home and moved to Tierra del Fuego, and told the investigator over the phone that he does not want to return and testify. P again offers a transcript of W1's first-trial testimony. Ruling, if D again makes a hearsay objection?

Ans. Overruled. Following the issue outline:

1. *First-hand knowledge.* W1's former testimony ("I saw it all") satisfies this requirement.

2. *Unavailability.* The investigator's affidavit satisfies Rule 804(a)(5). (Look up Tierra del Fuego in a world atlas.)

3. *Nature of prior proceeding.* Almost any kind of prior proceeding will do. A trial certainly will.

4. *Identity of adverse party.* D was a party at the first trial, where W1 testified; she is a party again at the current trial.

5. *Motive to examine.* The issue about which W1 testified at the first trial (who ran the light) is the same as at the second. D presumably had just as much reason (i.e. a "similar motive") to discredit W1's testimony at Trial # 1 as she has at Trial # 2.

6. *Opportunity to examine.* Unless the judge at the first trial improperly restricted D's chance to cross-examine W1, D has no basis to object here.

7. *Offering the testimony.* P need only offer a certified copy of the trial transcript, or call the stenographer, or satisfy Fed. R. Evid., Art. IX in some other way.

[b] "Opportunity and Similar Motive"

[i] "Similar Motive"

A number of factors must be considered to determine whether the adverse party (i.e. the party against whom the former testimony is now being offered) had a "similar motive" to develop W's testimony at the prior proceeding as that party would if the witness testified at the current proceeding:

1. *Factual issue.* The key factual issues on which W's former testimony is now being offered must have been important issues at the former proceeding as well: did D run the red light (*see* [a], *above*; Q. 1); did D boast to W1 about how he was cheating V (*see* Questions 3–5, *below*). If the key issues at the prior and present proceedings are different, however (*see*, Q. 9), the former testimony should not be admitted.

2. *Same side.* The adverse party must have been on the same side of those factual issues at the former proceeding as it is now in the current proceeding. If subsequently discovered evidence has forced the party to change its cause of action or defense, so now it wishes to prove certain facts it previously sought to disprove, it is unlikely that it had the same motive to develop W's testimony at the former proceeding as it would now.

3. *Comparative importance of the issue at the two proceedings.* Even assuming the former testimony passes the first two tests, some courts are sympathetic to a party's objection that it did not have a "motive to develop the witness's testimony" at the former proceeding if the issue just was not as important then as it is at the current proceeding. The test must turn not only on whether the questioner is on the same side of the same issue at both proceedings, but also on whether the questioner had "a substantially similar degree of interest in *prevailing* on that issue i.e. "whether the party resisting the offered testimony at a pending proceeding had at a prior proceeding an interest of *substantially similar intensity* to prove (or disprove) the same side of a substantially similar issue." (emphasis supplied) *United States v. DiNapoli,* 8 F.3d 909, 912–914 (2d Cir. 1993) (en banc).

A number of factors may effect whether the adverse party had "a substantially similar degree of interest" at the two proceedings:

a. *The nature of the proceedings.* If the former and current proceedings were both trials, there is a substantial likelihood that the "degree of interest in prevailing" was the same at the first trial as it would be at the second. If the former proceeding was of a less significant kind—a grand jury proceeding, a deposition, a preliminary hearing in a criminal case—this weighs against sufficient "similarity of motive" to "develop the [witness's] testimony."

b. *The burden of proof at the two proceedings.* In a grand jury or at a preliminary hearing, a prosecutor need only establish probable cause of a defendant's guilt; at trial, the burden is to prove guilt beyond a reasonable doubt. Thus, the prosecutor may not have as strong a motive to cross-examine and impeach an adverse witness at those earlier proceedings, particularly if doing so would reveal information or sources of information best kept hidden until trial. Similarly, a defense attorney at a preliminary hearing generally knows in advance that the judge will find probable cause. As a result, many defense attorneys simply try to get state witnesses to testify in as much detail as possible. This serves two purposes. First, it enables the defense to conduct some discovery of the state's case;[1] second, the more a state witness testifies at a preliminary hearing, the greater the likelihood that his testimony will contain inconsistencies about which the defense attorney can cross-examine him.

[ii] "Opportunity"

So long as the adverse party had a reasonable opportunity at the prior proceeding to conduct direct, cross or redirect examination of a scope similar to what would be permitted at trial, the requirement

---

[1] Unlike civil cases, in which litigants routinely depose all of the witnesses before trial, there is comparatively little discovery in criminal cases.

is satisfied. Perhaps a major development intervening between the time of the former testimony and the current proceeding might overcome the rule's bias toward admissibility: the adverse party could argue that the changed circumstances makes the motive to develop W's testimony different, or that she never had an opportunity to develop W's testimony in light of the new development. But if the adverse party, because of tactical considerations, chose not to examine the witness as extensively as she would now like, she will simply have to live with her choice.

Questions

Q. 3. V, a business man, sued D, his former accountant, claiming D embezzled company funds. During pretrial discovery, V, in accordance with the Federal Rules of Civil Procedure, deposed W1, who had been living with D while D worked for V. W1 testified that D had boasted to her about how he was cheating V.

At trial, V offers the transcript of W1's deposition into evidence. D objects: hearsay. Ruling?

Ans. Sustained. V has made no showing that W1 is unavailable.

Q. 4. Out of the hearing of the jury, V calls W2, his investigator, who testifies that he has learned that an anonymous benefactor gave W1 $20,000, which W1 is spending on a world cruise that set sail a few days before trial started. V again offers W1's deposition transcript. D objects: hearsay. Ruling?

Ans. Overruled. First, W1 is unavailable, per Rule 804(a)(5). (If I had to guess, I'd say W1's "mysterious benefactor" was probably D, who is better off by her absence—she isn't around to testify against him. Thus, the final clause of Rule 804(a) does not apply here because W1's absence was not procured by *V*, the party now proffering W1's former testimony.) Second, W1's former testimony satisfies Rule 804(b)(1).

Note, by the way, that technically, this is a triple-hearsay issue. D made statements to W1; W1 testified at the deposition; the stenographer wrote down what W1 testified to. But P can easily overcome each level of hearsay:

a. *D's statement to W1.* D's statement to W1 isn't hearsay at all; it is an admission per Rule 801(d)(2)(A).

b. *W1's former testimony.* W1's former testimony fits within Rule 804(b)(1):

1. *First-hand knowledge.* W1 testified at the deposition that she heard what D said.

2. *Unavailability.* Rule 804(a)(5).

3. *Prior proceeding.* W1's testimony was given "in a deposition taken in compliance with law in the course of the same . . . proceeding."

4. *Identity of adverse party.* D was a party to the litigation when W1 was deposed; he is a party now.

5. *Motive to examine.* A pretrial deposition is conducted primarily for discovery, but arguably D had as powerful a motive to cross-examine W1 at the deposition as he would now at trial, if W1 were available.

6. *Opportunity to examine.* There are no meaningful restrictions on direct and cross-examination during pretrial depositions.

c. *Stenographer to transcript.* As to the final level of hearsay (the stenographer's act of recording W1's deposition testimony): if D is unwilling to stipulate to its accuracy and admissibility, V need merely call the stenographer or some other "qualified witness" to have the transcript authenticated as the stenographer's business record, under Rule 803(6).

Q. 5. A jury returns a judgment for V. Thereafter, D is indicted for embezzlement. The prosecutor calls W1 (who is back from her extended sojourn abroad) as a witness. W1, proudly displaying a wedding band, says, "I refuse to testify against my husband," and produces a wedding certificate showing that she and D were married a week before the trial began. The prosecutor offers W1's deposition transcript from the earlier civil ligation. D objects: hearsay. Ruling?

Ans. Overruled. Even though this is a criminal case and the prior litigation was a civil suit, the situation here is really quite similar to the previous question. Our analysis of issues 2–5 differs slightly from that in Q. 4, but this does not change the outcome:

2. *Unavailability.* Most jurisdictions recognize a privilege which entitles a person not to testify against his or her spouse. W1 is therefore unavailable pursuant to Rule 804(a)(1).

3. *Prior proceeding.* W1's testimony was given "in a deposition taken in compliance with law in the course of . . . *another* proceeding," because the deposition was part of a civil case while the current trial is a criminal prosecution. This is not a problem, however; Rule 804(b)(1) explicitly permits this.

4. *Identity of adverse party.* The parties aren't completely identical in this problem, the way they were in the previous problems. The deposition was taken in the case V v. D, but is now being offered in the case *United States v. D.* This is no bar to admissibility, though, because the rule only requires that the party *against whom* the testimony is offered (in this case, D) must have been a party at the prior proceeding.

5. *Motive to examine.* Even though the ultimate issues at the civil and criminal cases are somewhat different (civil liability v. guilt), as far as what W1 testified about, the issues are the same: did D make the statements W1 said he made, or was W1 fabricating to get back at him for jilting her? Thus, D's motive to cross-examine (and impeach) W1's testimony at the time of the deposition is probably the same as it would be now if she were a government witness at the criminal trial.

D can argue, with some plausibility, that a civil litigant's motive to cross-examination for *discovery* purposes at a pretrial deposition is very different than would be a criminal defendant's motive at trial. The underlying issue in each case was the same, however—did D embezzle money from V or not, and, as to W1, was she telling the truth or lying about what D allegedly said to her about it. Unless D can demonstrate some fundamental unfairness about using the transcript, a judge is likely to admit it, rather than force the prosecutor to forego the evidence altogether. And given that it was the defendant's own action (in marrying W1) that rendered W1 unavailable, D should not expect a judge to be overly sympathetic.

In fact, the prosecutor might have an interesting argument that by marrying W1, he forfeited his right to assert a hearsay objection, as per Rule 804(b)(6) (*see* § 9.17[2]).

Q. 6. Police seize several kilograms of cocaine from an apartment, and arrest D1, the tenant, and D2, D1's alleged supplier. At a pretrial motion to suppress challenging the search and seizure, D1 takes the stand and testifies that (among other things) D2 paid half of D1's rent in exchange for D1 letting D2 use the apartment as a stash pad. D2 does not cross-examine.

The judge denies the defendants' motion to suppress, and D1 pleads guilty. At D2's trial, the prosecutor offers D1's suppression hearing testimony against D2, who makes a timely hearsay objection. Ruling?

Ans. Sustained. The prosecutor has not demonstrated D1's unavailability.

Q. 7. The prosecutor calls D1 as a witness, but D1 tells the judge, "I don't want to testify, because I'm afraid for my family." Does this suffice to establish D1's unavailability?

Ans. No. To be "unavailable" even though he is on the witness stand, D1 must validly claim a testimonial privilege (Rule 804(a)(1)), or "persist in refusing to testify . . . *despite an order of the court to do so*" (Rule 804(a)(2)). The prosecutor must ask the judge to order D1 to testify; only if he still refuses is he "unavailable."

Q. 8. Pursuant to the prosecutor's request in Question 7, the judge orders D1 to testify. D1 testifies fully about his own involvement with the apartment and the cocaine, but when the prosecutor asks him "Who brought the cocaine to the apartment?" D1 responds, "I don't remember." He gives this same answer to all similar questions about who his supplier was. When asked, "Do you know this man sitting here?" (i.e. D2), he again responds, "I don't remember." Does this establish D1's "unavailability"?

Ans. Yes, finally: Rule 804(a)(3). Even though D1 has testified with regard to part of the "subject matter of [his] statement," his professed inability to recall other important details renders him "unavailable" as to those details.

Q. 9. Now that we've finally shown D1 to be unavailable, is his suppression hearing testimony admissible against D2?

Ans. No. The facts in this problem satisfy all but one of the requirements of Rule 804(b)(1). If you don't already know which one, re-read Q. 6, and remember what you learned in your course in criminal procedure about "standing" to challenge a search and seizure.

The key issue here is requirement # 5, *motive to examine.* At a motion to suppress, the legal issue is very different than it is at trial. At a motion to suppress, a defendant must demonstrate his standing to challenge the legality of the search. Often this requires a defendant to offer evidence connecting himself to the contraband and to the place where it was seized. Thus, at the suppression hearing, D2 had absolutely no reason to impeach D1's testimony, because, in the context of a suppression hearing, D1's testimony *helped* D2.

At D2's trial, by contrast, D2 wants to challenge any evidence the government offers tending to connect him to the apartment or the cocaine. His motive to cross-examine D1 at trial, therefore, would be very different than it was at the suppression hearing.

Objection sustained.

Q. 10. In a breach of contract trial, P v. D, P called W1, expecting her to testify that P complied with his contractual obligation to deliver 500 class-A midget widgets to D. To P's surprise, though, W1 testified that the midget widgets P delivered were of inferior quality and didn't meet contract specifications. Flustered, P's attorney floundered a bit, asked a few clumsy and ineffectual questions, and muttered, "Nothing further." Delighted, D proclaimed, "Your Honor, we have no questions of this obviously truthful witness."

It becomes necessary to retry the case. At the second trial, D offers a transcript of W1's first-trial testimony. P objects: hearsay. Ruling?

Ans. Sustained. D has not shown that W1 is unavailable.

Q. 11. D submits an affidavit from W1's doctor attesting that she is unable to testify. Does this suffice to show that W1 is unavailable? If so, is W1's testimony now admissible under Rule 804(b)(1)?

Ans. Yes; and yes. W1 is unavailable per Rule 804(a)(4). The judge has discretion to accept such an affidavit, or even a simple letter, as proof that a witness is unavailable.

This question differs from the preceding ones because here, *P* called the witness at the first proceeding, while *D* is offering the testimony at the new proceeding. This is no bar to admissibility, however. Go through the checklist again. The key issues are:

4. *Identity of adverse party.* P was a party at the prior trial; he is a party at this one.

5. *Motive to examine.* W1's testimony related to the same issue at each trial: whether P complied with his contractual obligations.

6. *Opportunity to examine.* Even though P conducted direct examination of W1 at the first trial and would be cross-examining W1 if she testified at the second trial, this is no bar to

admissibility. Rule 804(b)(1) requires that the party against whom the testimony is now being offered (i.e., P) "had an opportunity and similar motive to develop the testimony by direct, cross or redirect examination." P had his opportunity; he just blew it.

P may argue that he didn't really have the opportunity, because he was taken by surprise. Similarly, P may argue that he didn't really have the same motive in Trial #1 as he would in Trial #2: having called W1 as his own witness in Trial #1, he decided as a matter of tactics to get her off the stand as quickly as possible, whereas if D called W1 in the second trial, P would go at her, hammer and tongs. P has a legitimate complaint here: the tactical situation *is* rather different.

But the judge has to make a choice here: if she saves P from the impact of his own tactical choice, she deprives D of valuable evidence not otherwise available. In all likelihood, P's objection will be overruled.

§ 9.04 Objections

Can the party against whom the prior testimony is now being offered object to portions of the transcript, if objections could have been made at the prior proceeding, but were not?

The best, and prevailing, approach divides such objections into two categories:

(1) Objections that go to substantive evidence issues, such as those addressed in Article IV of the Federal Rules, may be made for the first time at the new proceeding at which the former testimony is being offered.

(2) Objections that go primarily to form, in contrast (leading questions, unresponsive answers, answers more in the form of opinion than fact), cannot be made at the current proceeding if they were not made at the prior proceeding. The rationale for this approach is that the first category addresses whether the evidence is inadmissible per se; no one would be unfairly disadvantaged if inherently inadmissible evidence is excluded from the new proceeding. The objectionable aspects of evidence falling into the second category, by contrast, probably could have been corrected at the prior proceeding if a timely objection had been made, so it is unfair to exclude it at the new proceeding.

Questions

Q. 12. At a civil negligence trial, P offers the following passage from a transcript of the direct examination of Ms Jones at a pretrial deposition. Which of these exchanges should be excluded if offered under Rule 804(b)(1), assuming all other requirements of Rule 804(b)(1) have been satisfied? How should the judge rule on each?

Example (a):

Q. Miss Jones, when you first saw the red car, it was halfway up the block, is that right?

A. Yes.

Q. And you noticed immediately that it was weaving from side to side as it approached the intersection?

A. Yes.

Example (b):

Q. What happened when the red car neared the intersection?

A. Well, Charlie told me later that it started to slow down but then picked up speed again as the light turned red.

Example (c):

Q. What did the blue car do as the light changed?

A. The red car was definitely going too fast.

Example (d):

Q. Did you try to settle this thing without going to court?

A. Well, I figured, —

Q. Didn't you offer my client $500 if he'd forget the whole thing and not sue you?

A. Yes, I did. I didn't realize he was gonna make a federal case out of it.

Ans.

(a) The attorney asked leading questions, which is perfectly proper if this was cross-examination but is improper (barring unusual circumstances) if it was direct examination. Nevertheless, this objection goes to form, not substance. Objection overruled.

(b) The answer is hearsay; unless P can convince the judge that "Charlie's" statement to the witness comes within a hearsay exception, it should be excluded. A hearsay objection will be sustained.

(c) The answer is unresponsive to the question, and is worded more as an "opinion" than a "fact," but is otherwise admissible (the witness had first-hand knowledge, the information is relevant, etc.). Objection overruled.

(d) This should be excluded. Evidence of attempts to compromise potential lawsuits are excluded by Rule 408. An objection on that basis will be sustained.

§ 9.05 "Predecessor in Interest"

The original Advisory Committee draft of Rule 804(b)(1) would have admitted former testimony so long as the party against whom it was offered, or a party "with motive and interest similar" to his, had an opportunity to develop the witness' testimony at the former proceeding. The House Judiciary Committee rejected this language, reasoning:

> [I]t is generally unfair to impose upon the party against whom the hearsay evidence is being offered responsibility for the manner in which the witness was previously handled by another party. The sole exception to this, in the Committee's view, is when a party's predecessor in interest in a civil action or proceeding had an opportunity and similar motive to examine the witness.

Congress amended the draft of Rule 804(b)(1) to reflect the House Committee's position.

Courts have taken a variety of approaches to interpreting the "predecessor in interest" clause. One approach is to read the phrase "predecessor in interest" in the traditional, narrow sense of privity. Under this interpretation, X would be Y's "predecessor in interest" in a lawsuit only if Y "inherited" the suit from X. Examples:

- X brought a breach of contract action against Z. After pretrial depositions, X died, and Y, X's executor, continues the lawsuit on behalf of X's estate. Y is X's "successor in interest"; X was Y's "predecessor in interest." Thus, X's handling of depositions, etc. is attributable to Y for purposes of Rule 804(b)(1).

- X Co. and M, Inc. merged, to form Y Corp. Shortly before the merger, a lawsuit brought by P against X Co. resulted in a judgment. After the merger, that judgment was reversed, and a new trial was ordered. This time, P is suing Y Corp., because Y now "owns" not only X's assets but also its potential liabilities. X was Y's predecessor in interest; hence, the manner in which X's attorneys examined witnesses in the previous litigation is now attributable to Y Corp.

Some courts, by contrast, have substantially ignored the clear congressional intent to limit "predecessor in interest." The leading example is *Lloyd v. American Export Lines, Inc.*, 580 F.2d 1179, 1185 (3d Cir.), *cert. denied*, 439 U.S. 969 (1978).

In *Lloyd*, the Third Circuit essentially nullified Congress' revision of the Advisory Committee draft of Rule 804(b)(1), by defining the phrase "predecessor in interest" to mean "community of interest." Alvarez and Lloyd were crewmen on a ship operated by American Export. They fought, and each sued American Export, each alleging that the company negligently failed to protect him from the other. The two civil suits were consolidated into one case for purposes of trial.

Prior to the trial of these civil actions, however, the Coast Guard brought a proceeding against Lloyd, charging Lloyd with assaulting Alvarez. At the Coast Guard hearing, Lloyd testified, and was cross-examined by counsel for the Coast Guard, about the fight and other relevant matters. (Neither Alvarez nor American Export were parties at the Coast Guard proceeding.)

Lloyd subsequently disappeared, so only Alvarez' suit against American Export went to trial (although the case retained the formal title,"*Lloyd v. American Export Lines, Inc.*"). American Export sought to offer in evidence Lloyd's testimony at the Coast Guard hearing. Alvarez interposed a hearsay objection; American Export cited Rule 804(b)(1). The trial judge sustained the objection, reasoning that because Alvarez had not been a party to the Coast Guard proceeding, he had had no opportunity to cross-examine Lloyd, that the Coast Guard was not Alvarez' "predecessor in interest", and that Lloyd's prior testimony therefore did not satisfy Rule 804(b)(1).

The Third Circuit reversed. The Coast Guard, the court pointed out, had the same goal in cross-examining Lloyd at the earlier hearing as Alvarez would have to cross-examine Lloyd if Lloyd were available at the civil trial. The main issue in each case, after all, was whether the altercation was Lloyd's fault or Alvarez'; the Coast Guard was attempting to place the blame on Lloyd at the hearing, just as Alvarez would try to do at trial. Because Alvarez and the Coast Guard shared a sufficient "community of interest," the court reasoned, the Coast Guard was Alvarez' "predecessor in interest" for purposes of Rule 804(b)(1).

Judge Stern's concurring opinion accused the *Lloyd* majority of ignoring the intent with which Congress revised the original draft of Rule 804(b)(1). He also pointed out that because the Coast Guard did not represent Alvarez, its attorney's choice of issues, tactics and strategy might differ substantially from those Alvarez might use at trial.

Some courts have attempted to define a middle ground between strict "privity" and "community in interest," permitting former testimony to be offered against a party in the current trial so long as that party had some formal ties with a party who in the prior proceeding with "similar motive" to develop the witness's testimony.

In applying Rule 804(b)(1), therefore, you should be aware of the different approaches courts may take in applying the "predecessor in interest" clause: the "strict privity" approach, the "Lloyd-community of interest" approach, and the "formal ties" approach.

Questions

Q. 13. Several cars collide when a tractor-trailer overturns on I-495. P1 suffers a bruised shoulder; his car sustains $1200 in damages. P2, in another auto, is terribly burned and will require intensive medical treatment for the rest of her life.

P1 and P2 each sue D Co., which owned and operated the truck. The key issue is whether D's truck overturned because D's driver failed to pay attention, as plaintiffs claim, or, as D insists, was the truck suddenly cut off by a red sports car, forcing D's driver to swerve suddenly to avoid crushing that car but tragically, to overturn and involve several other vehicles.

P1 retains C, an attorney fresh out of school (not *your* school, but your cross-town or cross-state rival). C brings an action against D in state court seeking $5,000 for pain, suffering, expenses and lost wages. Meanwhile, P2's family has retained G, a leading personal injury attorney; G files an action in federal district court seeking $14 million in actual and punitive damages.

Because C has very few cases while G is juggling a heavy calendar, P1's action moves a bit more quickly than P2's. At a pretrial deposition, C deposes W1, D's driver, and W2, an apparently impartial eyewitness. C's inexperience is apparent throughout the proceeding, but D, who is anxious to do the right thing if it doesn't cost too much, ultimately settles with P1 anyway.

Shortly thereafter W1 dies and W2 quits his job to fulfill a lifelong ambition to backpack from Lisbon to Tierra del Fuego. When P2's case comes to trial, D offers the deposition testimony from P1's suit; P2 objects on hearsay grounds. Ruling?

Ans. W1 and W2 are both unavailable under Rule 804(a).

Even so, under Rule 804(b)(1) as the House Judiciary Committee intended it to be applied, the objection would be sustained. Although P1 and P2's claims arose out of the same accident, they are involved in completely separate lawsuits. There is no privity between P1 and P2; therefore P1 was not P2's "predecessor in interest." Accordingly, P2 should not be held accountable for how P1's attorney handled the examination of W1 and W2.

Under the *Lloyd* approach, however, P2's hearsay objection would be overruled. The factual issue in P1's suit was the same as in P2's suit (i.e. what caused D's driver to swerve, resulting in the tractor-trailer overturning). P1's interest in developing the testimony of W1 and W2 is the same as P2's interest: to cast doubts on D's version of events and if possible substantiate plaintiffs' theory. Therefore, according to *Lloyd*, P1 *was* P2's "predecessor in interest," and P2 is stuck with C's unartful and unsuccessful attempt to examine W1 and W2.

§ 9.06   Rule 804(b)(2): Statement Under Belief of Impending Death

[1]   In General

Fed. R. Evid. 804(b)(2) provides:

> **(b) Hearsay exceptions. The following are not excluded by the hearsay rule if the declarant is unavailable as a witness:**
>
> * * *
>
> **(2) Statement under belief of impending death. In a prosecution for homicide or in a civil action or proceeding, a statement made by a declarant while believing that the declarant's death was imminent, concerning the cause or circumstances of what the declarant believed to be his impending death.**

The usual justifications underlie what is commonly called the "dying declaration exception": necessity and reliability. Where the declarant is deceased, necessity is obvious (although in civil cases the offering party need only show that the declarant is "unavailable" under Rule 804(a), not that he or she is deceased). Reliability in olden days was predicated on the belief that no one would be willing to die with a lie on his lips, for to do so would condemn his soul to eternal damnation or, at least, an extensive stay in purgatory. Society has "progressed" since then, to the point that reliability today is predicated on the perhaps less certain hope that knowledge of impending death produces, even in a nonbeliever, a powerful psychological impulse to speak only the truth.

The application of Rule 804(b)(2) imposes the following requirements and raises the following issues.

1. The declarant (DL) must have had first-hand knowledge of the facts asserted in his statement.

2. The declarant must be unavailable, as defined in Rule 804(a).

3. DL must have believed his death was imminent and certain at the time he made the statement.

4. The statement must have concerned the cause or circumstances of [what DL believed to be] his impending death.

5. *Use in civil litigation.* In civil litigation (e.g. in a personal injury suit for damages), a litigant may use Rule 804(b)(2) even if DL did not in fact die, so long as DL is "unavailable" under 804(a).

6. *Use in criminal litigation.* In criminal litigation, either the prosecution or defense may use Rule 804(b)(2) in a prosecution of the defendant for unlawfully killing DL.

7. *Sixth Amendment Confrontation Clause.* The exception applies in criminal cases only if the declarant is dead. In *Ohio v. Roberts*, 448 U.S. 56, 66 (1980), the Supreme Court cited dying declarations as an example of a "firmly rooted exception." Thus, any statement that satisfies this exception also satisfies the Confrontation Clause.

[2] Satisfying the Requirements

Often the statement itself will provide the necessary proof that DL had first-hand knowledge of the facts asserted in the statement and believed that death was certain and imminent. You've probably seen this scene in one western or another:

Lance comes upon his friend Jim lying on the ground, hand clutched to his stomach.

Lance: Jim! What happened?

Jim: I know I'm a goner; not even a miracle could save me now. It was that low-down varmint Clyde what done it. He walked up behind me, tapped me on the shoulder, and when I turned around to face him he just smiled and unloaded his six-shooter in my belly. Tell Lu-Ann I always loved her. Tell her I never blamed her for loving you more'n she loved me —

(As Jim dies, his head cradled in Lance's arms, the camera catches the conflicting emotions on Lance's face—sorrow at the loss of his friend, a grim determination that Clyde will be brought to justice, and wonderment at learning that Lu-Ann, whom he had secretly loved since they were children, might actually love him too.)

Jim's statement satisfies each of the Rule 804(b)(2) requirements:

(1) Jim saw who shot him, so he had first-hand knowledge of the what he told Lance.

(2) Jim is dead, which establishes his unavailability.

(3) He believed his death was imminent and certain ("I know I'm a goner").

(4) The statement concerned the cause of his impending death.

(5) (not applicable).

(6) The statement therefore should be admitted a prosecution of Clyde for killing Jim. (Clyde could, however, exclude the portion of Jim's statement relating to Lu-Ann, since that statement does not "concern the cause or circumstances of what [Jim] believed to be his impending death.")

These requirements can also be satisfied in other ways. For example:

Lance: Jim, the doc says you can't hold on much longer. Tell me who did this to you and I swear I'll see him hang for it!

Jim: I didn't see who done it. I didn't know anybody else was there! But then I heard somebody behind me. One of his boots squeaks real loud. I was 'bout to turn around to see who it was when BAM! he shot me in the back. . . . Find the varmint with a boot that squeaks real loud, Lance! He's the one—

In this variation, Lance's statement to Jim ("Doc says you can't hold on much longer") establishes that Jim was aware that death was certain and imminent; and while Jim was unable to identify the perpetrator, his statement demonstrates first-hand knowledge that the man who shot him in the back wore a very squeaky boot. When Lance notices, a few days later, that D (who had been attempting to force farmers like Jim off their land) has a squeaky boot, Jim's dying declaration becomes admissible circumstantial evidence that D is the killer.

Questions

Q. 14. D is on trial for murdering his wife, DL. The state has presented evidence that DL became violently ill on May 20. She was rushed to the hospital and, after several days on the critical list, seemed to be recovering, only to suffer a relapse on June 1; she died on June 3. The state presents forensic evidence that her death was caused by ingestion of arsenic, together with related medical complications. Next, the prosecutor calls W1, a nurse who cared for DL in the hospital. W1 will, if permitted, testify:

DL said, "If I die, tell the police it was my husband. He poisoned the vanilla extract I keep behind the hat boxes on the shelf in my closet!"

Would this testimony be admissible under Rule 804(b)(2), if D interposes a hearsay objection?

Ans. No. Although DL's statement to W1 satisfies the second and fourth requirements (DL is unavailable and the statement concerns the cause of her subsequent death), it is does not satisfy the first or third requirement. It is doubtful that she had actual *knowledge* of who poisoned the vanilla extract; the statement sounds more like speculation than a recitation of something she observed. Moreover, the evidence does not show that DL believed her death was certain and imminent; she said "*If* I die," not "When I die."

Q. 15. P sues for personal injuries suffered when a moving vehicle struck him as he was crossing the street. No one saw the incident, and P suffers from partial amnesia and can no longer recall anything about it. An ambulance attendant will testify that, as P was being rushed to the hospital, he kept muttering, "I'm not gonna make it, I'm not gonna make it. It was a green station wagon. Maryland plates, XYZ—couldn't see the rest. Oh, no, why did this have to happen now, two weeks before the Superbowl! I'm not gonna make it. . . ." Does Rule 804(b)(2) overcome D's hearsay objection?

Ans. Perhaps. P will argue that each of the Rule 804(b)(2) requirements are satisfied:

(1) P had first-hand knowledge of the facts he asserted—he saw the style, color and partial plate of the vehicle that struck him.

(2) Even though P is alive, because he can no longer remember what happened, he is "unavailable" (*see* Rule 804(a)(3)).

(3) At the time, P believed his death was imminent and certain ("I'm not gonna make it. . . .").

(4) The statement concerned the cause of what P believed to be his imminent demise.

(5) Rule 804(b)(2) may be used in civil litigation even though P is still alive.

D will argue, on the other hand, that P's comment about the Superbowl suggests that P was not really convinced of his impending death: someone who is about to die wouldn't be worried about a mere sporting event (although, to paraphrase the late Vince Lombardi, to some people the Superbowl "isn't a matter of life and death—it's more important than that").

A judge could go either way, depending on whether she is a pro football fan.

§ 9.07 Rule 804(b)(3): Statement Against Interest

[1] In General

Fed. R. Evid. 804(b)(3) provides as follows:

(b) Hearsay exceptions. The following are not excluded by the hearsay rule if the declarant is unavailable as a witness:

(3) Statement against interest. A statement which was at the time of its making so far contrary to the declarant's pecuniary or proprietary interest, or so far tended to subject the declarant to civil or criminal liability, or to render invalid a claim by the declarant against another, that a reasonable person in the declarant's position would not have made the statement unless believing it to be true. A statement tending to expose the declarant to criminal liability and offered to exculpate the accused is not admissible unless corroborating circumstances clearly indicate the trustworthiness of the statement.

The justification for this provision is that a person is unlikely to say something that is against her own best interests (i.e. that might later be used against her), unless what she says is true. The key to this exception is that the statement must have been against the declarant's own interests *at the time she made the statement.*

At common law, the "statement against interest" exception included only statements against the declarant's financial ("pecuniary and proprietary") interests. Rule 804(b)(3) also includes statements that tend to expose the declarant to criminal prosecution, although as to the latter, the Rule imposes a corroboration requirement. Not surprisingly, Rule 804(b)(3) has been invoked quite often in criminal cases; its use in civil litigation has been comparatively rare.

It is best to approach Rule 804(b)(3) as if it was three separate rules. The first covers declarations against financial, proprietary, litigational or penal interest in *civil* cases; this use of the Rule is comparatively rare. The second covers a criminal defendant's use of the declarant's statement against penal interest as evidence of the defendant's innocence, as where a declarant says, in words or substance, "D did not commit that crime, *I* committed it." The third covers a prosecutor's use of a declarant's statement against penal interest as evidence of the defendant's guilt, where a declarant says something that tends to incriminate himself and also tends to incriminate the defendant.

[2] Use in Civil Litigation

Application of Fed. R. Evid. 804(b)(3) imposes the following requirements and raises the following issues:

1. Declarant must have had first-hand knowledge.

2. Declarant must be unavailable, as defined in Rule 804(a).

3. *"Interests" included within the Rule.* The Rule covers only pecuniary, proprietary, litigational and penal interests. Statements contrary to other "interests" are not admissible within the exception (*see* § 9.07[3]).

4. *"Tends . . . against interest."* The statement need not be unequivocally disserving; it suffices that it "tends" to be against the declarant's pecuniary, proprietary, litigational or penal interest. Remember that we must determine whether it was against the declarant's interest at the time he made the statement. This depends upon the factual context in which the statement was made (*see* § 9.07[4]).

5. *Individual declaration or narration as a whole.* In *United States v. Williamson,* 512 U.S. 594, 602–604 (1994), the Supreme Court held that when a prosecutor offers a statement that was against the declarant's penal interest as evidence against a different defendant, it is necessary to examine each declaration within an utterance to determine whether it was sufficiently against the declarant's interest, rather than considering the declarant's narrative as a whole (*see* § 9.12). It is unclear whether this approach to the meaning of "statement" will apply to other aspects of Rule 804(b)(3).

6. *Relationship to other rules.* Rule 804(b)(3) is sometimes confused with Rule 801(d)(2), "admissions of party opponent" (*see* § 9.07[5]).

[3] "Interests" Included Within the Rule

Fed. R. Evid. 804(b)(3) covers statements that were contrary to the declarant's "pecuniary or proprietary interest, or . . . tended to subject the declarant to civil or criminal liability, or to render invalid a claim by the declarant against another." A statement acknowledging a debt ("I owe X $ 5,000") could be against declarant's pecuniary interest; as could a statement acknowledging that a debt has been paid ("Y has paid me everything he owes me"). A statement acknowledging nonownership of real or personal property could be contrary to proprietary interest ("I don't own the Porsche, I borrowed it from my brother-in-law"). Q. 16 offers an example of a statement tending to expose declarant to civil liability. A statement conceding contributory negligence would tend to "render invalid a claim by the declarant against another."

The Advisory Committee proposed that Rule 804(b)(3) also include statements that tended to "make [declarant] an object of hatred, ridicule, or disgrace." Congress, however, rejected this language, reasoning that such statements simply lack sufficient indicia of reliability.

[4] "Against Interest"

Fed. R. Evid. 804(b)(3) is based on the assumption that people do not make statements which they know are damaging to themselves unless they are satisfied for good reasons that the statements are true. Thus, to fit within the Rule, a statement must have been *dis*serving, not self-serving, when the declarant made it. This requires the judge to examine the factual context in which the statement was made. If a statement appears on its face to be disserving, it is safe to assume it was against the declarant's interest unless the party against whom it is offered can persuade the judge otherwise. DL's statement, "I owe X $5,000," appears to be disserving (and therefore appears to fit within Rule 804(b)(3), assuming the Rule's other requirements are satisfied), because declarant is acknowledging a debt. But if DL made the remark during a dispute over whether she owed X $5,000 or $10,000, her statement was actually self-serving, and could not satisfy Rule 804(b)(3).

Statements sometimes contain self-serving *and* disserving elements. A motorist, for example, might say after a collision, "I admit I was doing 65 in a 55 mph zone, but the other guy must have been doing 85!" The statement is disserving in part ("I admit I was doing 65") but its overall thrust is self-serving. In such cases, where the disserving and self-serving parts of the statement are easily severable, the judge can simply redact the self-serving aspects and allow in only the disserving parts (unless, of course, the self-serving part of the statement satisfies some other provision of Article VIII). If the judge believes this would unfairly advantage one side over the other, however, she can exclude the entire statement. Where it is impossible to redact the self-serving part, the judge must assess whether, overall, the statement was more disserving or self-serving when the declarant made it, and rule accordingly.

[5] Contrasting Rule 804(b)(3) and Rule 801(d)(2)

It is important not to confuse Rule 804(b)(3), "statement against interest," and Rule 801(d)(2)(A)–801(d)(2)(D), "admission by party-opponent." Under 801(d)(2), we focus only on who made the statement and who is now offering it in evidence: the statement qualifies whether it was self-serving, disserving, or neutral, so long as:

(a) The declarant who made or adopted the statement is now a party to the litigation, or was an agent, when he made the statement, of someone who is now a party to the lawsuit; and

(b) The statement is being offered by the other party (i.e. the declarant's opponent, or the declarant's principal's opponent) in the lawsuit (*see* §§ 5.01–5.03, 5.07, 5.12).

Under Rule 804(b)(3), by contrast, it is irrelevant whether the declarant had any relationship to any of the parties to the current lawsuit, and either party to the lawsuit can invoke the Rule. Instead, the Rule requires that:

(a) The declarant must have had first-hand knowledge of the underlying facts when he made the statement;

(b) The declarant must be unavailable to testify at trial; and

(c) The statement must have been against the declarant's pecuniary, proprietary, or litigational (or penal) interest *at the time he made the statement.*

Questions

Q. 16. On June 1, P brings his car to be serviced by D service station. X, a mechanic, is assigned to work on the brakes. On June 3, X quits his job. On June 5, the brakes on P's car fail, and P is seriously injured. On June 6, X learns of P's accident. "That was my fault," X tells W, a friend. "I was drunk that day and forgot to finish reinstalling P's brakes."

P sues D, alleging that X's failure to service the brakes properly caused the brake failure and P's injuries. At trial, P calls W to testify about X's statement. D objects: hearsay.

a. Is X's statement to W admissible against D under Rule 801(d)(2)(D)?

Ans. N. By the time X made his statement, he was no longer an employee or agent of D (*see* § 5.14; *see also* Q. 12).

b. Is X's statement to W admissible against D under Rule 804(b)(3)?

Ans. No. P has offered no evidence that X is now unavailable.

c. P calls an investigator who testifies that he has searched high and low for X, but that no one has seen him for several months and that he left no forwarding address. Is X's statement to W admissible against D now under Rule 804(b)(3)?

Ans. Yes. X had first-hand knowledge of whether he was drunk and of whether he completed the job; he is also unavailable. His statement "tended to expose him to civil liability," because P could have sued him, as well as D; hence, it is unlikely "a reasonable person in [X']s position" would have made the statement "unless believing it to be true."

Q. 17. P's store burns to the ground, and she files a claim with FIC, her insurance company, seeking to recover the value of the building, the inventory that she claims was destroyed, and other assets. FIC refuses to pay, alleging that P hired X to burn the building down.

At trial, after P rests, D calls X, but X asserting his Fifth Amendment privilege, refuses to answer any questions. D next calls W, a long-time friend of X, if permitted, testify that a few days after the fire, X told W, "D hired me to torch her store. A couple of firemen got hurt fighting the fire. I feel real bad about that." (W acknowledges that he decided to come forward and testify after he heard about the $25,000 reward FIC offered to anyone who could prove that the fire was caused by arson.) Is X's statement admissible per Rule 804(b)(3)?

Ans. Apply the issue checklist.

1. *Declarant's first-hand knowledge.* X presumably had first-hand knowledge as to whether D in fact hired him to burn the building.

2. *Declarant's unavailability.* X is unavailable per Rule 804(a)(1).

3. *"Against interest."* X's statement to W was against his penal interest: it tended to expose him to prosecution for arson. Rule 804(b)(3) permits a civil litigant to use a declarant's statement against penal interest.

4. *"Tends . . . against interest."* Even though X assumed his friend W would not repeat what he said, X had to know there was a possibility that W would do so.

Note that there is nothing disserving about *W*'s decision to testify: he hopes to reap a $25,000 reward. But W is not the declarant, X is. The "against interest" requirement is satisfied so long

(Matthew Bender & Co., Inc.)

as it was against the *declarant*'s interest to make the statement at the time he made it, even if it is very much *in* the witness's best interest to repeat the statement at trial.

As you will see shortly, there are several complications that must be addressed when either a prosecutor or a criminal defendant seeks to use a declarant's declaration against penal interest in a criminal case. These complications do not apply, however, if plaintiff or defendant seek to use such a statement in a *civil* case.

§ 9.08 Declarations Against Penal Interest: Use by Defendant in Criminal Cases

When a defendant seeks to use a declarant's statement against penal interest as evidence of his own innocence (such as "D didn't commit the crime, *I* did"), the following issues must be addressed:

1. Declarant must have had first-hand knowledge.

2. Declarant must be unavailable, as defined in Rule 804(a).

3. "Interests" included within the Rule: Penal interest is recognized by the Rule.

4. *Tends . . . against interest.*" The statement need not be unequivocally disserving; it suffices that it "tends" to be against the declarant's penal interest. Remember that we must determine whether it was against the declarant's interest at the time he made the statement. This depends upon the factual context in which the statement was made.

5. *Corroboration requirement.* The last sentence of the Rule provides: "A statement tending to expose the declarant to criminal liability and offered to exculpate the accused is not admissible unless corroborating circumstances clearly indicate the trustworthiness of the statement" (*see* § 9.09).

6. *Individual declaration or narration as a whole.* In *United States v. Williamson*, 512 U.S. 594, 602–604 (1994), the Supreme Court held that when a *prosecutor* offers a statement that was against the declarant's penal interest as evidence against a different defendant, it is necessary to examine each declaration within an utterance to determine whether it was sufficiently against the declarant's interest, rather than considering the declarant's narrative as a whole (*see* § 9.12). It is unclear whether this approach to the meaning of "statement" will apply to other aspects of Rule 804(b)(3).

§ 9.09 The Corroboration Requirement

A lone gunman shot and killed X, and D was indicted for the crime. At trial, after the prosecutor presents her case, D offers an alibi defense, but the jury appears highly skeptical. Then, just as things look their darkest, D calls a surprise witness, W. "I was hangin' out a couple of months ago," W testifies, "tellin' my friend Eddie how worried I was about D gettin' indicted, when Roger Overnout, this guy I know from the neighborhood, says, D didn't kill X; he couldn't have, 'cause *I* killed X.'" When the prosecutor makes a hearsay objection, D's attorney informs the court that Overnout is unavailable—he died of a drug overdose three weeks ago. D's attorney argues that Overnout's statement is therefore admissible under Rule 804(b)(3) as a statement against Overnout's penal interest.

This is an example of a statement "tending to expose the declarant [Overnout] to criminal liability and offered to exculpate the accused [D]" (to quote from the last sentence of Rule 804(b)(3)). Evidence of this kind is ridiculously easy for a defendant or his associates to manufacture. All it takes is someone (W) who is willing to invent a conversation with someone else who "confessed" to the crime D is charged with—preferably someone else who, like Mr. Overnout, is not available to deny having made the incriminating statement.

At common law, such statements were inadmissible, because the "declaration against interest" exception to the hearsay rule covered only statements against the declarant's pecuniary or proprietary interest. The Advisory Committee and members of Congress wrangled considerably over whether to include declarations against penal interest within Rule 804(b)(3). The final text represents a compromise. The Rule includes declarations against penal interest, but directs that "[a] statement tending to expose the declarant to criminal liability and offered to exculpate the accused is not admissible unless corroborating circumstances clearly indicate the trustworthiness of the statement." Unless the judge is satisfied that the defendant has offered sufficient corroboration, the statement is inadmissible hearsay.

This leaves us with several questions. First, what must be corroborated? Second, who must be corroborated? Third, how much corroboration is enough?

1. What must be corroborated?

The last sentence of the Rule directs that the defendant must demonstrate that "corroborating circumstances clearly indicate the trustworthiness of the statement." In assessing trustworthiness, some courts look only at the statement itself and the circumstances surrounding the making of the statement; others also consider whether the *content* of the statement (i.e. what the declarant said) has been corroborated by other evidence.

a. The making of the statement.

The circumstances surrounding the making of the statement can tell us a lot about whether it is likely to be true. Z's boast to friends at a party ("I was the guy who broke into the school last week and stole all the computers") may not rate too highly on the reliability meter, if Q, later charged with being the burglar, seeks to have someone testify about Z's statement. People have been known to falsely claim to have committed a well-publicized crime in an effort to boast about how "bad" they are.

By contrast, suppose X and D are arrested for a bank robbery committed several days earlier in which X committed the actual robbery while D drove the getaway car. After being given the *Miranda* warnings, X admits, "Yeah, that was me who robbed the bank. But listen, D had no idea what I was doing. He's just some poor schmoe I talked into giving me a ride. He thought I was just going into the bank to make a deposit."[1] The circumstances surrounding this statement make it appear to be reliable for at least three reasons:

(1)   Unlike Z's statement in the previous paragraph, this statement does not merely "tend" to expose the declarant to criminal liability; it is an outright confession of guilt to the police. The greater the likelihood the statement *will* hurt the declarant, the more reliable it probably is.

(2)   Unlike Z's statement in the previous paragraph, X apparently has nothing at all to gain by making the statement.

(3)   If, as X said, D was no more than a casual acquaintance, then we can discount the possibility that X was falsely exonerating D out of loyalty, friendship or fear. Therefore, if D is charged with being X's accomplice, the circumstances under which X made his statement exculpating D have strong indications of trustworthiness.

b. The contents of the statement.

Some courts also look to whether the defendant has offered "extrinsic" corroboration (i.e. evidence), independent of the statement itself, that tends to corroborate its truth. In the school burglary example, suppose Q, the defendant, calls several witnesses to testify that a few days after the burglary, Z, who had no previous known access to computers, went around offering to sell several computers, of the same kind taken from the school, at a ridiculously low price. This requires us to look at Z's statement at the party in a new light. What might otherwise be seen as just an attempt by Z to impress others with his supposed "badness" now looks a great deal more credible.

---

[1] As you recall from your criminal law course, to convict D of being X's accomplice in robbing the bank, it is not enough for the prosecutor to prove that D in fact helped X commit the robbery by driving him away from the bank; the prosecutor must also prove that D did so knowing and intending to help X commit the crime.

2. Who must be corroborated?

Must the corroboration pertain only to the declarant's statement (assuming he said it), or also to the testimony of the witness to whom the declarant allegedly made the statement?

Remember that hearsay evidence usually involves the credibility of at least two people—the witness and the declarant:

(1) The *witness*. Is the person who claims to have heard the statement testifying truthfully and accurately? In other words, was there, as W claims, a declarant; did he make a statement; and if so, is W accurately repeating what the declarant said?

(2) The *declarant*. Assuming W is telling the truth, (i.e. there was a declarant and he made the statement W will testify to), was declarant's statement truthful and accurate?

Fed. R. Evid. 804(b)(3) clearly requires the judge to exclude the statement unless the defendant can show "corroborating circumstances clearly indicat[ing] the trustworthiness of the statement." This focuses on the statement and, to an extent, on the credibility of the *declarant*. Although *witness* credibility is almost always considered strictly a jury issue, some courts have read the legislative history of Rule 804(b)(3) as requiring the trial judge to exclude the statement unless the defense can corroborate the *witness's* testimony as well, by offering additional evidence, besides just one witness's testimony, that the declarant *made* the statement.

3. How much corroboration?

The defendant must offer some evidence supporting the truth of the declarant's statement. As to how much, the only clear answer is, "more than a little." The legislative history makes it clear, for example, that the mere fact that the defendant takes the stand and denies committing the crime is insufficient corroboration to secure admissibility of the (alleged) declarant's (alleged) self-incriminating, defendant-exculpating statement.

Questions

Q. 18. A lone gunman shot and killed X, and D was indicted for the crime. At trial, after the prosecutor presents her case, D offers an alibi defense, but the jury appears highly skeptical. Then, just as things look their darkest, D calls a surprise witness, W. "I was hangin' out with a couple of guys a couple of months ago," W testifies, "tellin' my friend Eddie how worried I was about D gettin' indicted, when Roger Overnout, this guy I know from the neighborhood, says, 'D didn't kill X; he couldn't have, 'cause *I* killed X.' " When the prosecutor makes a hearsay objection, D's attorney informs the court that Overnout is unavailable—he died of a drug overdose three weeks ago. D's attorney argues that Overnout's statement is therefore admissible under Rule 804(b)(3) as a statement against Overnout's penal interest.

What kind of corroboration would suffice to secure admission of the statement Overnout allegedly made to W?

Ans. *W's testimony* that Overnout made the statement could be corroborated (if such corroboration is deemed necessary) if "friend Eddie" also testifies that he heard Overnout make the statement, or if other witnesses testify that the heard Overnout make similar statements.

The *circumstances surrounding the making of the statement.* Here, I think, we have a bit of a mixed bag. Overnout probably did not expect his statement to be used against him, which tends to detract a bit from the trustworthiness of the statement. On the other hand, he knew that W was a friend of D's, so presumably he realized there was some risk that W might go to the authorities and accuse Overnout to get D off the hook. A judge might decide this is enough, but it would certainly be within judicial discretion to hold that it is not.

The *contents of Overnout's statement* might be sufficiently corroborated by some combination of the following. (a) A witness testifies that she saw Overnout near the scene of V's murder shortly before V was killed. (b) Evidence demonstrates that Overnout had a motive to kill V, or that a strong enmity existed between V and Overnout. (c) Overnout was arrested in possession of an item of property that other witnesses placed in V's possession shortly before V's death (assuming the circumstances of V's death suggest V was robbed by his killer).

No particular formula applies; the ultimate question is whether D has introduced enough direct or circumstantial evidence to "clearly indicate" that Overnout's statement (that he, not D, killed V) was "trustworthy."

Q. 19. D and V had feuded for months. Shortly before midnight on the evening of June 1, on Girard Avenue between 14th and 15th Streets, things came to a head: they had words, they pushed and shoved each other, and finally D shot and killed V. Charged with murder, D pleaded self-defense, insisting that he pulled and fired his own pistol only after V had pulled a gun and pointed it at him. Several people can attest that V owned, and often carried, a pearl-handled .32 caliber revolver. Unfortunately for D, no revolver was found on V or at the scene.

On July 1, in a different part of the city, someone robbed a branch of the First City Savings and Loan. A few days later, X was arrested for the robbery, and was interrogated by Detective W. X confessed to the robbery. As part of the confession, X told Detective W that he found the gun he used in the robbery. "I picked it up off the street about a month ago right after a guy got shot on Girard near 15th Street."

At D's murder trial, D calls X as a witness; but X, who has since pleaded not guilty in his robbery case, asserts his Fifth Amendment privilege. D therefore calls Detective W, hoping to elicit testimony relating X's statement.

a. How is X's statement relevant in D's murder trial?

Ans. From X's statement, it is reasonable to infer that X picked up a handgun off the street shortly after D shot and killed V. This tends to make D's self-defense claim more believable, because it explains why the gun, which D claims V pointed at him on June 1, was never found. Therefore, it has some tendency to "exculpate the accused."

b. The prosecutor makes a hearsay objection. Is the testimony it admissible under Rule 804(b)(3)?

Ans. Apply the list of requirements and issues:

1. *First-hand knowledge.* X, the declarant, presumably has first-hand knowledge of where he found the handgun.

2. *Unavailability.* X is unavailable, pursuant to Rule 804(a)(1).

3. *Interest.* "Penal interest" is recognized by the Rule.

4. *"Against interest."* Although X's statement about finding the gun did not in and of itself incriminate him (unless he is in a state that requires all handguns to be registered), it is so closely connected with his confession to the robbery which clearly *was* against his penal interest that it satisfies this requirement.

This situation differs from the typical defense use of Rule 804(b)(3), because here the declarant's statement incriminates him in a crime different from the one D is accused of. But in and of itself, this is no bar.

5. *Corroboration*

a. *Circumstances surrounding the making of the statement.* A post-*Miranda* confession is a fairly reliable "circumstance," particularly where the declarant has nothing to gain from lying about where he obtained the gun and has no known relationship to D that might prompt him to lie on D's behalf.

b. *Contents of the statement.* It would be useful if D could find some extrinsic corroboration of X's statement. For example, if X (or a witness in the bank) described the gun X used as "fairly small in caliber, with a white handle," and other witnesses described V's handgun the same way, that might well suffice.

c. *Witness credibility.* There is little reason to question Detective W's testimony: why would a detective lie to provide a possible defense to someone charged with murder?

d. *Declarant credibility.* X's lack of any apparent motive to lie about where he got the gun strongly supports his credibility here.

§ 9.10 Declaration Against Penal Interest: Use by Prosecutor

When a prosecutor seeks to use a declarant's self-incriminating statement against the defendant in a criminal trial, the following issues are presented:

1. Declarant must have had first-hand knowledge.

2. Declarant must be unavailable, as defined in Rule 804(a).

3. *"Interests" included within the Rule*: Penal interest is recognized by the Rule.

4. *"Tends . . . against interest."* The statement need not be unequivocally disserving; it suffices that it "tends" to be against the declarant's penal interest. A 1994 Supreme Court decision, *Williamson v. United States*, 512 U.S. 594, 599 (1994), defined the word "statement" in a way that will sometimes make it difficult to satisfy this requirement (*see* § 9.12).

5. *Relationship to other rules.* Two other rules should be considered, as well as Rule 804(b)(3), whenever a prosecutor offers a declarant's self-incriminating statement in evidence against a defendant: the coconspirator exception, Rule 801(d)(2)(E), and the "second-party *Hillmon*" aspect of Rule 803(3) (*see* § 9.13).

6. *Guarantees of trustworthiness and the Confrontation Clause.* Even though the Rule as written does not require a *prosecutor* to offer any "guarantees of trustworthiness" as a prerequisite to using a declarant's self-incriminating statement against a defendant (the corroboration-trustworthiness clause in the Rule explicitly applies *only* when a declarant's statement against interest is offered by a *defendant* to *exculpate* the defendant), most courts have held that unless the prosecutor does so, the statement must be excluded by the Confrontation Clause (*see* § 9.14).

§ 9.11 "Against Interest"

X is arrested for narcotics trafficking. After *Miranda* warnings, Detective Washington shows X photographs depicting X handing drugs to an undercover officer; he also plays tapes of X's drug-related conversations. He reminds X that, given his two prior felony convictions, if X goes to trial he faces life without parole. But, Washington adds, if X confesses, and names his supplier, maybe the D.A. will cut him a break. "O.K., O.K., you got me good," X replies, "that's me all right. I've been dealin' pretty regular for the last couple of months. I get my stuff from this guy named D. Now about this break you mentioned. . . ."

D is subsequently indicted. When the prosecutor calls Washington to testify about what X said, D makes a hearsay objection, and the prosecutor cites Rule 804(b)(3). Ruling?

Objection sustained. When X made his statement to Washington, he did so hoping to help himself by currying favor with the authorities. Hence, from X's perspective, his statement was self-serving, rather than against his interest.

The basic point is that the fact that someone confessed to a crime, or pleaded guilty, or testified about his own wrongdoing before a grand jury, does not, by itself, satisfy the "against interest" requirement. You must examine the factual context in which the statement was made. If X made his admission (incriminating D as well as himself) as part of a deal with the authorities, or in the hopes of striking such a deal, the statement cannot satisfy Rule 804(b)(3).

§ 9.12 *Williamson*: Individual Declaration or Narration as a Whole; "Collateral" Statements

In *United States v. Williamson*, 512 U.S. 594 (1994), police caught a man named Harris with 19 kilograms of cocaine in the trunk of his car. He told the police several different versions of how he came to possess the drugs; in each version he admitted knowing the cocaine was in the trunk and that they belonged to Williamson. At Williamson's trial, the Government called Harris as a witness, but he refused to testify even after being granted immunity. The trial court then admitted Harris' final statement against Williamson, per Rule 804(b)(3). The Supreme Court unanimously held that Harris's allegations against Williamson should not have been admitted, but left more confusion than clarity as to how the rule it enunciated should be applied in subsequent cases.

The basic issue was, how should a court read the word "statement" in Rule 804(b)(3)? In essence there are two choices:

(1) The first is to assess the declarant's narrative as a whole. If, on the whole, the declarant's narrative was against the declarant's penal interest, then it qualifies under Rule 804(b)(3). Although clearly exculpatory (self-serving) portions should be redacted, neutral collateral declarations within the narrative could be admitted along with the clearly self-inculpatory portions.

(2) The second approach to the general policy question is to examine each individual declaration within the narrative. Only those declarations that were against the declarant's interest qualify under Rule 804(b)(3); collateral neutral declarations as well as exculpatory (self-serving) declarations within the narrative must be excluded.

A six-justice majority, per Justice O'Connor, concluded that Congress intended that when applying Rule 804(b)(3) to a prosecutor's use of a declarant's statement against penal interest, a court must examine each declaration within a narrative to determine whether that particular declaration was sufficiently against the declarant's interest, rather than considering the declarant's narrative as a whole. Only those individual declarations within the narrative that were self-incriminating qualified as being against the declarant's penal interest. Exculpatory, mitigating and even neutral declarations within the narrative are not against the declarant's penal interest, the majority held; therefore they would not qualify for admission under Rule 804(b)(3).

The difficulties in applying the Court's general policy ruling is demonstrated by the fact that the six-Justice majority could not agree on how to apply that ruling to the facts. Four Justices, per Justice Ginsberg, concluded that *no* aspect of Harris's statement to the police qualified as a declaration by Harris against his penal interest. According to Justice Ginsberg, everything Harris said, including his admission that he knew about the cocaine in the trunk, was a self-serving attempt to curry favor with the authorities or was so closely intertwined with that attempt as to not make any difference.

Justices O'Connor and Scalia, the other two members of the majority, concluded that although those portions of Harris's narrative directly incriminating Williamson appeared to be an attempt to curry favor and did little to subject Harris to criminal liability and therefore should not have been admitted, other aspects of Harris's statement, such as admitting he knew about the cocaine in the trunk, "would clearly have been admissible under Rule 804(b)(3)." They concluded that the case should be remanded for further proceedings to determine which particular declarations within Harris's narrative could be admitted against Williamson. Because Justice Kennedy, the Chief Justice, and Justice Thomas (the three "dissenting" judges on the general question) also voted for remand, the case was remanded for further action.

Williamson requires us to address two questions:

1. Does the holding apply only to cases in which a prosecutor relies on Rule 804(b)(3) to offer a declarant's statement against penal interest against another defendant; or does it apply to all statements offered under Rule 804(b)(3) (i.e. in civil cases and in criminal cases when the defendant, rather than the prosecutor is offering the statement?). Most likely *Williamson* will apply to all uses of Rule 804(b)(3), but it is too soon to be certain.

2. Under what circumstances will a declarant's statement against interest be admissible against someone else? Justices O'Connor and Scalia provided examples:

   a. If declarant's statement directly incriminated only himself, and did not name or significantly refer to (other) defendants, it would be admissible against other defendants (assuming it met the other requirements of Rule 804(b)(3) so long as it was relevant. For example, when witnesses testified that two men robbed a bank, declarant's statement "I was robbing the bank Friday morning" would be admissible against a non-declarant defendant accused of being declarant's partner in the robbery. (The statement would be relevant against the non-declarant defendant if other evidence made it such—when, for example, another witness testified that he saw defendant and declarant together just before or just after the robbery was committed.) (Justice O'Connor's majority opinion.)

   b. The harder question to answer is, when (if ever) would it be against the declarant's interest to specifically name other perpetrators? Justices provided two examples:

      • During questioning about a murder, DL tells police, "I hid the gun in Joe's apartment." This tends to incriminate the declarant, because it tends to connect him with the crime. Thus, it would be admissible against non-declarant defendants, assuming other evidence made it relevant. (Justice O'Connor's majority opinion.)

      • If a lieutenant in an organized crime organization spelled out how the organization committed extortion and protection, naming names and defining roles, at least some of what he says likely would be self-incriminating, and thus admissible against the other participants. (Justice Scalia, concurring with Justice O'Connor.)

§ 9.13   Rule 804(b)(3); Rule 801(d)(2)(E); Rule 803(3) ("Second Party *Hillmon*")

From a prosecutor's perspective, Rule 801(d)(2)(E) and Rule 804(b)(3)'s declaration against penal interest provision are closely related, because *each permits a prosecutor to offer a declarant's statement, which tends to incriminate the declarant, as evidence of a non-declarant defendant's guilt.* The same is often true for "second party *Hillmon*" statements, in jurisdictions that recognize that variation on Rule 803(3).

Turn back to §§ 5.17, 5.18 and review the prerequisites a prosecutor must satisfy to admit a statement under Rule 801(d)(2)(E).

You will recall that the prosecutor must establish five prerequisites and an important procedural requirement:

1. A conspiracy in fact existed.

2. The declarant was a member of the conspiracy.

3. The non-declarant defendant, against whom the statement is being offered, was a member of the conspiracy.

4. The statement was made "during the course" of the conspiracy.

5. The statement was made "in furtherance" of the conspiracy.

6. It does not suffice that these facts appear from the contents of the non-declarant defendant's statement itself. The final sentence of Rule 801(d)(2) directs that "The contents of the statement shall be considered but are not alone sufficient to establish . . . the existence of the conspiracy and the participation therein of the declarant and the party against whom the statement is offered under [801(d)(2)(E)]." In other words, the prosecutor must offer *corroborating evidence*, independent of the statement itself, as to the first three requirements; the statement is admissible only if it and the corroborating evidence satisfies the judge by a preponderance of the evidence that the prerequisites have been met.

In essence, these requirements are imposed to assure that the statement is sufficiently reliable to satisfy the policies underlying the hearsay rule—and Confrontation Clause.

Suppose NB is on trial for being a major drug supplier. The prosecutor calls W1 to testify that SD1, a low-level street dealer, once boasted to him, "I can get you all the heroin you want, cause me and NB, we're real tight; he gives me all the merchandize I can handle." If the prosecutor relies on Rule 801(d)(2)(E), she cannot admit the statement unless she can establish all five prerequisites, and corroborate the first three.

But if the prosecutor instead cites Rule 804(b)(3), there appears from the language of the Rule to be no corroboration requirement; so long as SD's statement was against his own penal interest, it is therefore admissible against NB.

Think about it. Almost any statement made during and in furtherance of a conspiracy will be against the declarant's penal interests. Does it make sense that Rule 804(b)(3) should throw open the door to just about any such statement that fails to satisfy Rule 801(d)(2)(E), so long as the declarant is unavailable?

Now re-read § 8.13, covering "second party *Hillmon*" statements. In essence such statements must satisfy the following requirements:

1. The statement must be one in which the declarant expressed an intent to do something with the defendant.

2. If offered to prove that the *defendant* later in fact committed the act with the declarant, the prosecutor must offer evidence independent of the statement that *corroborates* it, (i.e. that tends to show that the defendant in fact did what the declarant claimed he and the defendant intended to do).

The corroboration requirement is imposed because without it, such a statement simply would not be sufficiently reliable to satisfy the purposes underlying the hearsay rule—and the Confrontation Clause. Suppose, in the same drug trial, the prosecutor calls W2 to testify that SD2, another street dealer, told him, "NB and I are going to pick up 20 kilos of pure tomorrow." As we have just seen, she cannot use Rule 801(d)(2)(E)) to admit SD2's statement against NB unless she can corroborate the existence of a conspiracy relationship between NB and SD2. She cannot use 803(3)-second party *Hillmon* unless she offer evidence tending to corroborate that in fact NB and SD2 picked up those two kilograms. But so long as SD2's statement tends to expose him to criminal liability (and it does), Rule 804(b)(3) appears to admit it against NB. Does it make sense that, so long as the declarant is unavailable, the prosecutor can do an end run around the 803(3)-second party *Hillmon* corroboration requirement, merely by citing Rule 804(b)(3)?

The *Williamson* rule, which requires a court to examine a declarant's utterance declaration by declaration rather than as an overall narrative, will probably prevent some statements of dubious reliability from being admitted under Rule 804(b)(3). The next section discusses how many courts have addressed similar concerns.

§ 9.14 Guarantees of Trustworthiness; Confrontation Clause

Prior to *Williamson*, many courts held that Rule 804(b)(3)'s declaration against penal interest provision is not "firmly rooted." They have therefore held that a prosecutor cannot rely on that provision to admit a statement unless the government can make a "particularized showing of [the statement's] trustworthiness." Some of these courts have held that in assessing trustworthiness, the judge should look only at the statement itself and at the circumstances under which it was made; other courts have held that the judge should also look at any extrinsic corroboration of the truth of the statement the prosecutor may be able to offer. In this respect, case law pretty much parallels the corroboration requirement that the rule explicitly imposes when a defendant seeks to use a declarant's declaration against penal interest as exculpatory evidence (*see* § 9.09).

In November, 1998, the Supreme Court granted certiorari in *Lilly v. Commonwealth*, 499 S.E.2d 522 (Va. 1998), a case that raises the question of whether declarations against penal interest are firmly rooted. Although the case involves state common law rather than Fed. R. Evid. 804(b)(3), it may also provide the Court with another opportunity to enlighten (or confuse) us about when a declarant's naming of the defendant as a participant in the crime is against the declarant's penal interest.

Questions

Q. 20. Two days after a bank robbery, DL tells G, his girlfriend, "X and I pulled that bank job they made so much noise about on the TV news the other night. We cleared $20,000 each!" May G, who by now is DL's *ex-girlfriend*,[1] testify as to this statement as a government witness at DL and X's joint trial for committing the robbery?

Ans.

a. G's statement clearly is admissible against DL: Rule 801(d)(2)(A).

b. Admissibility against X is unclear.

(1) Rule 801(d)(2)(E)

The prosecutor cannot rely on this Rule. Putting aside for a moment whether there is any evidence corroborating the existence of a conspiracy, or X and DL's involvement in it, a robber's boast to a girlfriend is not "in furtherance" of the conspiracy; moreover, it appears that the conspiracy to rob the bank was over when DL bragged to G about it.

(2) Rule 803(3)—second party *Hillmon*

Putting aside whether there is any corroborating evidence, the statement cannot satisfy Rule 803(3) because it looks backward to the past, not forward to the future.

(3) Rule 804(b)(3)

(a) Since DL is a defendant, the government cannot call him as a witness; to do so would automatically violate DL's Fifth Amendment privilege. Therefore DL is unavailable per Rule 804(a)(1).

(b) DL's statement that he himself was one of the robbers clearly was against his own penal interest. And unlike the *Williamson* case, DL wasn't trying to "curry favor with the authorities" when he identified X as the other perpetrator. But arguably *the fact that X was the other robber* does not, in and of itself, have any apparent tendency to incriminate DL. Thus, his naming X as his partner might be viewed as a "collateral, neutral" declaration outside the scope of the rule. If so, the most the prosecutor could use would be a redacted version: G could testify, "DL told me he was one of the robbers." On the other hand, some federal courts have rejected the notion that *Williamson* automatically excludes a statement in which the declarant names the defendant as another perpetrator in the crime.

(c) *Williamson* aside, if the Rule 804(b)(3) penal interest provision is not firmly rooted, the prosecutor will have to make "particularized showing of [the statement's] trustworthiness." There is nothing particularly trustworthy about the circumstances surrounding the making of this statement, and there is no evidence of extrinsic corroboration of it.

Q. 21. Suppose a few days after DL dumped G, she went to the police and told them what he had told her—including that DL had also told G, "I used my sawed-off shotgun and X used his pearl-handled .45-caliber pistol." Suppose further that press reports about the robbery had not specified weapons the robbers used, but several witnesses had described them as a sawed-off shotgun

---

[1] When I was a prosecutor, it surprised me at first how often criminals boasted to their girlfriends about their crimes, then treated them shabbily and dumped them. After awhile, the only surprising thing about this pattern was that the criminals were surprised at how willing and even eager their ex-girlfriends were to testify against them.

and a pearl-handled .45. When G comes to court to testify at trial, is DL's statement admissible against X?

Ans. Rule 801(d)(2)(E) or Rule 803(3) second party *Hillmon* still do not help the prosecutor, for the reasons outlined in the previous answer. As to Rule 804(b)(3):

a. DL is still unavailable, as per the previous question.

b. It is difficult to see why this statement gives the prosecutor a better *Williamson* argument than the previous statement did, except to the extent that the statement appears more trustworthy.

c. As to trustworthiness, however, the prosecutor has a much better argument—assuming a judge is permitted to look at extrinsic corroboration in assessing trustworthiness.

(1) That DL had "insider information" about the type of guns used by the robbers greatly enhances the trustworthiness of his (declarant's) statement. We no longer need be concerned that when DL claimed to have been one of the robbers, he was lying to G to impress her.

(2) The fact that *G* knew the kinds of guns the robbers used also makes it very difficult for X (or DL, for that matter) to claim that G was lying on the witness stand to get back at DL for dumping her. Thus, this tends to corroborate the *witness's* credibility, too.

Q. 22. Reconsider Q. 16 (the faulty brake job question). If *Williamson* applies to Rule 804(b)(3) in civil cases, is X's statement still admissible against D?

Ans. Yes. X's statement is directly disserving only to himself. It becomes relevant against D only through the tort law doctrine of *respondeat superior*. This poses no *Williamson* problem.

Q. 23. Reconsider Q. 17 (the arson case). Assume D and X are charged with arson. Is W's testimony about X's statement admissible?

Ans.

a. W's testimony is admissible against X per Rule 801(d)(2)(A).

b. Regarding Rule 804(b)(3):

(1) X had first-hand knowledge of whether he set the fire and who paid him to do so.

(2) X is unavailable per Rule 804(a)(1).

(3) X's admission that he burned the building clearly was against his penal interest.

(4) Does X's naming of D satisfy *Williamson*, or is D's identity as the person who paid X merely a "collateral, neutral" fact? We don't know for sure.

The prosecutor can argue that, unlike *Williamson*, declarant X here was not seeking to "curry favor" with anyone; he was expressing guilt and grief to a friend. The prosecutor will also argue that the fact that D (the owner of the building) paid him to burn the building *is* an incriminating fact, because that fact provides X's motive to burn the building. The defense can argue that the statement is just as incriminating against X if it is redacted to, "*Someone* paid me to burn the building. . . ."

(5) Relationship to other rules: Neither Rule 801(d)(2)(E) nor Rule 803(3) second party *Hillmon* admit X's statement against D, because the statement was not in furtherance of any conspiracy and was backward looking.

(6) Guarantees of trustworthiness.

(a) Circumstances surrounding the making of the statement. Suppose X testifies that he and W have long been good friends and that they regularly confided in each other, that W noticed after the fire that X began acting depressed and distracted, and that X told W about setting the fire only after W coaxed and nudged him to "tell me what's eating you." A judge might reasonably conclude that this offers sufficient "guarantees of trustworthiness."

(b) Extrinsic corroboration. (1) Suppose a fire insurance company salesman testifies that D significantly increased his fire insurance just a few weeks before the fire. (2) Officials at companies that supplied D with mechanize testify that D had a great deal of difficulty selling their goods. (3) Other witnesses testify that they saw D moving his most expensive merchandize and a few prized personal belongings out of the building the night before it burned. (1) and (2) suggests that D had a powerful motive to hire someone to burn down his building. (3) tends to suggest that D expected his building to burn down. This is the kind of evidence that would lend extrinsic circumstantial corroboration to X's testimony.

§ 9.15   Rule 804(b)(4): Statement of Personal or Family History

[1]   In General

Fed. R. Evid. 804(b)(4) provides as follows:

(b) Hearsay exceptions. The following are not excluded by the hearsay rule if the declarant is unavailable as a witness:

(4) Statement of personal or family history. (A) A statement concerning the declarant's own birth, adoption, marriage, divorce, legitimacy, relationship by blood, adoption, or marriage, ancestry, or other similar fact of personal or family history, even though declarant had no means of acquiring personal knowledge of the matter stated; or (B) a statement concerning the foregoing matters, and death also, of another person, if the declarant was related to the other by blood, adoption, or marriage or was so intimately associated with the other's family as to be likely to have accurate information concerning the matter declared.

The Rule covers statements concerning two closely related subjects: statements by the declarant involving his own "personal history," and statements by a declarant involving someone else's "family history."

[2]   Rule 804(b)(4)(A): Declarant's Own Personal History

The only prerequisites for admissibility are that the declarant must be unavailable, and the statement must relate to his or her "personal history." Note that the exception explicitly requires *no* showing that declarant had first-hand knowledge. The reason is simple: while most people "know" who their parents, grandparents, aunts, uncles, cousins, etc., are, and "know" how they are related to each of them, it is the rare person indeed who was actually present at his own conception, let alone at those of his parents, grandparents, and other relatives. As to many such matters, first-hand knowledge is simply impossible to acquire; hence the Rule does not require it.

Unlike its common law antecedent, Rule 804(b)(4)(A) does not require that the statement must have been made before the controversy arose that resulted in the lawsuit.

[3]   Rule 804(b)(4)(B): Statement Concerning Family History of Another

This Rule imposes three requirements: the declarant must be unavailable; the statement must relate to the family history of another person (which may include the circumstances of his death); and declarant must have been either legally related to the other person, or must have been "so intimately associated with the other's family as to be likely to have accurate information concerning" the subject-matter of the statement. As with Rule 804(b)(4)(A), first-hand knowledge is not required.

Rule 804(b)(4)(B) differs from its common law predecessor in two respects. First, like Rule 804(b)(4)(A), 804(b)(4)(B) does not require that the statement must have been made before the controversy arose which resulted in the lawsuit. Second, Rule 804(b)(4)(B) expands the common law exception by including statements made by non-relatives who are "intimately associated with the other's family"; the family doctor or lawyer, for example, or a longtime neighbor or friend. (The party offering the statement has the burden of establishing that the declarant had an intimate enough association with the family "as to be likely to have accurate information concerning" the subject-matter of the statement.)

Note that even if this degree of intimacy cannot be shown, the statement may still win admission under Rule 803(19), which covers reputation as to personal or family history. Similarly, if the statement is in a document or record of some kind, it may be admissible as a business or public record, a family record (Rule 803(13)), a baptismal or similar certificate (Rule 803(12)), an ancient document (Rule 803(16)), or other hearsay provision.

§ 9.16   Rule 804(b)(5)

As originally enacted, Rule 804(b)(5) consisted of a residual exception provision, identical to Rule 803(24). Both have since been transferred to Rule 807. Case law interpreting and applying Rule 804(b)(5) is still relevant in applying Rule 807.

§ 9.17   Forfeiture by Wrongdoing

[1]   In General

Fed. R. Evid. 804(b)(6) provides as follows:

(b) Hearsay exceptions. The following are not excluded by the hearsay rule if the declarant is unavailable as a witness:

(6) Forfeiture by wrongdoing. A statement offered against a party that has engaged or acquiesced in wrongdoing that was intended to, and did, procure the unavailability of the declarant as a witness.

The Rule is basically self-explanatory. If a party bribes or threatens or kills a declarant, or hires or encourages someone else to do so, or "acquiesces" in such conduct, that party has in essence waived a hearsay objection as to that declarant's hearsay statements. The provision codifies a rule that emerged in the case law over the past two decades, mostly in criminal cases. In the discussion that follows, I am assuming that a prosecutor is offering a declarant's statement in evidence and claims that the defendant has forfeited the hearsay objection per this provision.

Issues likely to arise include the following:

1. *Wrongdoing.* Does the conduct that procured the declarant's unavailability amount to "wrongdoing?"

2. "*Acquiesce.*" The Rule covers not only active procurement of wrongdoing, but also "acquiescence" in such wrongdoing.

3. *Burden of proof; procedure.* (*See* § 9.17[4].)

[2]   "Wrongdoing"

Certain conduct clearly qualifies as wrongdoing: murder, assault, threats, bribery. If a party arranges for someone to offer the declarant a lucrative job out of the country so the declarant will not be around to testify, this also probably qualifies as "wrongdoing," even if the declarant is unaware that his good fortune was prompted by the party in the impending litigation. Occasionally, though, it may be questionable whether conduct that prevents a declarant from testifying can be classified as "wrongdoing." Suppose, for example, a defendant in a criminal case ups and *marries* the government's key witness, so he can assert the privilege (recognized in some jurisdictions) of preventing his wife from testifying against him. Is this "wrongdoing"?

[3] "Acquiescence"

The party seeking to offer the hearsay statement need not establish that the other party himself killed, bribed or threatened the witness, nor that the party actively hired or encouraged someone else to do so; it suffices that the defendant "acquiesced" in such wrongdoing by another. To "acquiesce" is "to accept or comply tacitly or passively." If an underling says to an organized crime boss about to stand trial, "It would be a real shame if X [the key government witness] had an accident" and the boss shrugs, does this constitute "acquiescence" to the underling's implied suggestion that he kill the witness? If a lawyer in civil litigation tells a client, "I'll try to persuade [Y, plaintiff's key witness] not to testify," does this constitute the client's "acquiescence" in the lawyer's subsequent bribery?

If the lawyer bribes the witness or an underling kills a witness without first getting the client's tacit, passive acquiescence, the hearsay exception probably does not apply.

[4] Burden of Persuasion; Procedure

The Advisory Committee Note to the exception states that, per Rule 104(a), the party seeking to invoke the exception must persuade the judge of the requirements for the exception (wrongdoing, acquiescence) by a preponderance of the evidence. Presumably this would be at a hearing in the absence of the jury, unless the facts underlying the witness's unavailability are otherwise admissible at trial.

CHAPTER

10

THE "RESIDUAL EXCEPTION": RULE 807

§ 10.01 In General

When Congress first enacted the Federal Rules of Evidence, in addition to the more-or-less specific provisions of Rules 803(1)–(23) and 804(b)(1)–(4), Congress included two identical provisions, Rules 803(24) and 804(b)(5), intended to afford the federal courts a limited amount of flexibility and discretion to admit hearsay which, although not fully satisfying any of the specific exceptions, has "equivalent circumstantial guarantees of trustworthiness" and which satisfies several other substantive and procedural requirements. In 1997 Congress combined these two provisions into an identical new provision, nominated Rule 807. No change in meaning was intended.

Fed. R. Evid. 807 provides as follows:

Rule 807. Residual Exception

A statement not specifically covered by Rule 803 or 804 but having equivalent circumstantial guarantees of trustworthiness, is not excluded by the hearsay rule, if the court determines that (A) the statement is offered as evidence of a material fact; (B) the statement is more probative on the point for which it is offered than any other evidence which the proponent can procure through reasonable efforts; and (C) the general purposes of these rules and the interests of justice will best be served by admission of the statement into evidence. However, a statement may not be admitted under this exception unless the proponent of it makes known to the adverse party sufficiently in advance of the trial or hearing to provide the adverse party with a fair opportunity to prepare to meet it, the proponent's intention to offer the statement and the particulars of it, including the name and address of the declarant.

For a statement to overcome a hearsay objection pursuant to Rule 807, five conditions must be met; and if a prosecutor seeks to use the exception, the Confrontation Clause must also be considered.

1. The statement must be "offered as evidence of a material fact." (*See* § 10.02.)

2. The statement must be "more probative on the point for which it is offered than any other evidence which the proponent can procure through reasonable efforts." (*See* § 10.02.)

3. The statement must have "circumstantial guarantees of trustworthiness" equivalent to the other Rule 803 or Rule 804 exceptions (*ee* § 10.02).

4. The trial judge must be satisfied that "the general purposes of [the Federal Rules of Evidence] and the interests of justice will best be served by admission of the statement into evidence."

(Matthew Bender & Co., Inc.)

(Pub.748)

5. The offering party must give the adverse party advance notice of the intent to offer the statement, and most courts require that the notice specifically refer to the residual exception. This alerts the adverse party to seek evidence to challenge the hearsay's admissibility or to refute it. Despite the seemingly absolute language of the advance notice clause, where the offering party only learned of the evidence during trial (and therefore could not give the required notice), instead of excluding the evidence, courts have given the adverse party a recess, adjournment or continuance to enable it to attempt to combat the evidence.

6. *Sixth Amendment Confrontation Clause. See* § 10.04.

These requirements should be interpreted in light of the legislative history of the residual exception. The Advisory Committee admonished that the residual exceptions "do not contemplate an unfettered exercise of judicial discretion"; the House Judiciary Committee sought to exclude them altogether; the Senate Judiciary Committee reinserted them into the Federal Rules of Evidence, commenting that in doing so, the Committee did "not intend to establish a broad license for trial judges"; rather, the residual exceptions should be reserved for "exceptional circumstances . . . and exceptional cases. . . ."

§ 10.02 "Material"; "More Probative"

Clauses (A) and (B) of Fed. R. Evid. 807 require that "the statement is offered as evidence of a material fact,"[1] and that the statement must be "more probative on the point for which it is offered than any other evidence which the proponent can procure through reasonable efforts." The latter requirement has been the focus of considerable judicial attention. Some generalizations can be drawn from this case law.

1. Courts consider live testimony more probative than hearsay statements. Where a party fails to call an available witness who presumably could testify about the same facts, attempts to offer hearsay through the residual exception are often rejected.

2. Courts tend to be fairly strict in applying the "reasonable efforts" aspects of the requirement: the residual exceptions do not excuse an attorney's laziness.

3. The "reasonableness" of the effort to be required depends to some extent on the importance of the evidence and whether it is offered on a contested issue.

Questions

Q. 1. D was accused of carnal knowledge of G, a girl less than 16 years old. His arrest was based on statements G made to a social worker. At trial G testified and was cross-examined, but the jury could not reach a verdict. By the time the case comes up for retrial, G is unavailable: she and her family have moved to a different state. Therefore, the prosecutor offers in evidence her statement to the social worker. When D makes a hearsay objection, the prosecutor cites Rule 807. Ruling?

Ans. The objection should be sustained. G's testimony at the first trial, admissible under Fed. R. Evid. 804(b)(1), is more probative than her statement to the social worker, because the first-trial testimony was under oath and subject to cross-examination. The statement to the social worker, therefore, fails to satisfy the "more probative" requirement.

Q. 2. P sued five asbestos manufacturers, alleging that exposure to asbestos caused his debilitating lung disease. At trial, after proper advance notice to the defendants, P invoked Fed. R. Evid. 807 to offer in evidence the deposition of Dr. W, who had been a staff physician and consultant for JMC, one of the five companies P was suing. Dr. W's deposition, which focused primarily upon what the asbestos industry knew about the health hazards of asbestos at various points in time, had

---

[1] The use of the word "material" is probably inadvertent, given the care with which the Advisory Committee eschewed its use elsewhere in the Federal Rules of Evidence (*see* Advisory Committees' Note to Fed. R. Evid. 401, discussing the definition of "relevant evidence"); probably "relevant" is what was intended, although some scholars argue that the word "material" was chosen deliberately to indicate that more than mere relevance is required to justify using the residual exception.

been taken prior to the trial of a different lawsuit brought by a different plaintiff against JMC; Dr. W died shortly after she had been deposed.

All five defendants in the current case interpose a hearsay objection. Ruling?

Ans. As to JMC, overruled under Rule 804(b)(1). The issue in P's suit is the same as in the prior suit; JMC had an opportunity and similar motive to conduct direct or cross-examination of Dr. W at the deposition as it would now if she were available.

As to the other four companies, overruled under Rule 804(b)(1) if the court follows the Third Circuit's broad definition of "predecessor in interest." (*See* § 9.05.)

Otherwise, overruled under Rule 807. Even though P could have obtained expert testimony from other witnesses, Dr. W's situation, having been employed as a doctor and consultant for one of the defendants, was particularly probative on the issues of what the industry knew and when it knew it; testimony from an "outside" expert would not have been as probative.

§ 10.03 "Circumstantial Guarantees of Trustworthiness"

No all-purpose checklist or mathematical formula exists to govern the assessment of whether a particular statement has "circumstantial guarantees of trustworthiness" that are "equivalent" to one of the specific exceptions. Courts have considered a variety of factors, including the following:

1. *First-hand knowledge.* As a general rule, this is a "must"; except in truly extraordinary circumstances, without it, the statement will not qualify.

2. *Was the statement a "near miss"?* Most courts have held that a statement that almost qualifies under a specific provision may need only minor additional "guarantees of trustworthiness" to satisfy the residual exception. Other courts, however, have held that "near misses" should *not* be admitted under the residual exceptions, lest the residual provisions subvert congressional intent in spelling out the requirements for the specific provisions.

3. *Credibility and condition of the declarant.* Is (or was) she someone likely to be truthful, or not? Is she a clergyperson, law professor, police officer, used car salesman, drug dealer, convicted perjurer . . . ?[1] Was the declarant drunk or under the influence of prescription or illicit drugs at the time she made the statement?

4. *The statement itself.* Does it demonstrate, or at least suggest, that declarant had first-hand knowledge? Is it clear or ambiguous? Is it plausible or implausible on its face?

5. *When, how, where and to whom the statement was made?* Any number of sub-factors may be relevant:

    a. Was it made under oath, or under other circumstances giving the declarant a particular motive to speak truthfully; or, to the contrary, did the circumstances give declarant a powerful motive to lie?

    b. Was the statement disserving, self-serving, or neutral?

    c. To what "audience" was it made—a grand jury, a parent or spouse, a diary, a business associate, a casual acquaintance, the Dr. Laura radio program?

    d. How much time elapsed between the events in question, and the declarant's statement?

6. *Other circumstances surrounding the making of the statement* may be relevant in assessing the probable truthfulness of the statement.

7. *Availability of declarant.* Some courts have considered it very significant if the declarant testifies at trial, on the theory that the oath, cross-examination and the jury's opportunity to watch declarant's demeanor on the witness stand all tend to guarantee trustworthiness.

---

[1] Reasonable people may disagree as to where to rank these professions on the scale of probable credibility (except, of course, that of law professor).

(Matthew Bender & Co., Inc.)

8. *Corroboration or contradiction.* Does evidence independent of the statement itself tend to confirm or contradict the statement? Note, though, that while courts may consider extrinsic corroboration in civil cases, the Supreme Court has held that this is not permissible when a prosecutor seeks to use the residual exception in a criminal case (*see* § 10.04).

9. *Credibility of witness.* Although the credibility of the witness who will testify that declarant made the statement is usually a question strictly for the jury, some courts have included this factor in the evaluation as well.

Questions

Q. 3. X, the intended recipient of a Social Security check, reported to the Social Security Administration's local office that her monthly check for $373 had not arrived. She filled out and signed a form ("exhibit 1") attesting under penalties of perjury that she had not received the check and had not given anyone permission to possess, endorse or cash it.

Two months later, D was accused of possessing, forging and uttering X's check. To convict, the prosecutor must prove (among other things) that D did not have X's permission to possess the check, to sign X's name to it, or to utter (cash) it.

X died before the case reached trial, leaving an estate that included more than $40,000 in bank accounts. At trial, the government called W, X's roommate. W testified that, so far as she knew, X did not receive the check in question. W also identified X's signature on the Social Security Administration form, exhibit 1. Exhibit 1 is authenticated by an employee of the Social Security Administration. The prosecutor then offers exhibit 1 into evidence; D makes a hearsay objection.

a. Is the form admissible under Fed. R. Evid. 803(6) or 803(8)?

Ans. No. X, the source of the information, was not an employee of the Social Security Administration, and therefore did not have a "business duty" or an "official" duty to provide the information.

b. Is it admissible under Fed. R. Evid. 807, assuming the government had given D advance notice of its intent to offer it?

Ans. The key issue is trustworthiness. Of the factors listed earlier in this section, the following are pertinent:

1. X had *first-hand knowledge* of whether she received the check or authorized D to possess, endorse or sign it.

3. *X's credibility.* Evidence about X's character may be relevant here. If you have studied Rules 404, 405, 608 and 609, you have an idea as to the kind of evidence that might be admissible to attack or defend X's character for truthfulness. Evidence about X's physical and, more important, mental condition at the time he signed exhibit 1 is also relevant. If she was forgetful and confused, that argues against its trustworthiness. If she managed her own affairs carefully and meticulously (paid her own bills, balanced her checkbook, looked after her investments, and so on), by contrast, that demonstrates her mental acuity and therefore the probable trustworthiness of the statement.

5. *When and to whom the statement was made.* X knew that if she lied about whether she received the check she could be prosecuted for a felony. This is a plus for trustworthiness.

6. *Other circumstances surrounding the making of the statement.* X had substantial funds in the bank, and therefore had no apparent motive to lie about whether she in fact received a modest Social Security check.

7. X, being dead, is *unavailable.*

8. *Corroboration.* Because the prosecutor is relying on Rule 807 in a criminal case, a court may not consider extrinsic corroboration.

9. *Credibility of witness.* The Social Security Administration official to whom X spoke and for whom X signed the form has no apparent stake in the case and no motive to lie.

In the case on which this problem is based, the court, properly in my opinion, admitted the form.

c. D also makes a Sixth Amendment objection.

Ans. It should be overruled. X is unavailable; and the same indicia of trustworthiness that satisfies Rule 807 also satisfies the Confrontation Clause trustworthiness requirement (*see* § 10.04).

Q. 4. A few days after a winter storm, several construction workers, including R, the crew supervisor, were sent by their company to make repairs to the roof of a building owned by D Co. The roof was surrounded by a five-foot high wall.

The roof could be reached from inside the building through the building superintendent's apartment, or from outside by climbing a flight of stairs. The opening at the top of the stairs was shut with a makeshift gate that had been wired to the wall around the roof.

After the work crew arrived, R had a conversation with S, the building superintendent. A few minutes later R told W, a member of his work crew, "The super says we can't go through his apartment, because he's afraid we'll track mud all over his carpets; and he won't let us take down the gate, because he lets his dog run around on the roof and if we take down the gate the dog might get down the stairs and run away." Thus, the only way the men could get on and off of the roof was to climb over the fence at the top of the stairs.

The men worked for several hours. As R was climbing over the fence to get to the stairs at the end of the day, the fence gave way, and R fell to his death.

P, R's widow, brought a wrongful death action against D Co., alleging that unsafe work conditions caused R's death; D Co. defended by claiming that R's own negligence (his failure to take down the gate) caused his death. Prior to trial, P served notice on D Co. that she planned to elicit testimony about what R had told W about R's conversation with S.

At trial, W testifies that there was a lot of slush and mud on the ground because of the previous day's storm, and also testified that there were dog droppings on the roof. Then P seeks to have W testify as to what R told him following R's conversation with S. (S is unavailable at trial.)

D Co. makes a hearsay objection.

a. How many levels of hearsay are there?

Ans. It appears that there are two (S to R and R to W).

As to the first level (S to R), the hearsay objection is easily overcome. P can argue, (1), that what S said to R wasn't an assertion of fact, it was a direction or imperative ("You can't go through my apartment"; "you can't take down the fence") (*see* § 2.05[4]); or (2) that because S was D Co.'s building superintendent, what he said is admissible against D Co. under Rule 801(d)(2)(D) (*see* § 5.12).

Thus, only the second level (R to W) poses problems.

b. What rules should P cite to overcome D Co.'s hearsay objection?

Ans. The two likely candidates are Rule 803(1), present sense impression, and Rule 807.

Rule 803(1). R's statement to W, in which he repeated what S allegedly had said to him, satisfies most of the requirements quite easily (*see* § 8.02.). R had first-hand knowledge of what S had said; the statement "described or explained" what S had said and also explained how the men would have to get to the roof. The time factor, though, may be a problem. W can't be quite sure how much time elapsed between the R-S conversation and R's statement to W—perhaps five minutes, perhaps 10, perhaps 15. To some courts, that may be a bit too much for Rule 803(1) (which requires that the statement was made "while the declarant was perceiving the event, or immediately thereafter").

Rule 807. P easily satisfies the first (advance notice), third (relevance) and fourth ("more probative") requirements. The key is the second: trustworthiness. Of the factors listed at the beginning of this section, the following are pertinent:

1. *First-hand knowledge.* R had such knowledge of what S had said to him.

2. *Near miss.* See the immediately preceding discussion of Rule 803(1) addressing this point.

4. *The statement itself.* It was a plausible explanation, by a supervisor to his work crew, of how they would have to get access to the roof and why.

5. *When, where, and to whom the statement was made.* R made his statement to W only minutes after his conversation with S, so it is unlikely he would have forgotten what S said. R had no motive to lie, because following S's instructions made the job more difficult and dangerous.

7. *Availability of declarant.* R is dead and S cannot be found.

8. *Corroboration or contradiction.* The mud and slush on the ground corroborate R's explanation of why S would not let the men enter the roof through S's apartment; the dog droppings on the roof corroborate R's statement as to why S insisted the men could not take down the gate.

Conclusion: R's statement is admissible under the residual exception.

§ 10.04 Confrontation Clause; Corroboration

In *Idaho v. Wright,* 497 U.S. 805, 817 (1990), the Supreme Court held that the residual exception is not "firmly rooted." It is doubtful, moreover, that a statement falling within the residual exception will automatically be afforded "independent evidentiary significance." Thus, to satisfy the Confrontation Clause, the prosecutor will (1) be required to make a particularized showing of trustworthiness, which imposes no extra burden because the government must already do so to satisfy Rule 807; and (2) may be required to call the declarant as a witness, or establish declarant's unavailability.

Use of extrinsic corroboration as evidence of trustworthiness.

In *Wright,* the Court also held that in assessing the trustworthiness of a statement offered by a prosecutor under the residual exception, a court may look only at the statement itself and the circumstances in which it was made; a court may not look at extrinsic corroboration. A mother was charged with assisting her male companion to sexually abuse her 5 and 2 year old daughters. In considering the admissibility of statements that the younger child made to a pediatrician, the trial court considered, among other things, physical evidence that the child was abused, testimony by the older child that she had seen the male molesting the younger child, and circumstantial evidence suggesting that the abuse occurred while the mother and her companion were in the house with the child. The Supreme Court, per Justice O'Connor, held that it was error for the trial judge to consider any of this evidence. Permitting extrinsic corroboration as proof of a statement's trustworthiness, a 5-to-4 majority concluded, "would permit admission of a presumptively unreliable statement by bootstrapping on the trustworthiness of other evidence at trial," which, the majority concluded, would be "at odds with the requirement that hearsay evidence admitted under the Confrontation Clause be so trustworthy that cross-examination of the declarant would be of marginal utility." Dissenting, Justice Kennedy pointed out the irony of excluding from consideration an entire class of evidence most likely to establish whether the statement was in fact trustworthy.

Some courts have held that extrinsic corroboration of a statement's trustworthiness may be considered, however, in civil litigation. Whether it may be considered when a defendant in a criminal case offers such a statement is uncertain.

INDEX

[References are to section numbers.]

I–1

[References are to section numbers.]

[References are to section numbers.]

(Matthew Bender & Co., Inc.)

(Pub.748)

[References are to section numbers.]

[References are to section numbers.]

(Matthew Bender & Co., Inc.)